THE MIND OF
EAST ASIA

Lily Abegg

THAMES AND HUDSON

LONDON · NEW YORK

Translated from the German
Ostasien Denkt Anders
by A. J. Crick and
E. E. Thomas

COMPOSED BY W. S. COWELL LTD IPSWICH
PRINTED IN GREAT BRITAIN BY JARROLD AND SONS LTD NORWICH

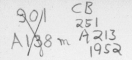
CONTENTS

INTRODUCTION

IT is one thing to discuss theoretically the contrasts between the East and the West; it is quite another thing to have long personal experience of them. I grew up in Japan and subsequently spent eleven years as a journalist in the countries of the Far East, from Japan to Siam, and so I had opportunities for getting to know the peoples of those countries reasonably well. From time to time I visited Europe and so was continually able to compare at first hand the occidental and oriental ways of life. Each time I travelled back and forth the process of re-adaptation was a difficult one; each time it required a conscious effort to get used to the other world.

In Europe I was always impressed by the industriousness of the people, their mental and nervous tenseness and their preoccupied expressions. Only a few persons manifestly possessed the gift for enjoying the present; the majority appeared to be concerned all the time about the morrow. To come here from East Asia was like suddenly exchanging a warm bath for a raw wintry landscape. In the East you have more time, are less preoccupied with problems of all kinds, and that is why in some way you experience the course of the day and current events more intensely. I have always thought of my years in the Far East as having been very full and consequently very long, while those spent in Europe seemed short and fleeting.

During the first few weeks of my visits to Europe it really seemed to me that the people here were slightly mad. How sullenly they went about their business and how they scurried around! Their entire happiness appeared to depend on whether or not they caught a particular tram or bus. No one here walked at a steady, dignified pace through the streets as the East Asians do and as I felt really befits a cultivated person. On fine spring days no one here sat out in front of his house contentedly sunning himself and looking at the first buds and flowers.

Instead, housewives were engaged—at least this was the case with us in Switzerland—in removing the last speck of dust from the most remote corner of the house. In the more intellectual occupations and in business life 'nervous breakdowns' resulting from overwork appeared to be no rare occurrences. Strange people, these Europeans! Not very gifted, somehow, as regards living!—that is how it struck the puzzled East Asian side of my nature. But gradually it changed. For if you happen to be of European descent you soon fall back into the habit of knitting your brow.

I should like to mention one particular incident which I shall never forget and which seems to me to bring out strikingly this fundamental feature of the European character. In December, 1939, I arrived in Naples from China and was, like all my fellow travellers, glad to have reached European soil safe and sound in spite of the war. Yet hardly had we gone ashore than we looked at each other with disappointment and surmise. What could have happened? Why did everybody look so worried? An accident? A cataclysm? Italy's entry into the war? Then I espied an acquaintance, who lived in Naples, and went up to him to inquire what it was all about. 'I don't follow,' he said, 'nothing special has happened here.' An elderly Englishwoman, who had spent thirty years in China, muttered to herself 'I forgot, we are in Europe, that's all!'

So that is how the 'sunny South' struck us, that Naples which, to the transalpine mind and even to the North Italian, spells a certain carefree atmosphere and *dolce far niente*. The fact is, we belong to a particular species, whether we happen to live in Sicily, Norway or Spain. For over two years all of us had seen in China nothing but war, bombs, destruction, flight and misery, and yet we felt Europe, where war had only just begun—even Italy, which was not yet involved—to be most depressing.

Here are several witnesses to testify that I am not exaggerating. Lafcadio Hearn,[1] that well-known writer on Japan, spoke of the fear with which the Japanese regarded the 'ill-tempered faces' of the occidentals. C. G. Jung,[2] the famous Swiss psychologist, says: 'The White man is without doubt nervous, hasty, restless, unstable and (in the eyes of the rest of mankind) filled with the maddest ideas . . .', while the German author Ernst Jünger[3] expresses the same thing in one simple sentence: 'The Orientals must think us mad.' Bertrand Russell[4] speaks of 'Western push and hustle', and thinks that in contrast with the Chinese way of life ours represents 'restless change, discontent and destruction.' The echo from the East replies in similar strain. The Chinese Lin Yutang[5] explains in his picturesque way that 'progress' clearly means 'more neurasthenia, more aspirin and more expensive illnesses . . . more softened brains and more hardened livers . . . more spleens, dilated hearts, and shattered nerves', while the Japanese Kakuzo Okakura[6] confirms that we are an 'abnormal species'.

On the other hand, it has often enough been suggested on our part that the East Asians do not represent normality; not in the sense that they are schizophrenic, but on account of their supposedly retarded mental development and alleged lack of natural talent.

The observations contained in this book are the result less of theoretical studies than of practical experience. Years spent as a journalist in East Asia, the obligation to report regularly on cultural and political phenomena in those regions, constantly confronted me with certain basic questions which for a long time I found puzzling and inexplicable, and to which the literature on the subject provided no satisfactory answers. My interest meanwhile tended to concentrate on the peculiar quality of the East Asian way of thinking, and it is from a progressively more intensive preoccupation with this problem that this book came to be written.

In investigating and analysing this way of thinking I happened inadvertently to discover its psychological determining factors, whereupon it became evident that the entire East Asian character could be reduced to a single denominator once the psychological key to it was found.

This book represents, then, an attempt to fathom the East

Asian character and at the same time to establish in what respects it differs most markedly from that of the West. Since in both cases we are concerned with civilizations which, each in its own way, are among the most highly developed and differentiated in the world, the undertaking is no easy one. The presentation will inevitably entail a certain amount of simplification, and it will not be possible to bring out in each instance the wealth and variety of these cultures or their inherent contradictions and paradoxes.

This is particularly true of my treatment of the character of the West, which is introduced into the argument only in so far as appears necessary to an understanding of the contrasts and in formulating cultural characteristics. In treating of the West I shall have to confine myself to establishing the dominant factors in our cultural development, even though I am well aware that this method is open to criticism because the dominant influences were invariably accompanied by powerful counter-currents.

This work confines itself entirely to East Asia and is not concerned with the contrasts between the West and the rest of Asia. Even this limited aim is most difficult to achieve because of the many existing differences between China and Japan. The variations within East Asian culture, however, are of no greater consequence than those to be found within the Western world. The East Asian cultural orbit can perhaps best be defined by equating it with the area over which the Chinese script has spread. This would include Japan, Korea, Manchuria, China, and also, to some extent, Indo-China. I shall concern myself, however, only with the two principal peoples, the Chinese and the Japanese.

During the past few years in particular the East Asians have shown us once again how very important they are both to us and as a factor in the entire international situation, whether it be as a friend like present-day Japan or as an enemy such as Communist China. By virtue of their great vitality these peoples compel our attention time and again, be it in a positive or a negative manner: the Korean war is sufficient evidence of the latter.

Our interest in the East Asians is twofold: firstly, we wish to know whether we can learn something from them, more particularly from their traditional ways which are diametrically opposed to our own; secondly, we should like to know what is really going on there and in what direction these countries are likely to develop. In Japan, westernization, and consequently a closer approximation to our own kind of existence, has made rapid strides in the post-war years, but do not let us delude ourselves! 'Approximation' is a very different thing from identification. The Japanese will, for example, never prove capable of transforming themselves into true democrats in the Western sense; on the other hand, they can certainly try to establish a new harmonious synthesis based on the more progressive Western influences and their own Asian proclivities.

What then is happening in China? What does Chinese Communism mean? This book tries to provide certain fundamental answers to questions like these. Of one thing I am certain, Chinese Communism is not to be regarded solely as a political phenomenon, but also as a mental and spiritual crisis. The Communists are trying to exterminate thousand-year-old traditions and to inculcate into the Chinese people something entirely new. But this new thing, Communist theory, has its origin in the West, even if it does not represent straightforward Western ideas but rather a Marxist debasement thereof, further kneaded and distorted by despotic concepts imported from Russia. At all events we are averse to describing present-day Communism as 'Western'; yet for Asia, too, it is something strange and novel. For, Asia—East Asia in particular—has never yet produced any rational ideologies (and this is what Communism is) of its own.

Will the Communists, those rationalists and worshippers of the exact sciences, then, succeed in suddenly turning the Chinese, who have hitherto been sceptical and indeed contemptuous of science and technology, into people who are capable of building machines and aircraft on their own? I believe that this process of re-education will take a very long time and that the economic and consequently the political and military strength of Communist China need not be rated too highly for the time being. Red China does not yet possess any genuine strength of its own; it merely seems to have it by reason of its collaboration with the U.S.S.R. and the backing which the Soviet Union provides.

The Korean war is of interest in connection with this book only in so far as it throws light on the aggressive spirit of Communist Chinese defence—in full accord with the wishes of the Soviet Union. Regarded from the point of view of historical development it is only the strategic and military part of a chapter in the story of the great events of the Communist revolution in China.

L.A.

NOTES

[1] Lafcadio Hearn, *Izumo*.
[2] C. G. Jung, *Aufsätze zur Zeitgeschichte*.
[3] Ernst Jünger, *Der Arbeiter*.
[4] Bertrand Russell, *The Problem of China*.
[5] Lin Yutang, *The Importance of Living*.
[6] Kakuzo Okakura, *The Awakening of the East*.

Chapter 1

CLEAVAGE AND TOTALITY

ALTHOUGH a notable and extensive literature about East Asia has grown up in the course of the past few decades we are as yet only beginning to gain a true understanding of that exotic cultural sphere. Why is this? How is it that we still cannot rightly comprehend the Chinese and Japanese even though we have been in direct contact with them for a considerable time? It is mainly due, as this book tries to show, to the fact that the East Asian and the Westerner are entirely different, particularly in their psychological constitution.

Up to now we have been only vaguely aware of our peculiar psychological features; we have taken it quite for granted that our way of thinking and feeling was normal and we judged the rest of the world from the Western point of view. For a long time we failed to discover our mistake; indeed, we worked on the assumption that we were objective and possessed a special gift for getting to know and understand foreign peoples, which was made all the easier for us because of our world-wide interests. The sinologues, for example, regarded Chinese history in exactly the same way as our historians treated Western history, known as the 'history of the world', paying most attention to lines of historical development. If we try to approach East Asia, however, with preconceptions based on the usual ideas of development we shall get to know nothing of the essentials of its culture, nor shall we gain any new and valuable experience.

*

Before embarking on a psychological analysis of the contrast between East Asia and the West it is perhaps well to mention a few of the principal theses which have been put forward on this subject.

Most modern authors try to express the contrast in terms of the formula 'dynamic versus static'. Others talk about Western activity as opposed to Asian passivity. Hegel for his part saw the main difference in the antithesis between freedom and despotism, while in Oswald Spengler's view the Chinese degenerated into a mere 'fellaheen people' some 2,000 years ago. Others contrast youth and age, worldliness and other-worldliness. Some authors—in particular the East Asians themselves—over-simplified the problem by contrasting their own culture, as one governed by 'feeling', with ours, as one ruled by the 'intellect'. The foremost Japanese philosopher of our day, Kitaro Nishida, is an example.

The contrast between 'dynamic' and 'static', though at first glance it may appear satisfactory, does not bear critical examination. How, for example, are the rapid rise of Japan and her truly 'dynamic' offensives early in World War II to be fitted into such a scheme? The rejoinder that the Japanese had changed so completely as a result of their contact with the West is not sound, for the East Asians have had notable accesses of dynamism in earlier times. We need only remind ourselves of the deeds of the Mongols, a kindred people. When the famous German geographer, Ferdinand von Richthofen, established in the last century that the rise of Japan could be characterized as the transformation of 'latent into kinetic energy', he was doubtless correct, but it should be added in amplification that similar changes had also happened earlier on. With what élan did the Japanese under Hideyoshi, the great 'Taiko', press forward to the very frontiers of China in the sixteenth century! Not without justification is Hideyoshi described as 'the Japanese Napoleon'. It is quite legitimate to point out that East Asia's dynamism is of a different kind from our own—but that fact is in no way expressed in the formula 'dynamic versus static'.

There is yet another objection to this formula, on the grounds of possible misunderstanding. The East Asians themselves frequently take an entirely opposite view when they treat the problem on a philosophical plane and describe their own culture as dynamic and ours as static. East Asians are obsessed by the thought of eternal change, and in consequence time rather than space is the real element in which they live. 'Today' has no meaning for them except in that it is linked with the eternal Yesterday and the eternal Tomorrow. Space is nothing but a fleeting aspect of the fleeting present. This concept of change, otherwise described as the universal dynamic principle, is one of the fundamentals of East Asian philosophy. Our culture, on the other hand, is dominated, as the Japanese Kitayama[1] explains, by a 'desire for space'. He thus sets our 'space' culture against the East Asian 'time' culture. And so in this way we come to a direct reversal of the 'dynamic-static' theory!

It is equally dangerous to maintain that the East Asians, in contrast to ourselves, are generally passive, since these peoples have for ages been characterized by their industry and zeal. Did not Confucius say 'Man must be up and doing'? And is not East Asian Buddhism largely imbued with the idea that man has to realize himself by actions? The peoples of tropical Asia can be described as passive, but never the East Asians. It is worth observing at this point, however, that their activity viewed psychologically, is of a different character from our own.

It is perhaps unnecessary, in view of the events of recent years, to go further into Hegel's thought on the subject. It shows clearly how dangerous it is to elaborate differences purely on the basis of contemporary facts and trends, without touching on the deeper reasons for the antithesis.

Spengler admittedly says, in his *Decline of the West*, that our way of looking at history has hitherto been too narrow and false, and that it is therefore necessary to consider world history from new points of view. Yet you will find only very little about China in his two large volumes and practically nothing about Japan; above all, nothing which does not fit into his pattern of cultural morphology. He aims, of course, at the full conspectus, but in practice falls back mainly on the West and on that family of peoples who, like the Arabs, have always been in association with us. His thesis of the growth and decline of cultures has

2

certainly provided us with valuable suggestions, but nothing more, since it is questionable even as applied to the Western orbit. Applied to large parts of Asia and principally to East Asia, moreover, his theory completely falls to the ground. The reason lies in the fact that Spengler, although he does not base his thought on the concept of progress, once again proceeds from the idea of development, and with this alone it is simply not possible to get the measure of East Asia. For him, as for many Westerners, the idea of meaningful existence is absolutely identical with that of 'History' and so too with that of 'historical development'. According to his pattern Chinese history came to an end as far back as the Han period or some 2,000 years ago, the Chinese thereafter slipped 'once more into the zoological ebb and flow of the primitive era', and their culture subsequently no longer had any 'soul'. The remarkable ink drawings of the Sung period were therefore 'soulless' and the construction of the Imperial Canal would properly have to be treated in *Brehm's Zoology*. If China, as Spengler maintains, had in fact sunk into insignificance at such a very early stage there would have been nothing for us to admire in Chinese culture except the teachings of some mystics and moral philosophers, and a collection of old folk-songs. What Spengler failed to grasp, however, was that the value of Chinese culture lies in the very fact that it has *not* developed but has maintained its character and its validity for thousands of years. Whether, and to what extent the Communist Revolution constituted a break with these traditional events, will be discussed later.

If we confine ourselves to a consideration of Western history, in which peoples and cultures have in fact taken the lead more or less in rotation, we can easily become pessimistic and arrive at the conclusion that we too must suffer 'decline and fall'. If, on the other hand, we survey the history of all mankind, we must ask ourselves why we should learn nothing from the past and fall into decline, while the Chinese and the Indians have survived and remained active for thousands of years and still continue to do so.

In putting forward the antithesis of 'youth' and 'age' it is necessary to make so many reservations that in the end nothing very positive emerges. In the first place the Japanese, who did not move into the limelight of history before the fifth century of the Christian era, are certainly no 'older' than we are. While it is correct to state that the Chinese are old, we need to qualify this by adding that they are nevertheless still young. They are in fact both—and that is one of the refreshingly illogical facts of East Asia.

The formulae 'worldliness—other-worldliness' or 'materialism-spirituality'—the latter a variation of the former—are useless, since these terms do not express opposites in East Asia as they do with us. There is really no such thing as a 'beyond'; rather is it the case that 'here' and 'the beyond' are strictly speaking merely two different aspects of the same thing. One must think of East Asia in 'complementary' terms, in the same way as the most recent developments in physics demand of us; whereupon we briefly encounter for the first time the phenomenon that some of the most ancient East Asian concepts may perhaps be regarded as extremely 'up-to-date' as judged in the light of our present-day science.

The East Asians, to be sure, with their great pleasure in material things, at times display such joy in living that it is tempting to think of them as more materialistic and worldly than the Westerners. At other times, however, when they bear great sorrows and die with equanimity, they tend rather to give the impression that they are living in 'another world'.

The East Asians themselves have hitherto been generally inclined to typify our culture as a purely materialistic one, which is understandable to some extent, since they came into closer contact with us in a decidedly materialistic age. The same time-factors are responsible for the contrast they make between Western culture of the intellect and their own culture of feeling, or for their regarding our orientation as 'rational', and theirs as deriving from the 'soul'. The leading minds of East Asia are now beginning to sense that the Occident can be comprehended only in the totality of its history and development. We, for our part, are on the point of realizing that there is no need to take a negative view of a people holding fast for 2,000 years to truths long perceived.

In World War II the fight against 'Western materialism' formed the basis of Japanese propaganda. Japan wanted to free the good, virtuous children of Asia from the foreign devil of a materialistic culture. Many, even among the intellectuals, believed in this crusade. We cannot altogether blame the Japanese for adopting this slogan, for we find ourselves after all engaged in a conscious struggle against the materialism of our time. This propaganda, in so far as it was produced by the government, had of course other closely related purposes; it was necessary to stamp the technical superiority of the Americans as trivial in the eyes of the people, and at the same time to direct their attention to the ultimately inevitable victory of mind over matter. The suicide pilots who hurled themselves at enemy targets were intended to serve as models of this superiority of the spiritual principle over technical efficiency. At all events this war-cry was effective not only in Japan but in the rest of Asia, for the Asians are not lacking in a certain spiritual pride any more than we are.

*

Such attempts to typify the antithesis between East and West as have been mentioned above give us of course certain pointers, but they do not really go to the heart of the matter. Even the view which maintains that the main difference lies in diverse kinds of religious feeling offers no true solution, since these in turn are determined to a large extent by a differing psychic constitution. It is therefore necessary to define briefly the main features of this psychic dissimilarity.

The psychic development of Western man consisted above all in the progressive differentiation of his psychic functions. Feeling, intellect, the will and sensations went their several ways and accomplished those remarkable feats peculiar to each of them. Deep religious feeling and abstract philosophy, miracles of technology and marvellous harmonies of music, the conquest of the earth and the conquest of the atom—all these things we have experienced and accomplished in the course of our development. Things such as these are not found in East Asia or anywhere else in the world.

Our differentiated functions happened originally to find themselves more or less in a state of balance, which only then gradually disappeared as the functions steadily developed more and more independently of one another. Now, the over-emphasis of a single function could easily lead to a severe disruption of the 'total equilibrium' which was becoming steadily more unbalanced and complex. The last function to make itself independent in our case was the will. The emancipation of the will from the totality naturally led to the creation of the most dangerous tensions. We have already experienced one example of the collapse of the 'total will', but the crisis has nevertheless yet to be overcome. For this reason the necessity for the control of the functions is today already widely recognized. Our psyche has thus 'further developed' in the true sense of the word, in that the structure of the soul has been steadily further subdivided.

The term 'development' is misleading if applied to the East Asian soul; it is better in this connection to speak of an 'unfolding'. The East Asian soul is much closer to 'totality'; the individual functions have not become so distinct and independent with them as they have in such marked fashion with us.

The difference can be visualized perhaps in the following way. If we think of spiritual totality—of which every healthy person has something—as a straight line, then our various psychic functions are projected in enormous curves from this base line. At the present day, it appears—to maintain this simile—that those curves, on whose boldly projected lines lay our great achievements, are once again returning to the base line. In the East Asian psyche there are no such great parabolas, only numerous small ones which are ever emerging anew and always returning to the base line. Thus we may speak of 'little developments' succeeding one another, and in playing their part the functions never move far away from their 'native' totality.

It is perhaps worth quoting a few witnesses who can confirm our theory, although most of their statements are not very clearly formulated in the psychological sense. 'Thinking and feeling, which in the West exist as separate entities, here operate as a single force', says the Japanese Kitayama,[2] and he continues: 'The centre of gravity of spiritual activity in East Asia lies less in systematic comprehension of the universe and universal history than in real experience of totality through an intuitive perception of that essence in which all mental and sensuous functions combine.'

Another Japanese, Yoshiro Nagayo,[3] expresses himself in this way: 'The orientally viewed soul training is not usually included in the mental culture of the Occidentals. Apparently the Westerners have three things—faith, morality, sciences-arts. . . These three things are severally secured in recognition of their different values and attributes; and so they are not combined to form one inclusive method of human training—the comprehensive discipline of life. Herein can be perceived the special reason for the development of occidental culture as such.'

The well-known Japanese buddhist writer, Professor Daisetz Suzuki[4] says: 'Different though the teachings of Shintoism, the poetic art, and of Confucius may be, they all aim ultimately at the comprehension of the Single Heart. (One heart, the wisdom of Buddha and motionless perception are names for one and the same thing.)' Among Western investigators, C. G. Jung[5] in particular has drawn attention to the 'total' character of the East Asians. According to him, the 'Chinese' were 'never capable of so sundering opposing elements of human character that they lost sight, to the point of becoming unaware of, one another. A warning that the modern European is not to be regarded as the normal human type can indeed already be found in the work of Jacob Burckhardt.[6] 'In man it never happens that merely one side exclusively is active, but always the whole, even though some sides of it are more feebly, unconsciously active. These things, moreover, cannot be judged in the light of the endless division of labour and specialization of our day, but rather by the standards of those ages when all things were still closely associated.'

The East Asian soul has, then, ascended in its 'totality' from stage to stage. This is the direct way of becoming conscious of totality, whereas we approach full consciousness by making a detour through the separated functions. At this point it is perhaps desirable to make an observation in order to avoid misunderstandings. When in this book reference is made to Western development and East Asian 'unfolding', only the dominant features are meant. For, just as in our case totality was always preserved to a certain extent, so too have the East Asians exactly like ourselves 'developed' in some degree. The dominant features are nevertheless decisive, since it is they that determine to what extent one culture differs from another.

The questions relating to the antithesis 'Totality and Cleavage' are today by no means academic; they belong in fact to the most burning questions of our time and therefore quite naturally do not merely concern those who have a special interest in East Asia. Rather does preoccupation with East Asia offer only one of several possible ways of approaching this set of problems, one which almost all thinking people come up against nowadays in some form or other. East Asia, however, offers a particularly favourable line of approach and field for preliminary investigation, since it offers us the possibility of studying totality in living people who are on a high cultural plane.

Before continuing, it is necessary, however, to define certain terms in order to elucidate what follows. The chief difficulty—a fundamental one—lies in the fact that our terms are those of the 'split' type of man, while the East Asian terms are those of the 'total' type. That is why reciprocal renderings so often give a distorted and misleading picture. Did we wish to be precise

we should have to explain to the East Asians on each occasion
what we understood by 'heart' or 'intellect' or 'development',
while we, for a proper understanding of certain Chinese 'characters', would really require in every case a long psychological
and philosophical commentary.

Naturally enough I find myself compelled to adhere to our
Western concepts; nevertheless, I shall try to indicate from
time to time when these concepts do not exist in East Asia, or
are comprehended in a different way. Generally, I shall adhere
to the definitions of C. G. Jung[7] with two important exceptions
which concern the concepts of thinking and growing conscious.

East Asian thinking does not consist in the pure activity of
the thought function which, according to C. G. Jung, is one of
the four basic human functions (Thinking, Feeling, Sensation,
and Intuition). In speaking of East Asian thinking we would
do better to talk of 'exercising' the entire psyche (including the
unconscious). For the unconscious also plays a part in the
thought process, though it can never be 'active'; rather does it
'happen' independently of our consciousness or will. The
expression 'exercising' is thus intended to convey a process
which can be at once conscious and unconscious.

So the inclusive term 'thinking' is here taken to embrace all
those operations of the psyche from which conscious images,
concepts or perceptions result, without presupposing that these
are necessarily expressible in speech or writing. This conception
of thought is thus an extraordinarily broad one. But here one
is faced with the following alternatives. If I take this concept
in its narrower sense, I must conclude that the East Asians are
poor thinkers and that thinking in their case merely plays a
secondary rôle. If, on the other hand, I take the concept in its
broader sense (as I have done here), we come to the conclusion
that they are very deep thinkers. In making this decision, considerations are involved which are not perhaps strictly pertinent
but can at least be regarded as instructive. Objective persons
who have neither conscious nor unconscious preconceptions
will be indifferent to the sense in which I employ the concept

'thinking', provided that I define precisely what I mean by it. In practice, however, it is different. If I say that somebody 'thinks badly' it is naturally taken as a negative assessment. Furthermore, if the East Asians, according to our definitions do not 'think', in what then does their mental activity really consist? How shall we term this activity? Perhaps we might say they 'ponder'. This—rather old-fashioned—word, handed down from a time when we 'thought' rather less, would in fact meet the case fairly well. But feeling for language and common usage militate against it. One simply cannot say that the East Asians are bad thinkers but good 'ponderers'. Let us therefore stick to the accepted word 'think'.

The functions are not entirely 'fused' amongst the East Asians, but one may say with some justification that the attainment of this fusion is their aim. In the East Asian's view it is not the 'total' manner of thinking but, on the contrary, that which treats the thought *function* as something separate—that does not take 'the entire man' as starting-point—which is the more primitive. The East Asian has known at first hand enough psychic differentiations to be well aware of the dangers of such cleavages and of the problems they create, and he has therefore constantly striven for the opposite, namely the reconquest of totality.

Thinking, according to Jung, is composed of an active contribution (directed thought, intellect, rational function) and a passive one (intuitive thought, intellectual intuition, irrational function). East Asian thought can comprise all these kinds of thinking without one or several of them becoming predominant. The same is true of the 'laws peculiar to the function of thinking', which can likewise operate to some extent in East Asia. As we shall see in the following chapter, however, 'total' thinking, which may well at present appear to be very vague and ill-defined, is also fully equipped with its own set of laws.

We shall now consider the concepts of consciousness and cognition, and in so doing I shall abide by C. G. Jung's definition:[8] 'By consciousness I understand the relatedness of psychic contents to the ego in so far as they are perceived as such by the ego. In so far as relations are not sensed as such by the ego, they are unconscious. Consciousness is the function or activity which maintains the relation of psychic contents with the ego. Consciousness is not identical with *psyche*, since, in my view, psyche represents the totality of all the psychic contents, and these are not necessarily bound up directly with the ego, i.e. related to it in such a way that they take on the quality of consciousness . . .'[9]

Broadly interpreted, this means that we can grow conscious alike from positive activity and from letting things alone, from the free working of the entire psyche. Consciousness is the 'higher' the more it 'knows' of (senses) the entire psyche, and the 'lower' (the more primitive), the less it knows about it. The higher consciousness thus absorbs more of the unconscious into the ego than does the lower consciousness. The latter, for example the intellectual consciousness, knows little of the unconscious and even tries to deny it. Jung, indeed, also speaks of 'the superstition of the dissolution of the subconscious by the intellect'. Jacob Burckhardt[10] had already said: 'Even a further upward development of the intellect must be subject to doubt, since, as culture progresses, the division of labour might well result in a steady narrowing of the consciousness of the individual.'

The concept of consciousness is often taken in a narrow, rational sense; it is taken to mean knowledge of the things of this world, in fact the 'Sciences'. As a result, even such a notable figure as Alfred Weber[11] can accuse the Chinese of 'an inadequately clarified consciousness'. Once again we have here exactly the same criticism as that which the East Asians are generally in the habit of directing at us.

Our consciousness developed in an extravert, that of the East Asians in an introvert manner.[12] The East Asians followed the inner way and reached a high level of consciousness relatively early; whereas in their knowledge of the world they remained far behind us. They know man better, and we are better acquainted with the world. That is how those mutual accusations of defective knowledge, which are made with complete justification by each side, come about.

Now that we have described the sense in which the fundamental concepts 'thinking' and 'consciousness' are each to be interpreted, it must be emphasized once again that all our concepts, in so far as they are applied to East Asia, must be used with great caution. Chinese reasoning is different from ours in that it is based on the 'totality' of man and not on ratiocination; it is not, therefore, disturbed by contradictions in logic. The eighteenth century was mistaken when it took the Chinese conception of reason to be the same as that of the West. Because of the transient similarity between both concepts of reason, produced by the prevailing circumstances, their totally different origin was overlooked, and it was not suspected that they would have an equally different future.

We must keep these differences in mind even when we say, for example, that the Japanese are more influenced by feeling and the will than the Chinese. Japanese culture based on the will, in however extreme a form it occasionally may manifest itself, is of a different kind from its Western counterpart; it is never the outcome of a detached and independent function.

*

It will perhaps become clearer how little our traditional concepts can be applied to East Asia if we for the moment consider in turn some East Asian conceptions. The French sinologue Marcel Granet makes it very plain in his book *La Pensée Chinoise* how easily misunderstandings can occur if Chinese-written characters are rendered by Western expressions. He says, among other things:

> Il convient donc de rompre avec la tendance, qui prévaut encore, de rendre ces emblèmes, lourds de jugements de valeur où s'exprime une civilisation originale, par des termes empruntés (après une assimilation rapide et qui ne tient point compte de la

divergence des mentalités) au vocabulaire—conventionel lui aussi mais visant expressément à une précision impersonnelle et objective—des philosophes d'Occident.

We shall attempt by producing several examples to explain ourselves without including illustrations of Chinese-written characters, even though this, too, creates certain difficulties. They have a character which often occurs in Confucius and which has generally been translated up to now as 'virtue', but is rendered by Richard Wilhelm as 'magic'. One therefore reads in the Wilhelm versions not of the virtue of the holy man or sage but of his magic. In our view Wilhelm's rendering is nearer the mark, since it does more justice in the first place to a certain lack of conceptual exactitude among the East Asians, and secondly because our word 'virtue' is far too narrow in meaning and has a moral connotation. It is just this moral complexion of which the Chinese concept, and for that reason the Japanese also, is totally devoid. Roughly what is meant by it— to explain it in the briefest possible way—is that a personality influences naturally by way of example; not so much through teachings and words, as simply through its existence. This is, of course, presupposing that the personality of the holy man, the ruler, or even an ordinary person is 'good', so that his influence also is good. In any case we are here concerned with a concept which comes out of quite another world and for which we have no equivalent.

Another written character which frequently occurs in philosophical writings, and which is most frequently rendered as 'element', but sometimes also as 'energy', is equally significant. Richard Wilhelm has translated this character as 'state of transformation'. The dualistic distinction between energy and matter is quite unknown to the Chinese, a fact which Granet too has brought out very clearly. Western translations up to now may be said to have corresponded to the dualistic universe of the mechanistic-scientific age. The progress of science in recent times and the resulting expansion of our own view of the universe help us today, even though it is little realized, to get a better understanding of the old Chinese conceptions.

There is no need to introduce at this point the word 'Tao', which is usually translated as 'way', 'meaning' or 'logos', since the meaning of this term even in China itself was subject to modifications in the course of history. But let us think, for example, of the Chinese 'Sin' (Japanese Shin, Kokoro), which, it is true, literally means 'heart', but which, when thus translated without qualification, can be most misleading. ('Sin' incidentally does not signify the physical heart; this latter is expressed by another character which however includes as a component the symbol for 'Sin'.) For us the concept 'Heart', if we employ it figuratively, always signifies something appertaining to feeling. For the East Asian, however, that is not always the case. 'Sin' means for him much rather consciousness or even centre, spirit or soul. If the East Asian wants to express anything pertaining to feeling, he does not talk of the heart but rather of the bowels. One's entrails for example are 'torn with grief' or 'tied in a hundred knots'. Yet almost every translator on reading in the Chinese 'My entrails are torn', renders this image with 'My heart breaks', for fear that his readers would otherwise not understand it or think it ridiculous. Through such renderings, however, the impression is unintentionally conveyed that the Chinese understand 'Heart' in the same way as we do.

It is customary, moreover, particularly for the East Asians themselves, to use the word 'God' where 'Heaven' or the 'Gods' occur in their texts. The Japanese in particular, when talking to foreigners, speak almost without exception about 'God' when in reality they mean their Gods or the Divine. In such cases there is no linguistic justification, since an exact translation is easily possible; but familiarity with a foreign language makes it easy to get into the habit of making superficial use of the concepts of that language.

This is only an extremely small selection from the wealth of expressions whose translation and understanding create extraordinary difficulties. It is, indeed, not a mere handful of Chinese written characters, but the great majority, which cannot be adequately or accurately rendered in European languages. Translations of Chinese classical writings can turn out to be so very different from each other that one might sometimes doubt whether these works were indeed based on the same originals.

NOTES

[1] Junyu Kitayama, *West-östliche Begegnung*.
[2] Ibid.
[3] Yoshiro Nagayo, 'Beauty in Contrast' (Contemporary Japan).
[4] Daisetz Suzuki, *Zen und die Kultur Japans*.
[5] Richard Wilhelm and C. G. Jung, *Das Geheimnis der Goldenen Blüte*.
[6] Jacob Burckhardt, *Weltgeschichtliche Betrachtungen*.
[7] C. G. Jung, *Psychologische Typen*.
[8] Ibid.
[9] About the ego Jung says: 'By "ego" I understand a complex of ideas which constitutes the centre of my field of consciousness and appears to me to possess a high degree of continuity and self-identity. Hence I also speak of an ego-complex. The ego-complex is as much a content as it is a condition of consciousness, since I am aware of a psychic element in so far as it is related to my ego-complex. But inasmuch as the ego is only the centre of my field of consciousness, it is not identical with the whole of my psyche, being merely one complex among others. I therefore distinguish between the ego and the Self, in that the ego is only the subject of my consciousness; the Self, that of my total psyche, which incorporates the unconscious . . .' C. G. Jung, *Psychologische Typen*.
[10] Op. cit.
[11] Alfred Weber, *Abschied von der bisherigen Geschichte*.
[12] C. G. Jung distinguishes between the extraverted culture of the Western mind (*abendländische Geisteskultur*) and the introverted culture of the Eastern mind (*Geisteskultur des Ostens*). Cf. *Die Beziehungen zwischen dem Ich und dem Unbewussten*.

Chapter 2

THOUGHT WITHOUT LOGIC

You do not have to stay long in East Asia to discover that the Chinese and Japanese on almost every occasion behave differently, feel and think differently from the way we would in the same situation. If we wish to obtain an idea of how the East Asians will react to any particular event, our best plan is to imagine what would be their most logical response, and to expect precisely the reverse. Those who set great store by logical thinking, or who hate contradictions, will not find themselves at home in East Asia. Whoever carries on a discussion with the Chinese, and tends to take seriously the rational and logical expression of his own views, need not be at all surprised if they regard him as an extremely limited sort of person. Educated Chinese admit nowadays that our mode of thought is suitable for explaining, say, an aero-engine; but to speak of human affairs in such a way appears to them simply puerile and primitive.

A Chinese can discourse for half an hour or so about the good qualities of the Communists, their modern ideas and their incorruptibility, and at the end he will arrive quite unperturbed at the 'conclusion' that he cannot stand the Communists and is in favour of Chiang Kai-shek. He can also assert that the Americans are now the most wonderful people and the leading nation of the world, and in the same sentence add the remark that he profoundly hopes that the Chinese will never sink to such depths as those very Americans whom he has just been praising. This does not mean that the Chinese has no opinion— such pronouncements often border on intellectual play, for the Chinese is fond of talking,—but it does mean that he is reluctant to form an over-hasty or superficial opinion, merely because it happens to be 'logical'. He has more respect for human affairs than we have and does not like to 'clear up' those matters which by reason of their nature or their state at the time are in fact changeable, unclear and ambiguous. By taking this view he often gets much closer to the truth than we do with our so-called clear conceptions.

Whoever conducts negotiations with Chinese or Japanese may readily despair, since he has the feeling that he is not making the least progress. After four weeks he can still be just as much in the dark about the intentions of the person with whom he is negotiating as he was on the first day.

*

Before we attempt to explain the East Asian mode of thought it is desirable to give some account of what has been said about it up to the present. The net result is, it is true, not very impressive, and if I should nevertheless quote the rather meagre pronouncements on the subject I do so not least because they all point in *one* direction. The most thorough exposition of Chinese thought which we possess is the work of Marcel Granet,[1] which has already been mentioned. What Granet offers us is a description, in minute detail, of the anti-causal and anti-conceptual Chinese way of thinking and of the thought forms resulting from it; in so doing he draws attention at the same time to the decisive significance of analogies and associations in the world of Chinese thought. Nevertheless, Granet does not go into the question of *why* the Chinese think in this manner and what are the psychological or other explanations of their mental attitude. In general, therefore, his work is more in the nature of a description than an explanation of the peculiar quality of the Chinese, and so of the East Asians.

Richard Wilhelm in his short *Chinese Philosophy*, describes thought in the age before Lao Tse and Confucius as 'pre-logical' and then, in treating the various philosophers, speaks frequently of 'magic thinking', of 'meditative absorption' and the 'mystical experience of oneness', just as he indicates the beginnings of discursive thought and those of the logical and dialectical kind. In our view, the fundamental difference in the nature of Chinese thought generally finds too little expression in this small book. Anyone who is not previously well aware of the deep gulf between the East Asian way of looking at things and our own might even get the impression from reading his work that the Chinese are after all in many respects very much like us, and thus fall into that very error against which Granet gives such clear warning. Other books, too, about East Asia, particularly those about China, often create this impression in the minds of people who have never been there. Thus it is hardly to be wondered at that philosophers, historians, sociologists and others who concern themselves with China should find themselves after all their efforts constantly faced with the 'puzzle' as to why these extremely intelligent, gifted and sensible Chinese have not developed any science and technology and no 'proper' philosophy, and why they are to such a large extent caught in the dark toils of necromancy.

The well-known Chinese writer Lin Yutang[2] explains, after his usual assaults upon logic and its uselessness, that the Chinese thinks in 'concrete analogies'. It seems to us that he is not quite correct in this, since the Chinese can employ abstract analogies just as well as concrete ones. (To be exact, the difference between abstract and concrete is by no means so sharp in East Asia.)

A description which really touches the heart of the matter, and is very much to the point, can be found in Keyserling's *Travel Diary of a Philosopher*. He is admittedly talking about Indians, but his findings are equally applicable to the East Asians. Keyserling says: 'The Westerner proceeds from thought to thought, inducing, deducing, differentiating, integrating; the Indian from state to state.'

The most extensive work on 'thought forms' is perhaps that of Leisegang,[3] who nevertheless, so far as East Asia is concerned, confines himself to a fairly brief mention of Lao Tse. Leisegang's exposition is of such fundamental importance that it is desirable to repeat it here at some length. It must be observed at the

3

outset that, in contrast to the usual practice, he equates 'logic' with 'method of thinking', and so does not understand by it only that method of thinking which is based on the thought laws inherent in rational thinking. In this book, however, we shall keep to the old concept of logic and would thus say: it is true that there are various thought forms and methods of thinking, but there is only one logic. Leisegang characterizes the 'circle of thought' process in the following way (the italics are mine):

I. The metaphysical soil from which this logic springs, the reality which it attempts to copy in the form of concepts, judgments and syllogisms, is the world of the mind, a world which coincides, however, with that of organic life. *Mind and Life are in essence the same.* The process of development of the mind is the same as the process of living. Life is taken in this context to be an independent force which concentrates itself in the seed, *emerges as an organism which gathers itself together again in its product, the seed, from which the new cycle begins.* Starting with the single organism, the basic idea is applied to the entirety of organic life in nature, then to mankind, and finally to the whole cosmos. So there originate these cycles of the development of the individual, of mankind, and the world, which run parallel to one another. The reproduction of this process in ideas and words leads to the logic peculiar to this form of thought.

II. LOGIC.

I. The concepts with which this system of logic operates in the main are no abstractions, no generic concepts, which embrace others, but those which bring to the fore the principal stages in the cycle of life and of the process of mind, particularly the beginning, the middle, the end: summer – winter; day – night; light – dark; one – all; spirit – flesh, and so on. *Each concept does not require other superimposed and subordinate concepts to make it understandable, but its diametric opposite.*

2. Judgments are arrived at by linking those concepts into a ring, in which A connects with Z, and Z is again linked to A; or, in those more complex chains of reasoning which involve more than two stages, A is linked to B, B to C, and so on until Z is again linked with A.

3. The process of proving is carried out by drawing the assertion which is to be proved into a closed ring of judgment, or by taking the assertion itself as a segment of a cycle and extending it, on the analogy of other rings of judgment, to form a complete circle of thought.[4]

To make things more easily understood one of Leisegang's diagrammatic illustrations is reproduced below. It illustrates the sentence of Heraclitus: 'Souls in death turn to water, but water turns in death to earth, but water out of earth comes, and out of water soul.'[5]

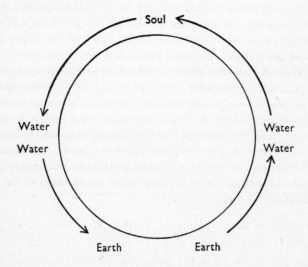

This illustration of cyclic thought applies equally well to East Asian thinking, in respect not only of the metaphysical basis but also of 'logic' and the forming of judgments. These explanations, however, are not sufficiently comprehensive to give the reader a real understanding of East Asian thought. We are not told, for example, how concepts are formed in this kind of thinking, concepts which Leisegang rightly describes as representing 'no abstractions, no generic concepts embracing others'. Neither is it explained how it is, in this kind of thinking, that the 'circles running parallel to one another', that is to say the analogies, necessarily come about. We can thus say that Leisegang's definition, as concerns East Asia, is accurate but incomplete.

Before daring to make our own attempt at describing Chinese thought, it is apposite to quote a further passage by C. G. Jung on the subject.

In the *Secret of the Golden Flower* which he edited in collaboration with Richard Wilhelm, he offers the following explanation, using the *I Ching*, the Book of Changes, as his starting point:

> The science of *I Ching* is based not on the principle of causality but on a principle which has not hitherto been given a name, since it does not occur with us; this principle I have attempted to designate as the *synchronistic principle*. My interest in the psychology of unconscious processes compelled me many years ago to cast about for another principle by which to explain things, since the principle of causality appeared to me to be inadequate for the purpose of explaining certain remarkable phenomena of unconscious psychology. I soon found, in fact, that there are parallel psychological phenomena which simply cannot be related causally to one another and must stand in some other relationship in the way they occur. This relationship seemed to me to be based essentially on the fact of relative simultaneity, hence the term 'synchronistic'.

This synchronistic principle applies, if I understand Jung correctly, rather to the thought content than the thought method, just as the causality principle was not the cause but the outcome of our thought. Of course, one might also put it this way: the Chinese discovered the synchronistic principle and the Westerners the causality principle, because they each possessed the corresponding thought forms. This explanation of Jung's, however, does not include any expression of his views on the East Asian thought process, and we shall therefore discuss the synchronistic principle at a later stage, in connection with the East Asian conception of things.

Jung's writings, incidentally, contain further isolated references to the East Asian mode of thought. For example, he makes the points that the Chinese concepts are 'not logical in our sense, but intuitive perceptions',[6] and that he suspects the great oriental philosophers of being 'symbolic psychologists, to whom one could do no greater injustice than to take them literally'—a remark which has received the express approval of Richard Wilhelm.[7]

In his psychology, however, Jung draws a distinction between extravert and introvert thought[8] and we must ask ourselves whether the latter does not coincide with the East Asian way of thinking.

Generally speaking, the antithesis between extravert Western culture and the introvert culture of East Asia holds good, but for want of suitable preliminary studies it is not yet possible to elaborate it thoroughly in all its aspects.

The terms 'extravert' and 'introvert' having up till now been applied only to Western man, introvert thought, interpreted in terms of our psychology, is essentially a Western concept. Whether extravert or introvert, the logic of thought remains unaltered, as Jung himself says.[9] It follows, therefore, that East Asian thought, which distinguishes itself by its totally different 'method of thinking', cannot be explained by those definitions of introvert thought which have been given us up to now.

The existing literature has provided us with the following distinctive attributes with which to characterize East Asian thought: magic, co-ordinating, analogizing, associative, cyclic, mystic, synchronistic. We gathered, moreover, that the East Asian, generally speaking, thinks neither logically, nor causally, nor analytically, nor architectonically. It was further mentioned that his mental activity progresses 'from state to state', that he thinks in written characters and allows himself to be led by them 'from the contemplation of one conceptual symbol to another'.

*

Where does it get us, then, this jumble of conceptions and terms, some of them philosophical, some psychological in origin?

Perhaps it is best to begin with the *total* character of this way of thinking, since this determines its other attributes.

Western thought, which has predominated in recent times, has direction; it is that type of thought which we define as directed thinking (active thought-activity, intellect). That part of our thought which is not directed (passive thought-activity, intellectual intuition) comes about in an irrational manner, but results, as the term 'intellectual intuition' testifies, in a comprehensible, intellectually palpable thought product. Which amounts to saying that this product is open to examination by directed thinking. But if we are concerned not with intellectual intuition but with intuition of a general kind, this latter sort, in the Western view, cannot in any way be classed as thought. Since *intellectual* intuition is thus also subject to the control of directed thought, we can state that our minds have been dominated in recent times by directed thought.

This thinking can be shown graphically as a straight line, thus:

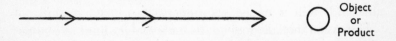

Object
or
Product

It would, indeed, be ideal if thought thus moved in a direct line (without obstacles) straight towards the object, the aim, or towards that product which emerges as the result of reflection. In such a case directed intellectual thought meets with success. This illustration applies in principle also to dialectic thought, which would also really follow a straight line, i.e. have a direction; in such a case, however, it would be necessary to visualize the straight line as provided with 'barbs' on both sides, representing thesis and antithesis (as in the diagram above).

The weaknesses of this kind of thought lie in the fact that the straight line which is prescribed by the laws of logic inherent in intellectual thinking, can either shoot past its target or be held up by obstacles. Diagrammatically it would look like this:

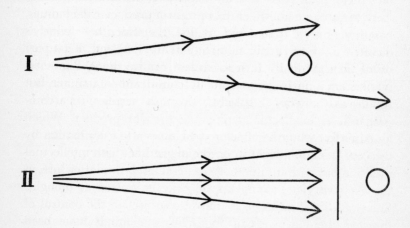

This kind of thinking is thus liable either to shoot past the object and pass on into infinity, that is to say to lose itself in fruitless speculation, or come up against obstacles which it is not sufficiently well equipped to surmount.

East Asian thought does not follow a straight line but consists of enveloping or encircling moves; shown diagrammatically, it appears something like this:

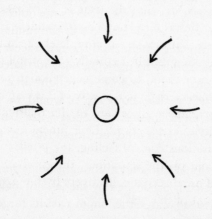

The East Asians at first make nothing more than small advances in no particular direction, and the arrows only then turn towards a definite centre, the aim or product of the thought, when they sense this centre. At first, therefore, there is only a cloud of arrows flying in all directions and following no pattern, until they gradually turn towards a central point. These advances are a mixture, psychically considered—partly intellectual, partly emotional, based partly on the senses and partly on the will.

A perfect example of such thinking is when all the arrows succeed in closing right in on the object like this:

In this case the object is not merely reached by the intellect or by feeling, but it is completely comprehended by the whole psyche. It is not enough, then, for only one or two arrows to hit the bull's-eye, for in such a case the object has not yet been completely attained.

This way of thinking possesses the advantage that one very quickly knows *roughly* what the issue is, but it also has the disadvantage that one rarely knows *exactly* what it is all about. It seldom happens that one shoots completely at random, as with intellectual thinking, but it is equally rare for all the arrows, or at least enough of them, to come near enough to the mark.

The chief characteristic of this way of thinking lies in the fact that it remains constantly aware of the relative value of the actions of individual functions. One function hereby controls the other; sensations control feeling, the intellect and the will, the intellect controls the sensations, the emotions the will and so on—and all are directed collectively by the psychical centre, the middle point of the 'self'.

From the physical point of view this centre is to be found, according to the East Asian conception, in the middle of the body, in the region of the navel. That is why it is not the head or the heart, nor even broad shoulders and strong arms which hold much significance for the East Asian, but for thousands of years it has been the middle of the body, the belly. Mental and physical strength are concentrated in this middle, and flow outwards from it. And that is why not only East Asian images of gods and of Buddha are frequently represented with a large paunch, but also the 'Sumo', the Japanese wrestlers, even nowadays cultivate such a paunch.

The East Asian does not think with the head, but with the belly. Just as the steady, firm movement of the brush or the sword thrust does not come from the heated brain, but rather from the 'Tandem', the centre of gravity of the body, so too do thoughts. In many meditational exercises the mental and physical attributes of the individual are combined in characteristic fashion, for the body is the repository of both the 'total' mind and of breathing. When air is inhaled, it is, in the East Asian conception, collected in the body and distributed from there to the very extremities. This is why cultivation of regular breathing has for ages been of such basic significance, for it serves to strengthen the belly and thus the entire man, including his mental powers.

'The custom of strengthening the abdominal portion of the human body is, spiritually speaking, what the Orientals call the training of the soul', says the Japanese, Yoshiro Nagayo,[10] who goes on to explain: 'If we put our whole emphasis on the brain in the sense of the word "intellect", the lower portion of the body would float in the air, our feet would be separated from the earth, our ideas would become abstract and our nerves would break down', thus, for the 'total' man and the 'total' thinker, the centre of the body is the most important area.

Now that we have tried to illustrate the pattern of the East Asian's thinking, certain peculiarities, which we observe in our dealings with East Asians or in their way of doing things, will be readily understood. We see now, for example, why they so often give vague information, and why it is so difficult to judge their decisions in advance. Where we would have a clearly developed piece of reasoning, a progressive train of thought, a clear concept, they often have nothing more than a misty picture composed of 'arrows'. In such cases the Japanese is in the habit of opening the conversation with a long-drawn 'Saa . . .', which means that he is not himself at all clear; while the Chinese utters a series of rapid phrases which similarly make it obvious that he has not yet formed any clear opinion on the subject. The lady who taught me Japanese in Tokyo once said despairingly, when I insisted on a more precise explanation of some Chinese character: 'Foreigners always want to know everything so exactly—we are different. We think rather in clouds'. My Chinese teacher in Chungking, when speaking of a written character, stated that I would have to 'feel' its meaning.

Whoever has spent any length of time in East Asia soon realizes that he must be patient and let things 'simmer'. Energetic enquiries and continual fresh arguments merely do harm, for they create turbulence in the 'cloud formation' and prevent the discharge of the small 'arrows'. It is scarcely possible to accelerate this way of thinking and forming decisions to any real extent, since reasoning and the will do not in fact play a major part in the process. Indeed, it is stated in the Li Chi:[11] 'If he (the noble one) has asked and has not clearly understood, he waits until the Master is at leisure, and observes his mood; then he repeats the question. If this time also he fails to get an answer, he does not attempt to elicit it by insisting.'

The result is that when a decision is finally reached, we get the impression of something sudden and unexpected. A historic example of East Asian uncertainty and surprisingly sudden resolution was the attack on Pearl Harbour. Those who assert that Japan had already decided months earlier to enter the war on Germany's side are being wise after the event; nor are they adhering to the facts of the case. That Hitler would precipitate a war could have been forecast with reasonable certainty—it

was the logical outcome of Western 'development'—but that
Japan would participate in this fashion remained uncertain up
to late autumn, 1941. Pearl Harbour surprised us in Tokyo just
as much as the Americans.[12]

And did not the unconditional capitulation of Japan in
August, 1945, come just as unexpectedly as the earlier attack?
Was not the world amazed that this ostensibly so heroic people
surrendered unconditionally to the enemy while millions of its
soldiers who had never fired a shot were still under arms?

The fact that East Asian thinking is not to be hurried by the
exercise of energy and will, does not mean that it takes longer
than ours in every case. While it can be slower, it can also be
quicker, according to the subject, the capacity and also the luck
of the thinker. Thus, the East Asians are superior to us in com-
bining different ideas and in assessing complex situations (cf.
p. 273 *et seq.*). The East Asian mode is well illustrated, too, by
the traditional forms of Japanese sport such as fencing[13] and, in
particular, 'Sumo', a type of wrestling similar to the Swiss and
Icelandic varieties. The Japanese wrestlers do not immediately
attack one another when they are given the signal to begin, but
usually stand facing each other for some time and observe each
other closely. In the past it sometimes happened that both the
Sumo watched one another for as long as two hours without
a move, but nowadays the time limit is fixed at twenty minutes
for the spectators' sake and for practical reasons of business.
Sometimes, but only rarely, it happens that the wrestlers at once
get to grips with great speed. What is the reason for these tactics
which seem so strange to the foreigner? The wrestler waits for
the moment when, with gathered strength and in a state of inner
preparedness, and therefore with full concentration of body and
soul, he feels himself ready to attack; at the same time he tries to
discover a moment when his opponent is weak. The key to the
situation lies in the fact that a wrestler will only attack just after
inhaling, when he is in every respect most completely equipped
for action; conversely, he seeks to engage his opponent when the
latter is breathing out. Because of this extreme concentration on

the moment of attack, the fight is often settled in an instant. It is the fighting method of the total man, who undertakes something important only when he is fully concentrating on the matter in hand, with every fibre of his being, body and soul; in just the same way as he only comes 'to a conclusion' in his thinking, when all the small arrows have closed on the object. This, too, explains the contrast between uneasy quiet and concentrated action, which characterizes the old East Asian forms of sport. The exercises in concentration and meditation which used to be practised by East Asian artists and craftsmen—also by warriors in Japan before the start of battle—are based on the same peculiar habit of mind, the wish to produce a state of 'total' readiness.

*

Before returning to our description of East Asian thought, we propose to examine briefly whether the 'new thought form' which is now being talked about in scientific circles and which is regarded as a revolutionary departure from tradition, possesses some particular affinity to the East Asian way of thinking. The new mode of thought is based on the complementary principle, that is to say, on the fact that two diametrically opposed statements can be made about the same thing, both of which can be proved and are correct. The famous Danish scientist Niels Bohr was one of the first who, working on the basis of the modern quantum theory, established that 'between the space-time definitions on the one hand and the laws of causality on the other, there exists a complementary relationship of such a kind that each limits the validity of the other'.[14]

P. Jordan[15] speaks of the 'replacement of thinking in objective processes by the new complemental thought form', and K. von Neergaard[16] explains: 'only those descriptions which amplify each other in complementary fashion correspond to full reality or at least to a large segment of it. This modern thinking in physics—and it is already penetrating medicine too—is a profound experience for anyone who goes through it. It is a kind of thinking which is only seemingly of less precision and which is of incomparably greater elasticity and depth. Therein lies a possibility, by no means unimportant, of defeating the fateful, even deadly, doctrine of Relativism.'

We do not yet, however, regard these statements strictly speaking as a new way of thinking based on the complemental principle, but merely as confirming the existence of complementary factors. What, then, has really happened? The contradictions—now called complementary factors—were discovered by physics on the basis of calculations and experiments which quite naturally adhered strictly to the 'old' scientific logic and the causal principle. In other words, pure mathematics, logic and causality, consequentially applied, produced results which could no longer be understood in their own terms. We were thus faced with new results of our researches, which could no longer be comprehended by the old method of thinking. And so there arose, inevitably, the necessity of looking for another interpretation. Since the contradictions supplemented one another, it followed that reality was built up on the complementary principle. From this idea there developed a new scientific attitude which regards things *a priori* as complementary. But is this a new way of thinking? It is established that 'it' is so, but nobody can explain *what* is so, or why. Merely to establish the new set of facts neither requires, nor has required, a new way of thinking; this only becomes necessary if we ask what the complementary principle really states and what it is about. This question cannot any longer be answered by mathematics, by logical thinking or experiments, but only by—'philosophy' (in the broadest sense). In answering this question philosophy will, of course, make just as little progress as science, if it relies on the traditional logical and rational way of thinking. Otherwise we would be able to grasp the complementary principle, as hitherto, merely in a formal sense but not its content and meaning. This new mode of thought, which Jordan and Neergaard doubtless had in mind, is, however, as yet in its early stages; this is entirely new territory.

We are inclined to think that this mode of thought will prove to be 'total' in kind and resemble East Asian thought in structure. In making this supposition we rely above all on the fact that intellectual thought in the form of science has given proof that it will never be *able* to resolve the existing conflicts. According to the statements of leading investigators these logically produced contradictions *must* persist, or our whole scientific system is quite untenable.[17] Thus, if we look at the problem scientifically and not philosophically in the wider sense, it will never be possible in atomic physics to work otherwise than simultaneously or alternately with the wave idea *and* the particle idea. Other procedures are by reason of the structure of 'reality' and human thought, not only impossible but unthinkable.

If science itself proves that such contradictions must persist, then there is good reason to look about for a way of thinking which will help to interpret the results of modern research. Apart from our own—the thought form of highly differentiated Western man—we know of only one other mode of thought which is prominent and still alive today: that total way of thinking which is represented by the East Asians, and in a kindred sense also by the Indians. It is neither desirable, nor is it possible for psychological reasons, for us to turn our backs completely on our traditional way of thinking, but we should endeavour to set limits to it, and, venturing beyond these, to foster the 'total' element in ourselves, which we have neglected up to now. Of the problems arising out of such a synthesis we shall have something more to say towards the end of this book. At all events, efforts spent on maintaining the primacy of directed rational thought in all circumstances, and, when this type of thought does not manage to provide an explanation, on dragging in religion as a stop-gap, strike us as most unsatisfactory. This is little more than an attempt to evade the real problems. We must understand, for example, that feeling and intellect are not contrasts but 'complementary' functions—merely two ways of looking at one and the same thing. The ultimate principle, whether we call it God, the Absolute, or Buddha, cannot be fully comprehended or felt by one function alone, but only by the psychical totality of man.

When K. von Neergaard says the new way of thinking is 'seemingly of less precision, but of incomparably greater elasticity and depth' than our traditional way of thinking, he probably means to suggest that the admittedly often inexact formulations of modern physicists approach more closely to the truth than the earlier mechanistic pronouncements which, though they may have been exact, did not on that very account correspond to reality. Presumably Neergaard is thinking not merely of the complementary findings which result, for example, from the double nature of light and matter, or rather, as Jeans[18] calls them, the 'ghostly remains of matter', but also of the other imprecise statements of physics, particularly the new quantum theory. Weizsäcker explains that the quantum theory, in the formally logical view, 'employs several values of truth concepts, when in addition to the attributes "true" and "false" a statement can have the attribute "undetermined, and in fact with such and such a probability of being true".' From Weizsäcker's premises,[19] then, if 'A' is taken to represent a statement on a particular set of circumstances, we can reach such a conclusion as: 'Neither is A valid, nor is A invalid'. Also, with regard to the classical question about the finite or infinite nature of the world, science formulates occasionally such paradoxical statements as, for example: 'The world is not really finite, neither is it, on the other hand, really infinite.'[20]

Neergaard's words about 'seeming lack of precision' and 'the greater depth' could apply equally well to East Asian thought. Moreover, there is a striking and unmistakable similarity between the statements quoted above and common Chinese turns of speech, such as 'A is not right, but he is also not wrong'. Unmistakable, too, is the similarity to one of the innumerable sayings of the oriental sages, for example the Zen-Buddhist observation: 'All that exists is as it is, but it is at the same time void, it is neither real nor is it unreal.'[21]

Thus we are concerned in both cases with imprecise and paradoxical statements, but now we come to the interesting point: whereas in the first case it is a matter of drawing the final conclusion from formally logical premises, in the latter case it is a question of the results of a total view of things and total thinking. Modern physics arrives at these conclusions from the outside, the East Asian from the inside. Proceeding from plurality, modern physics thus finds itself faced with an incomprehensible unity and is compelled to make paradoxical statements about it, while the East Asian, proceeding from unity, has known for a very long time that it is not possible to make other than paradoxical statements about unity. It is perhaps therein that the deeper reason for our interest in East Asia is to be found, since we are here concerned with people who have never lost, and have never ceased to think about, that unity and totality which we are now on the point of rediscovering.

*

The East Asian mode of thought finds peculiarly characteristic expression in meditational exercises, the practice of which can be traced back to remotest antiquity and thus to a time much earlier than the introduction of Buddhism. The ultimate aim of these exercises was the attainment of a state of mystical union, of higher transcendental consciousness, and they cannot for this reason be equated in every case with those exercises practised in the Christian religion which are similarly called 'meditation'. The concentration-exercises of the present-day Catholic Church, particularly, for example, those practised by the Jesuits, do not serve to promote revelation and illumination, but rather the strengthening of faith and the will. The deeper possibilities of meditation are, it is true, occasionally explored in the West, but not as a general rule nor in a systematic way.

Whereas prayer is a primary feature of the Christian religion (if not in theory, at least in practice), meditation similarly characterizes East Asian religions. Viewed psychologically, this shows the difference between the religiosity of the 'divided', 'unintegrated' type of man and that of the 'total' type, for prayer has a strong emotional element, which explains references to 'fervent' prayer, while in the East meditation is a matter of total contemplation. Naturally, other conceptions as to the function of prayer have persisted in the West (the Roman Church, Thomas Aquinas), but let us not forget that we are here primarily concerned with the elaboration of the ways in which the dominant features of cultures differ from one another. Thus it can generally be said: we think *or* feel, we philosophize *or* pray, while the East Asian tries to combine the two.

Methods of meditation which can also be rightly called the 'technique of mysticism' need not be described by us here; we are mainly interested in drawing attention to the total character of these exercises. Let us cite a few examples to bring out our point.

We begin with the *Secret of the Golden Flower*,[22] a Chinese introduction to meditation, from which we quote some passages concerning the elimination of the consciousness and the vitalization of the original spirit. It is particularly emphasized that the way must be found from 'conscious action to unconscious inaction'. 'If you wish to preserve the original spirit, you must first subdue utterly the power of the intellect' and thus 'forget both body and heart'.[23] The following is said of the disturbing influence of 'reflection':

> Fixed contemplation is essential; it serves to confirm illumination. You must not remain rigidly seated when worldly thoughts break in upon you, but you must try to find out where this thought occurs, where it originated, where it fades away. By further pursuing reflection you do not come to an end. You must confine yourself to seeing whence this thought emerged, and you should not look beyond the point of origin; for you cannot consciously succeed in discovering the Heart (i.e. getting beyond consciousness with the aid of consciousness). Let us all bring the heart to a state of peace: that is true contemplation. . . . If the flight of your thoughts still continues without ceasing, you should stop and then resume

4

contemplation. You must contemplate, and then resume fixation. That is the two-fold culture of confirmation and illumination of the spirit.

Emphatic warning is also given against the dangers of indulging in fantasies while meditating, for 'that is the world of demons'.

There is the case, for example, when you sit down to meditate and see flames of light or many colours appearing, or see Bodhisattvas or gods approaching and other such fantasies. . . . Or, when you have sat for a long while, the images crowd in upon you, and you want to stop them, and cannot; you let yourself be carried along by them and feel lighter. In such cases you should not in any circumstances continue with your meditation, but you must stand up and walk about for a while, until your strength and your heart are once again in harmony; only then may you sit down again to meditate.

It is constantly stressed that nothing can be achieved by energy and the will; 'I do not say that you should make no effort, but the correct attitude is midway between being and non-being; if you purposely achieve purposelessness, then you have succeeded'. Absolute mastery, even mortification, of 'body and heart', of intellect, fantasy and the will is demanded so as to render possible concentration on the source of strength, the light, so that the 'Golden Flower' (a symbol of the 'transcendent great Oneness') becomes visible.

By meditating thus, the core of man, his inmost self, experiences and thinks, having cast off all psychical functions.

*

Lao Tse, Chuang Tse and many other Chinese sages and thinkers, as well as most Chinese and Japanese Buddhists, gained their wisdom from such mystic meditation. The way of thinking of the other East Asian philosophers, who did not lay the main emphasis on such exercises in concentration, is, however, also closely akin to this kind of mystic contemplation.

The assertion that Confucius was at heart a mystic admittedly sounds rather strange, but it is correct to say that he, too, thought mystically; that is, in a 'total' manner. Confucius' main interest was not in metaphysical and psychological revelations, but he showed great respect for Lao Tse and other mystics, and he himself did on occasion recommend meditational exercises.[24] In Confucius we see the greatest representative of that type of total thinker whose thoughts are directed especially towards practical and active living. It is almost unnecessary to point out that, in contrast to the Western philosophers, he has initiated no 'system', and that his teachings cannot be comprehended in a purely rational way. We used to consider him rational only because we were hardly capable of thinking of, or comprehending anything as being other than rational, and because many mistakes crept into the translations of his teachings on account of this preconception of ours.

What mattered to him was not knowledge or the development of abilities and skills but rather the state of the soul, and this is constantly emphasized in East Asia even today. This is the prerequisite for that existential mastery for which the East Asians have always striven. That is why we come across the thought time and again in Confucius, and later on especially among the Japanese, that man can only realize himself by 'doing'. This doing, however, could never result in activity for activity's sake, since it was only required in so far as it served to develop personality. According to the teachings of Confucius, and according to the Chinese view in general, man is intended to realize by activity not only himself but also the cosmic laws. That comes about when man acts aright; he then stands in harmony with the cosmos.

The total view is perhaps most consciously and most pronouncedly cultivated at the present day by Japanese Zen-Buddhism, which came originally from China (where it is called 'Chang'). Most of the other Chinese and Japanese Buddhist Sects also cultivate meditation, and lay stress on this kind of religious experience and thought; in no case, however, in such pure form as the followers of Zen-Buddhism. The Zen sects dispense entirely with books, dogmas and teachings, and merely try to help their followers by means of direction on meditation, so that they may reach the core of knowledge, the 'confluent experience of universal oneness'.[25] In the Zen contemplations it is usual to impose a paradoxical meditational exercise. Here is an example:

> A monk once asked the master Ummon: 'What is the purest form of truth?' Ummon replied: 'The hedge around the closet.' The monk asked further: 'How did it then come to that?' Ummon replied: 'As a shining golden Lion.'

These paradoxes are explained by Glasenapp[26] in the following way:

> The intention here is to show that the absolute is superior to all contrasts, and embraces alike what is most pure and what is most filthy. The golden lion symbolizes the leaping strength of truth, which is so powerful that it is able to take all contrasts within its embrace.

The Zen-Buddhists distinguish between Ushin, 'present heart' and Mushin, 'no-heart'.[27] (It is worth recalling in this connection that for the East Asians heart does not denote 'feeling' so much as consciousness, cf. p. 21.) Daisetz Suzuki says in this connection:

> If you are possessed by certain thoughts, then your heart is to that extent closed to other thoughts. If you are occupied, then you can neither hear nor see anything, but if you keep your heart empty, that is to say open, then you can take in everything which approaches you—that is what is called Mushin. If, however, you are only concerned with keeping your heart empty, this very condition of your heart will prevent you from realizing Mushin or the original heart. Herein lies the difficulty of attaining the state of no-heart. But when your practising reaches maturity, it comes about of its own accord. You cannot hasten this state of Mushin. As an old poem has it: 'Being mindful of not-thinking is thinking nevertheless. O that I were now beyond thinking and not-thinking!'

Zen, says Suzuki,[28] tries to achieve 'Prajna and Karuna'. Prajna and Karuna are Sanskrit terms; Prajna can be translated as transcendental knowledge, and Karuna as 'love' or 'compassion'. Whoever has acquired Prajna through enlightenment will, according to the Zen teachings, understand how to act aright. The Zen meditations have thus always been also a preparation for inner composure, for inner preparedness, for any kind of action. Herein lies the very reason for the exceptional success of the Zen Schools. Zen is, as Kitayama[29] says, a religion of action, for 'thinking and doing are one'. It is a method of 'getting the world in the right key'. Daisetz Suzuki[30] expresses it in this way: 'From the absolute void there springs the most wonderful unfolding of action.'

Not only priests and monks take part in the Zen exercises, but also many laymen who wish to study the methods of concentration. In Japan, particularly during the last war, these attracted large numbers from all sections of the population. This was mainly a patriotic urge; there was a need to compose and fortify oneself for the hard tasks of the war years. 'Asian self-realization', of which there was much talk from the time of the 'Manchurian Incident' (1931–2) onwards, also played a considerable part in this. Meditation was quite consciously felt to be a traditional and suitable form for this Asian return to the self. Not only officers, businessmen and ministers of state, but also postal officials, shop assistants, railwaymen, young schoolboys and many others, meditated. It went so far that even in training establishments, schools and also in many factories and other concerns a short period was set aside in the mornings for 'meditation' (of course not necessarily of a Zen-Buddhist kind!)

Zen meditations, or rather the exercises for learning successful meditation, generally take place communally in large halls, and the priests walk about and rouse those who have fallen asleep— and there are not a few of these—with vigorous shakes. Those who are meditating sit on the floor with their legs crossed; the eyes are open, the mouth is shut, and the tongue should lie against the roof of the mouth. Peaceful, light and regular breathing is of great importance, as is always the case with these exercises. Many, however, do not make much progress, many do not even achieve a state of true inner composure. The opponents of Zen (above all, *other* Buddhist sects), asserted as far back as the thirteenth century, that 'they just doze in their seats and think depraved wanton thoughts'.[31]

Even today you very often get a like impression. If you hear, for example, that the wealthy industrialist X has had a special pavilion built in his garden so that he may withdraw to it in the mornings for meditation, there arises the just suspicion that the great man goes there to think about business matters, about the education of his wayward son or the problem of how he may yet manage to finance the new Geisha with whom he has just become acquainted. Nevertheless, the method remains to all intents and purposes the same: composure with outward and inward peace in order to reflect on something. We should never lose sight of the fact, moreover, that even the 'reflection' of this business man is conducted in the East Asian manner already described; it is never purely a matter of mere rational cogitation.

Knowledge gained through 'total' thinking can rarely be explained rationally and is sometimes even quite impossible to express, or can at best be suggested by means of paradoxes. This knowledge consists, for the greater part, of total concepts, ideas in the fuller sense of the word, or symbols and images. Nevertheless it is conscious knowledge or preceptions with which we are here concerned (cf. our definition of consciousness, p. 17ff.).

The Buddhist thinkers resemble their Taoist counterparts in the brevity of their utterances. Anyone who has taken an interest in Buddhism will already be aware, through the Indian versions, of the sparse messages or the complete silence. In East Asia, as we have already hinted, the Zen sects in particular are characterized by their silence. This tradition is traced directly back to Buddha.

Gundert[32] says of it:

> An anecdote which describes in characteristic fashion the inception, and at the same time essential features of the Zen schools, and which was first recorded in Tang about the year 800, serves our purpose: Buddha sat surrounded by his pupils and silently turned a flower between his fingers. They all looked at him with a questioning expression, except for Kasyapas over whose face there passed a gentle smile. Then the exalted one said: 'The complete possession of truth fully perceived, the impalpable spirit of Nirvana, is mine. This do I give into Kasyapas' keeping'.
>
> This is 'the transmission from spirit to spirit' on which the whole Zen tradition is based. Dogma is discounted by it; its 'tradition lies apart from the teaching of schools'. For did not the Buddha himself, after forty years of preaching, explain when trying to affirm the uselessness of all instruction, that he had never spoken a word since his enlightenment . . .?

The *Book of Changes*[33] contains a revealing passage which reflects the old Chinese conception of the possibility of transmitting knowledge:

> The Master said: 'Writing cannot fully express words. Words cannot fully express thoughts.' Can one then not see the thoughts of the holy men and sages? The Master said: 'The holy men and sages recorded the images in order to express their thoughts completely, they made signs so as to express completely the true and the false. They then added their judgments and were thus able to express themselves in words completely.'

So here we find a positive view of the possibility of expression; and this possibility is in fact seen in the interplay of three factors: images, signs and judgments (words). 'Signs' are here intended to mean those symbols composed of whole and broken lines, which form the basis of the philosophy and the oracle of the I Ching.[34] And so images and symbols are here regarded as the original and basic means of expression, while judgments are included as amplification.

Naturally, therefore, particular stress is laid, in the I Ching and other ancient Chinese writings, on the idea that all culture had its origin in images, or as one might say, 'primal idea-images'. 'The discoveries of the various instruments of culture were not ascribed to clever reflection, but were traced back to original cosmic situations understood in a religious sense.' So we read, for example, in the I Ching:[35]

> When at the beginning of time, Pao Hsi ruled the world, he looked up and regarded the images in the sky, looked down and regarded events on earth. He considered the patterns on birds and animals and how they were adapted to their surroundings. He proceeded directly from his own self and indirectly from external objects. Thus he invented the Eight Signs (i.e. the hexagram of I Ching), so that he might become associated with the virtues of the bright gods and order the conditions of all living things.

Goethe[36] has left us a description of the 'pure contemplation' so closely related to the total mode of thought, and his description applies remarkably well to the East Asians. He says that 'pure contemplation of the outward and inward' is 'very rare', and that it expresses itself 'symbolically, principally in mathematics, in numbers and formulae, in speech originally, tropologically, as poetry of genius, as the proverbial wisdom of the human mind'. We have already observed that the Chinese express themselves symbolically; 'mathematics, in numbers and formulae' corresponds to the highly developed East Asian mysticism of numbers. Who does not recall, on reading the words 'in speech originally, tropologically', of Lao Tse and other sages ('tropologically' from 'trope', i.e. 'figurative expression')? And who does not think, on reading the expressions 'poetry of genius' and 'proverbial wisdom of the human mind', of the many short poems, the fragmentary notes, pages of diaries and aphorisms of the Chinese, who are so fond of recording their wisdom in this way? There is no need for irritation at the word 'mathematics'. It is here employed because it is conceived as a play of symbols and not as a logical science.

*

How, we must now ask, does the East Asian proceed with the products of his thought, with the ideas he has acquired? How are these views elaborated by total thinking?

Up to now we have proceeded from the contrast between directed thought moving in a straight line and thought based on envelopment. It is now necessary to explain more precisely the differences resulting from this basic dissimilarity. Thought in a straight line moves on from point to point; it cannot comprehend the whole at once, but only its individual parts. It is a 'one-way thought' which has to penetrate everywhere before it can build a picture of the whole. In other words, this kind of thought must start by analysing. After the process of analysis is finished, this thought reconstructs the whole from its various parts. In this sense it can also be called an architectonic, constructive kind of thinking. This mode of thinking is dangerous in that it overlooks the fact that the whole differs from the sum of the parts.

Thought based on envelopment first sees the whole, and the parts only subsequently find their place in this whole. In this kind of thinking every part belonging to the whole, the whole being already comprehended, must quite automatically have its place or its function in it. It is not necessary to analyse the details, for they are indeed already seen in their inter-relationship. The parts are allotted their respective places without analysis. It is thought of a synthetic kind.

How, then, does it come about that the parts are arranged within the whole? In the first place there was the whole, i.e. the idea and laws of the whole. The individual part, however, since it belongs to the whole, cannot conflict with the idea and the laws of the whole. It must have as its basis the same idea. In this way the idea and the law of the whole are conferred upon the parts.

There is no analysis before the analogy comes to be applied; nor is there, as in straight line thinking, any deduction or induction on the basis of analytical findings. Consequently no attempt is made to discover whether the idea and law of the component part in fact correspond to those of the whole, and so analogizing proceeds unchecked by criticism.

Here are a few more examples of thinking in analogies. The four prime attributes of heaven (creative, all-pervasive, generous and unshakable) have been equated for ages past with the four cardinal virtues of man. The *Book of Changes* has this to say on the subject:

> Creative power is the chief quality of natural goodness: the noble person embodies human love and can thereby become the most exalted among men. The totality of the excellent one is all-pervasive; the noble person combines so much excellence in himself that this excellence conforms to the rules of life and good behaviour. Generosity is the harmonious combination of the duties of life; the noble person has such a beneficial effect on creatures, that he combines the duties of life in a harmonious way. Unshakableness is the firm foundation of all doing; the noble person is unshakably firm, and that is why he can accomplish things. The noble one behaves in accordance with these four qualities; that is why (in the *Book of Changes*) reference is made to the creative, all-pervasive, generous and unshakable.

We need only remember that the Tao (way, meaning or logos) of heaven is identified with the Tao of man, or that, according to the Chinese conception, the odd numbers correspond to the heavenly powers and the even numbers to the earthly ones. This is carried so far that the following explanation is given in a Chinese text: 'It is these numbers with which the universe brings about changes and sets in motion the Kwei and the Sen (the evil and the good spirits).'

Not only single concepts, however, are related by analogy, but whole series of concepts or, more exactly, series of symbols which are felt to be analogous. In this way whole chains of associations or co-ordinations are formed. The points of the compass and the seasons of the year provide, as a rule, the basis for such associations. One of the best known is this:

East	Spring	Green	Dragon
South	Summer	Red	Phoenix
West	Autumn	White	Tiger
North	Winter	Black	Tortoise.

Here, then, the points of the compass and seasons are related to colours and symbolic animals. The following table, according to de Groot,[37] gives 'the whole basis of Chinese pathology and medicine':

East	Spring	Wind	Wood	Sour	Liver	Muscles and Heart	Anger
South	Summer	Warmth	Fire	Bitter	Heart	Blood and Spleen	Joy
Middle		Moisture	Earth	Sweet	Spleen	Flesh and Lungs	Thought
West	Autumn	Dryness	Metal	Sharp	Lungs	Skin, Hair and Kidneys	Care
North	Winter	Cold	Water	Salty	Kidneys	Bones and Marrow	Fear

The peculiar quality of Chinese thought, in particular the uncritical employment of analogies, finds vivid expression in this table. I therefore quote what de Groot has said of it by way of explanation:

The effect on man of the fivefold breath of the world Tao here sketched out, is called by the Chinese 'the rotation in five phases' or the 'cycle of breathing', and this is because the seasons, to which they correspond, are the annual cycle of Yang and Yen. The principle of the healing art has always been recognized as lying in this effect. . . . These influences are introduced into the human body by ingenious inhaling, and these then ensure, according to the season of the year, the health of the corresponding limbs and vital organs. In this elaboration yet more ancient lore and wisdom was dragged in, more especially the teaching that the five elements (or states of transformation—Author's note) affect one another partly in a destructive, partly in a creative sense; wood, for example, produces fire and conquers earth; fire produces earth (ashes) and conquers metal; earth produces metal and conquers water, and so on. The other factors contained in the table influence one another in a similar manner. Consequently, if one knows how to link all the factors of the macrocosm with those of the human microcosm in a sensible fashion and make shrewd use of their various combinations, it is by no means difficult to decide on the correct diagnosis for any illness and to get at the precise seat of the trouble or, in other words, to employ Chinese phraseology, to discover the organ which has been attacked by influences which are contrary to Tao. The diet of the patient, moreover, can be regulated according to the five types of taste . . .

Another authority on China, Marcel Granet,[38] has the following to say concerning ancient Chinese medicine:

Rien de plus raisonnable, pour un malade, que d'appeler en consultation un médecin disert et un sage fort en histoire. La physiologie et l'hygiène ou la morale se confondent avec la physique,—ou plutôt avec l'histoire, c'est-à-dire avec l'art du Calendrier; l'anatomie et la psychologie ou la logique se confondent avec la cosmographie, la géographie ou la politique. . . . Géomancie et calendrier, morphologie et physiologie communes au macrocosme et aux microcosmes, voilà le savoir total et l'unique règle.

In repeating the critical statements of de Groot and Granet concerning the philosophic basis of Chinese medicine (we are here concerned with the views, not of doctors, but of sinologues!), it is by no means my intention to make all Chinese medical practice appear senseless or even primitive.

The Chinese have acquired valuable experience in this field and worked out successful methods of healing which have aroused increasing interest in Western medical and pharmaceutical circles. In other words, 'cosmic' foundations are not so utterly 'wrong' as might appear from the table at a first glance; they are probably neither more nor less assailable than the ideas of our academic medical science have been up to now. Intelligent treatment of man and his illnesses is doubtless not possible without a good measure of 'total' thinking.

*

Total man, who sees something at once harmonious and organic in the world, feels a need to present the various series and combinations in a definitive and self-contained form. Since he thinks organically, he regards the changes as analogous to the cycle of the seasons, and to that of life.

Most of his association sequences can therefore be made to conform to circles. Here, for instance, is reproduced an old cyclic representation[39] of the 'nine points of the heavens':

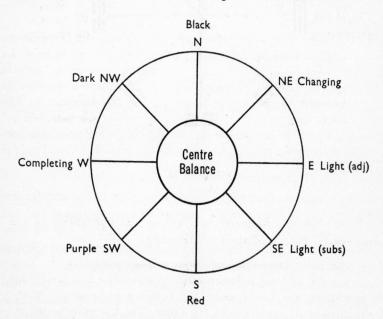

The following diagram is an arrangement on the basis of data given in the *Book of Changes*.[40] (This is only one of the possible arrangements. There are various others.) Here the south is shown at the top, as it is in most Chinese illustrations. The eight signs, which consist partly of whole, partly of broken lines, are, as has already been mentioned, the basic symbols of the I Ching. Their Chinese designations are omitted.

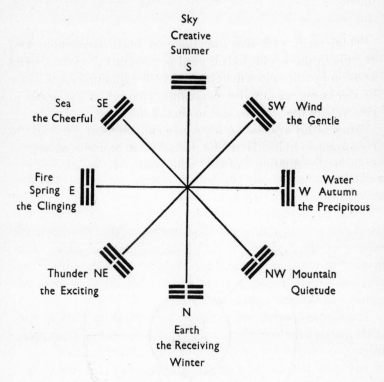

In the *Book of Manners*[41] we find an old description of the successive phases and their relationships:

The five changeable conditions exhaust themselves by their movement and succeed each other in turn. The five changeable conditions, the four seasons, the twelve months form a cycle, in that each emerges from the other. The five sounds, the six tubes, the twelve pipes provide the key-note in that order. The five types of taste, the six ways of cooking, the twelve sorts of food form in sequence the basis of meals. The five colours, the sixfold variegations, the twelve kinds of dress form in sequence the basis of clothing. Man is therefore the heart of heaven and earth and the germ of the five changeable conditions. He is fed by their taste, he clothes himself in their colours, he distinguishes their sounds, and lives by these things. In proclaiming his laws, therefore, the holy person constantly takes heaven and earth as his basis. . . .

We thus find, in accordance with Leisegang's definition, that the formation of cycles is an essential feature of East Asian thought. If concepts can be introduced into a cycle by the creation of analogies it is then 'proven' that they stand in their appointed place.

It is, therefore, right to regard the East Asians as 'thinkers in cycles'; we nevertheless prefer the expression 'total thinker', since this designation is more comprehensive and its fundamental structure, in the psychological sense, is suggested at the same time.

Much has already been said in the way of observations on the Chinese script and its relationship to the thought and culture of the Chinese. It seems to us, however, that their manner of writing is often regarded right from the outset too much as something independent and too little as a product and element in Chinese culture as a whole.

The Chinese script was probably created as far back as the latter part of the second millennium B.C., and has since been subject to certain changes, none of which have probably been of any very far-reaching consequence during historical time. It is better to talk of written 'signs' or 'characters', than of 'symbols', as is so often done. The symbol is the chosen expression, the best possible description or formula for a relatively unknown fact recognized or postulated as existing. With the sign, on the other hand, the chosen expression is intended to do little more than reproduce the simplified and abbreviated designation of a known fact. (In this sense the winged-wheel badge of the railway employee is not a symbol but a sign.)

It is also incorrect to talk of a picture-writing. Admittedly it was one in its earliest beginnings, but it had already largely lost this character at the beginning of historical time. Nowadays the written characters give expression to Chinese concepts which consist, however, not only of images and symbols but also of ideas in the fullest sense of the word. While it is thus incorrect to speak merely of written symbols or of a picture-writing, it can be fairly stated that this script *can* have a pictorial and symbolic character. The essential feature of these written characters lies in the fact that they represent entire words and not letters or syllables. The fundamental nature of this word-script is determined by the monosyllabic character of the Chinese language. Of the way in which the Japanese, whose language is polysyllabic, succeeded in dealing with this script, we shall have more to say later on.

The statement that the written characters represent Chinese concepts must be given greater precision by pointing out that in reality *only* the script and not the spoken word gives these concepts expression. What is the reason for this? Throughout historical time the characters have remained almost unchanged; for nearly three thousand years, their peculiar complexity and picturesqueness has remained unaltered. The spoken word, or the word written in syllables is fleeting; I can therefore work upon its meaning in an etymological fashion but not in such a concrete way as with the Chinese written characters.

It is here a question of an 'ideographic, as opposed to a scientific' use of the word. This ideographic use 'lacks the collateral security which lies in the discursive reference'.[42] The author of these words draws attention to the observation, so apposite from our own point of view, that according to Plotinus the Egyptian ideograms were more suitable for expressing intuitive knowledge than the letter characters. The East Asians, whether consciously or unconsciously are of the same view, and that is the deeper reason why they do not give up their script although they feel it at the present time as a most serious encumbrance.

Most peoples began to put down their thoughts in writing by using a kind of runic-pictorial script. From such beginnings the Western peoples developed syllabic scripts, the Chinese, however, a word script. The profoundly 'total' Chinese, indeed, took fright from the outset at the very idea of dissecting or analysing pictures which had been seen as such, and then put down in writing with such a strong element of draughtsmanship. Goethe's saying[43] that 'image and word are correlates which are forever seeking each other', is most apt in this instance.

Since the Chinese kept to the original written images and created no new writing by adopting the analytical approach, they had no choice but to extend their mode of writing in a synthetic fashion as their culture advanced. The old picture-signs soon sufficed no longer. It was necessary to find further signs for new philosophic and religious views, concepts and ideas; for new things in the arts and crafts, and in everyday life. To this end, the old picture-signs were constantly being put together in different ways, so that the signs used nowadays usually consist of two or three, and frequently, too, of four or more of the old signs. (As this went on, the original character of the signs came to be so modified by simplifications, writing habits and practical requirements, that the old pictorial sense can in most cases hardly be recognized.) As this process continued, the old signs were employed not only according to their sense but also according to phonetic principles. The word 'cypress', Chinese 'pe' is a good example. The character for this word is composed of the sign for 'tree' and that for 'white' which is also pronounced 'pe'. (Quite often in place of the sign for 'white', that for 'hundred' is used, and this is also 'pe'.) In other words: this character denotes a tree which is called 'pe'. Therefore the character for 'pe'—whether it is the one for white or that for a hundred—is used, not on account of its meaning but because of its sound. In this way something like 10,000 written characters gradually evolved, the vast majority of them consisting of composite signs. This enormous number is really the result of the fact that the Chinese, working synthetically, have steadily extended their script instead of analysing word and script so as to discover their basic elements, which would have led inevitably to a simpler mode of writing, as happened in other cultures.

5

Even though this gives a psychological explanation of the evolution and retention of Chinese script, it is perhaps well to indicate some other elements which have served to confirm this conservative tendency. Originally the scripts of most peoples were associated with holiness and magic, since they were invented by priests or magi; the other members of the tribe were not able to master the art of using signs and in the early stages did not even understand them. In East Asia, writing has retained something of this magic even up to the present day. In the first place, the number of illiterates has always been very large in China because of the great difficulty of learning the characters, which alone takes several years. Over half the population is still illiterate even now, and the number of those who can read more than the signs in commonest everyday use and who can write a letter by themselves probably does not comprise more than ten per cent of the population. It is these illiterates who see in the written characters a mysterious art, and this fact has always been exploited by those who have learnt to write, so that they may raise their status and their power. The educated had no interest in simplifying the script. A Chinese of rather old-fashioned views once said: 'Why should we, then, do away with our old written characters? Why, every blockhead and every foreigner would then be able to read our books!' So esoteric motives also play their part in the culture of East Asia.

*

How does the Chinese use his written characters, how does he in fact 'write'? Compared with ours, the Chinese language is an ungrammatical one; this is not to say that it has no grammar, but that it is of a different kind and less pronounced than our own. The following statement is generally true: the Chinese does not compose a sentence by building up the words into a logical grammatical structure; instead, he forms chains of words without declining or conjugating them. In Chinese one says something such as: 'You Shanghai go, I no Shanghai go, you no Shanghai go, I Shanghai go', which is intended to mean: 'If you go to Shanghai, I shall not go there', and conversely, 'If you are not going to Shanghai, I shall go.'[44]

Now, the Chinese behaves in very much the same way when he writes. In speaking he sometimes uses, it is true, a variety of auxiliary words and adjectives so as to express what we regard as the most elementary grammatical necessities. As a result of recent efforts to approximate the written language to everyday speech this trend is also noticeable in modern literature, while the lack of grammar is a particular feature of the classics and older writings. Thus writing originally influenced thinking in an anti-grammatical sense, that is to say in an anti-logical and also anti-discursive way. It is easy to see why this happened. The written character for a word always stays the same, it cannot be 'declined'. The auxiliary words, on the other hand, can likewise be represented by word characters, and this has also happened to some extent. Yet there has at the same time always been a kind of aversion to the increasing prevalence of these auxiliary words expressed by written characters. The reason for this is that every character is of the same size and occupies the same amount of space. It conflicts with the sense of style and the thought, especially of the 'total' man, to have to place next to the important signs for Harmony, Virtue, Tao and so on, the unimportant signs for 'of' or 'through' or 'on' in equally large dimensions. In other words, it does not look right and it distracts attention from the main concepts. These main concepts which lack 'the collateral that lies in the discursive reference', are in fact always predominant in total thinking. In speaking, I can always make the auxiliary words recede into the background by putting less emphasis on them, but in writing, I cannot do this, for here I require a whole written character for each of them.

When he writes, the Chinese plays, as it were, a kind of game of dominoes. Since the written signs, in contrast to the spoken word, possess a character of their own and lead a life of their own, they are able on their own 'initiative' to play an active part in the formation of the sentence and in the creation of meaning. The written character combines sense-structure with aesthetic composition. I can employ a sign in writing because it is balanced, harmonious and graceful. I therefore try to arrange my thoughts so that the sense of this written character fits in well with them. In such a case it is feeling and artistic sense which are the controlling factors, for it is by using this particular character that a special tone is set. Characters are frequently so employed in aphorisms and poems. In such cases, however, the actual structure of the character also plays a part; that is to say, not only the sense of the entire character but also the meaning of each of its component parts. It can be most helpful to me in my context if, in the composition of the character which I wish to use for rendering a particular concept, the signs for tree or jewel or sun occur, for example. For in certain circumstances definite associations and moods are created thereby.

As an example we can give the opening words of the first of the famous Seventeen Articles of Shotoku Taishi, the great Japanese Crown Prince Regent and statesman, who lived at about the turn of the sixth century. They are as follows: ' "Wa" is of the highest importance.' (Or: ' "Wa" is the one thing that matters.') The word 'Wa', which is of such weight in both Chinese and Japanese, means roughly: co-operation, self-realization, harmony, concord. Now, the old name for Japan, namely Yamato, is written with the same character (Wa), which is usually preceded by the character for 'great'. It might thus occur to one to read as follows: 'Yamato is the one thing that matters.'

Such associations are, so far as Japanese literature is concerned, often the finest, the truest essence of what the writer, and also the reader, has in mind—associations, however, which we often cannot establish with certainty. There are certain allusions and intimations which are indeed operative, but not sufficiently clearly to bear discussion.

Moreover, there is sometimes play on characters. For example, two words which are composed of two signs each are so selected that the two middle signs, considered together, themselves form a word. The same thing can also occur with two individual signs, in that the lower part of the first and the upper part of the second, if taken together, also form a sign word. (The East Asians write from top to bottom and not from left to right).

Whoever falls into the clutches of a 'Western-educated' East Asian language teacher will only with great difficulty, if at all, manage to get the spirit of Chinese writing. These teachers attempt by every means to extract the logical and grammatical elements (which are everywhere present in elementary form) from the Chinese and Japanese language and script, and use a 'method' which has been cleverly worked out on Western lines. The East Asians themselves never learn, and never have learned, the written characters by following a 'method', but simply imitate them and learn them by heart. In this way the meaning becomes gradually apparent to them, entirely without any methodical explanations about the derivation and employment of the 'roots' and the other components of the characters. It is also worth remembering that neither the Japanese nor the Chinese ever knew that they possessed a grammar, or even what was meant by grammar, until we told them about it.

Script and thought in China have exercised a mutual influence. The Chinese psyche created the former and has clung to it from an inner need. In contrast to the letter scripts, it possessed a life of its own quite independent of the language. Like an iron framework or a corset, it has had the effect of strengthening and preserving the conservatism of an already, in essence, highly conservative Chinese culture. It provides the 'total' mystic with an ideal vehicle for expressing his ideas in writing. We must not forget, furthermore, that it has helped to maintain the old forms in Chinese culture by handing down faithful renderings of ancient works.

*

The Japanese write and think in essentially the same way as the Chinese. But their language, which is polysyllabic and possesses more grammar than Chinese, can never be wholly reproduced by Chinese script. In consequence, the Japanese have, for about the last thousand years, made use of a syllabic script which, to be precise, can be written in two different ways. (This syllabic script, incidentally, is supposed to have been invented not by a Japanese but by a Chinese.) It serves in particular to reproduce those numerous declinations and conjugations, as well as the auxiliary words, which are to be found in Japanese. Many of the more educated can also write pure Chinese, but such cases are now rare, and it must be learnt by the Japanese in the same way as we learn Latin. (In the secondary schools Confucius is read in the original.)

It is not so much this simultaneous use of two scripts which makes the Japanese mode of writing so complicated. The reason is much rather that the Japanese took over many Chinese words at the same time as they adopted Chinese writing, with the result that roughly half the Japanese language today consists of words of Chinese origin. In consequence the characters can be read in a Japanese way, or in a Chinese, i.e. a 'Japanized' Chinese way. And so it happens that it is frequently impossible to tell—and the Japanese themselves are likewise often at a loss to know—how a character, the meaning of which is perfectly familiar, should be read or pronounced in a particular context. Since Japanese is polysyllabic and two, if not three, Chinese characters are usually needed to reproduce a Japanese word, it is the general rule that all the characters which constitute a word must be read only in one way, namely all in the Japanese or all in the 'Chinese' way. There are, for example, two characters which are always read in the Japanese fashion and are then pronounced 'Shina-mono', which means 'wares'. Yet if these two signs stand in the reverse order, they are pronounced not 'mono-shina' but have to be read Chinese fashion and are pronounced 'buppin', which also means 'wares'.

What is more, the Japanese often select Chinese characters merely on the phonetic principle. Thus, if one does not know the whole word, it is impossible either to read it or grasp its meaning, even when the sense of each individual sign is fully appreciated.

These are only a few indications of the great difficulties of the Japanese mode of writing which, it is true, draws on the aid of a syllabic script but in spite of this is in all probability more difficult to learn than the pure Chinese writing normally used in China. Memory, not understanding, affords the greatest help in learning it.

Though it is not proposed to go any further into the general question of East Asian syntax, we shall cite one other example which throws a vivid light on the difference between the East Asian way of thinking and our own. We have said that the Japanese in contrast to the Chinese have more grammar, but it is a collectivist grammar, so to speak, in contrast with our individualistic kind. In the Japanese, just as in the Chinese sentence, there is frequently no subject, but in Japanese it is possible also to have several subjects in one sentence. It is often difficult for the logically thinking foreigner to grasp the meaning of such sentences. A Japanese professor once tried to explain to me such a sentence in a 'philosophical' way. He said: 'The feeling persisting unnoticed (i.e. the feeling emanating from the first subject) is transformed continuously into other feelings (which emanate from the other subjects), but it nevertheless persists as the same feeling.' The syntax of such a sentence thus has to be 'felt' rather than 'understood'. The sentence, moreover, has to be viewed and taken in *as a whole* (because of the first subject which 'persists' to the end 'as the feeling', and the meaning or 'feelings' of the other subjects which are fitted in to that whole). The 'total' way of thinking is again reflected in the construction of the sentence: it is not necessary for me to arrange the individual parts (the other subjects) in logical sequence within the whole.

The question is always being asked: Why don't the East Asians at last jettison their old script? For several decades now attempts have been made to modernize it, but they have failed to gain ground. Why is this?

We think we have already given the real answer to this question. The reason lies ultimately in the close connection between the East Asian ways of writing and thinking. The East Asians feel that to abandon the old script system would not be a matter of mere technicalities, but that something more would be sacrificed. Inevitably the introduction of a purely syllabic or letter script would profoundly influence their traditional way of thinking, which in any case is already subject to gradual changes as a result of contact with the West. A change in their system of writing would thus be a step fraught with the most serious consequences and one which they have hitherto been afraid to take.

In consequence, every Japanese child—there is no illiteracy in Japan—and every Chinese child, provided it attends school, has to continue to cram its memory with hundreds of written characters. In the Chinese primary schools the following has hitherto been the established minimum requirement: the learning of some 1,500 signs which one must be able to write, and of some 2,500 which can at least be read. In Japan the corresponding numbers are about 1,200 and 2,000 respectively. This, however, is only true of the primary schools. Compulsory primary education suffices in Japan, for example, to provide for reading of ordinary novels and of the news and advertisement columns of the newspapers. Theoretically it should also be adequate for the reading of editorials in the papers or difficult books and treatises. In actual fact, this is not the case without further effort and education.

*

So the old heritage continues to be dragged along despite the fact that the East Asian mind, which at the present day has to master so many other tasks, is completely overburdened by it. How much more freely and more successfully could the East Asians think and work if only they would not fritter away their best years with the study of their script! But it is not just in recent times that the East Asians discovered the fact that it is possible to write in a different and simpler way. The Chinese have for ages been acquainted with Pali and Sanskrit, and the Japanese have used for the past thousand years a syllabic script of their own in addition to the Chinese written characters. The Chinese themselves also possess a kind of syllabic script which they occasionally use in conjunction with the proper characters, but only for phonetic purposes. Never, since it has been known, has this kind of writing been wanted. The most celebrated Japanese novels were written in the tenth century entirely in the syllabic script (because they were written by women, and at that time women had not yet for the most part learnt the Chinese characters). So the possibilities were recognized; nevertheless, the pure syllabic script did not manage to establish itself.

It is often asserted that the transcription of East Asian languages is impossible and that that is the reason why the East Asians have stuck to the old way of writing. This idea is surely wide of the mark, even if it has to be admitted that transcription poses some difficult, though not insoluble problems. Firstly, a great amount of Chinese and Japanese has been rendered into syllabic scripts and into Latin script (with the use of supplementary phonetic signs), and all these texts are thoroughly understandable. Secondly, there are languages which have to contend with exactly the same phonetic difficulties as Chinese and which despite that fact have always been written with letters or syllabic signs. In Siamese, for example, there are eight vowel sounds, as there are in South China; whereas there are only four vowel sounds in classical Peking Chinese. Yet the Siamese used script derived from Pali. Why then should that be impossible in East Asia? It is due, not to their inability, but their lack of *will* to transcribe.

In both China and Japan attempts are constantly made to get over the present situation by means of a compromise; that is to say, the Chinese characters are not to be done away with, but the number of characters in common use is to be reduced to a minimum. But these efforts have never achieved satisfactory

results, because the officially or unofficially established minimum, which neither in China nor in Japan ever came to less
than 1,200 written signs, always showed a tendency steadily to
increase again. It was not only the Ministries of Education or
idealistic reformers but also, and not least, the Press in both
countries, which had a great interest in keeping down, so far as
possible, the number of written characters in current use. All
the same, they never really succeeded. Why was this? The
answer partly lies in the fact that modern times, particularly
where technology, science and economics are concerned, introduce new words and expressions, some of which have to
be translated from foreign languages, and characters have to be
found to match their meaning. Quite frequently, characters
which are rarely used are dragged from oblivion for this purpose.
It once happened in Tokyo that within a few months the
number of characters which had been 'abolished' by the Ministry of Education was equalled by those employed in the
registration of inventions at the Patent Office alone. Another
decisive factor, for example, is that the leading topics treated in
the Press and in literature continue to change year by year.
During the War a large number of relatively unknown written
characters were used in Japan, because they were indispensable
in connection with technical and military matters and strategic
subjects. After the defeat, most of these expressions and characters, which had been learnt with no little effort, could be
forgotten, but in their place the Japanese now have to get used
to a fresh set of signs connected with Democracy and Parlia-
mentarianism. It can be seen that despite every effort this will
remain a knotty problem so long as there is reluctance to take
the great plunge and break with tradition.

NOTES

[1] Marcel Granet, *La Pensée Chinoise*.
[2] Lin Yutang, *The Importance of Living*.
[3] Hans Leisegang, *Denkformen*.
[4] Ibid.   [5] Ibid.

[6] Richard Wilhelm and C. G. Jung, *Das Geheimnis der Goldenen Blüte*.

[7] Ibid.

[8] C. G. Jung, *Psychologische Typen*.

[9] Ibid.

[10] Yoshiro Nagayo, 'Beauty in Contrast' (Contemporary Japan).

[11] Li Chi, *The Book of Manners*.

[12] There were bound to be doubts, since even within the Japanese Government no one knew for certain up till November 1941 whether it would come to war. It was manifest that the new Prime Minister Tojo—who was friendly towards the Axis, and had replaced the peace-loving Prince Konoye in October 1941—and his circle would in certain circumstances risk war. But it was still uncertain whether such a set of circumstances, dependent as they were on the negotiations with the Americans which were still in the balance, would ever materialize. There was also the question as to whether Tojo even then would be able to prevail against the powerful anti-war elements who were in part closely associated with the Emperor. Japan did not embark upon this war in the same wanton spirit as did Hitler. Months—indeed, years—of political jockeying, of counselling for and against, of plot and counter-plot preceded this decision. Japan was not *gleichgeschaltet* the way Germany was. There was no '*Führer*', but many leading personalities, who all had differing viewpoints. Everyone who was in Tokyo during the months before Pearl Harbour can testify as to how uncertain was the outcome of these inner political wranglings. A complete switch-over in Japan's foreign policy against the Axis was—despite the Three-Power Pact signed only a year before—still held to be possible by well-informed persons in the summer and autumn of 1941. The despatch to Washington that autumn of the two Japanese special envoys Nomura and Kurusu represented a well-intentioned attempt on the part of Konoye and the peace party to come to terms with the United States. It had not originally the aim of misleading Washington as to Japan's real plans. The fact that Tojo's government subsequently deceived not only the United States Government but also its own envoys is a different matter; and opinion can equally well be divided over the fact that the Japanese High Command—Army and Navy—was in any case preparing all the while for an armed conflict. But we must clearly differentiate the rôle of the Army—personified by General Tojo—as a political, and in this case also a war-waging power.

[13] Japanese fencing (in which the protagonists hold the sword in both hands) has been banned since the American occupation as being a warlike sport. On the other hand, the Sumo contests—probably the most popular sporting events in the Island Kingdom—are held as before, in the spring and autumn.

[14] As quoted by Bernhard Bavink, *Ergebnisse und Probleme der Naturwissenschaften*.

[15] As quoted by K. v. Neergaard, *Die Aufgabe des 20 Jahrhunderts*.

[16] K. v. Neergaard, *Untergang im Relativismus?*

[17] Cf. in particular C. F. v. Weizsäcker, *Zum Weltbild der Physik*.

[18] Sir James Jeans, *Physics and Philosophy*.

[19] Op. cit.

[20] Ibid.

[21] Daisetz Suzuki, *Zen und die Kultur Japans*.

[22] Op. cit.

[23] About the original spirit (*Urgeist*) we read: 'The true essence is the primal spirit. The primal spirit is essence and life, and if one accepts what is real in it, it is no less than the primal power.' Again: 'This primal spirit is without consciousness and knowledge, but is able to regulate the formative processes of the body.' Op. cit.

[24] J. J. M. de Groot, *Universismus*.

[25] Robert Schinzinger, 'Japanische Philosophie' (Mitteilungen der Deutschen Gesellschaft für Natur- und Völkerkunde Ostasiens).

[26] H. v. Glasenapp, *Der Buddhismus*.

[27] Robert Schinzinger, op. cit.

[28] Op. cit.

[29] Junyu Kitayama, *West-östliche Begegnung.*

[30] Op. cit.

[31] Quoted from G. B. Sansom, *Japan: A Short Cultural History.*

[32] Wilhelm Gundert, *Japanische Religionsgeschichte.*

[33] *I Ching.*

[34] It was originally a matter of whole and broken wands (yarrow stalks), such as today are still used for consulting the Oracle in accordance with the I Ching. Detailed explanations are contained in R. Wilhelm's translation of the I Ching, to which we have had frequent recourse, and which contains copious annotations.

[35] Op. cit.

[36] *Maximen und Reflexionen.*

[37] Op. cit.

[38] Op. cit.

[39] *Li Chi,* op. cit.

[40] *I Ching.*

[41] *Li Chi.*

[42] Erich Brock, *Das Weltbild Ernst Jüngers.*

[43] Op. cit.

[44] Heinrich Hackmann (*Der Zusammenhang zwischen Schrift und Kultur in China*) testifies to the fact that the lack of grammar, particularly in the language of Chinese literature, is largely responsible for divergencies in rendering Chinese texts. By way of example, he quotes five different translations of the well-known first paragraph of Chapter 39 of the Taoteking—each sinologically unexceptionable.

Stan. Julien: 'Voici les choses qui jadis ont obtenu l'Unité. Le ciel est pur parce qu'il a obtenu l'Unité.'

H. Borel: 'De dingen, die eertijds de Eenheid hebben verkregen zijn: de Hemel, die puur is door de Eenheid.'

R. Wilhelm: 'Die im Anfang das Eine erlangten: Der Himmel erlangte das eine und ist rein.'

Thos. Kingsmill: 'Originally there was only the monad. Heaven grasped it and became intelligent.'

L. Grill: 'Was es für eine Bewandtnis damit hat, dass Dinge von alters (von jeher) teilhaben am (schlechthin) Einen (am Tao): der Himmel ist Kraft des Einen rein.'

In this connection Hackmann comments: 'Those are just a few of the translators. In meaning, they scarcely differ from one another. The point to be noted, however, is the manifestly free manner in which the Westerner logically arranges and formulates his adaptation of the Chinese text. One uses a relative clause, where another chooses a causative one. The third elects to use a co-ordination of two main clauses. The fourth prefers a preposition used with a noun. Such variations are only possible because the original is insufficiently moulded grammatically.'

Chapter 3

THE WORLD OF MYSTIC REASON

WHAT is it that the English refer to as 'The Call of the East', about which there is so much talk in regard to India and East Asia? Wherein lies the power of attraction which entices back to East Asia so many of those who have spent some time there?

Many reply that it is the 'atmosphere', without being able to explain at all clearly, however, what this atmosphere comprises and to what it can be attributed.

We may assume that it is the tenor of life in East Asia which by its enchantment gradually captivates all those who manage to disregard all those things which upset us there—Chinese dirt and callousness, Japanese superiority or inferiority complexes and many other strange and even disgusting things. Whoever is seized by that enchantment escapes from it only with difficulty, no matter how culture-conscious a Westerner he may be. It is not even necessary to be conversant with one of the East Asian languages, or to give oneself up to the study of Eastern philosophy or of Buddhism, to be thus captivated. The whole atmosphere exudes this influence, along with the commonplaces of everyday life: the way in which people cry, laugh, travel and move about, conduct business, die, play with children or endure aerial bombardment.

It is the East Asian feeling of oneness with the world and life which creates this frame of mind: the inner calm, philosophic resignation, the joy in the outside world, together with humility in the face of the inexplicable and the eternal, cheerful industriousness and activity combined with consciousness of the transience of all action, joy in material things and indifference to their loss or destruction. It is the feeling that man is never isolated, for he forms a community with the living and the dead, with the spirit of the universe and with nature, in which gods, spirits and demons still move and have their being as in ancient times.

East Asia knows neither devil nor sinners, neither excessive individualistic responsibility nor penitential sense of guilt. There is, moreover, no morbid quest for what is new and no undignified haste, unworthy of human beings. Is it to be wondered at if the Westerner, oppressed by responsibility, problems and cares, is sometimes assailed there by a sense of emancipation, a suspicion that there is also another way of doing things than our own? At about the turn of the century Lafcadio Hearn[1] wrote in Japan of the 'physical satisfaction which the Westerner feels, comparable only to that release which the nerves detect when one escapes from the oppressiveness of a close atmosphere into thin, free, clear air'.

Let us, however, remain critical. The reaction to East Asia has by no means always been of the kind which we have just described. Those who were borne up by optimistic confidence in Western perfection and Western achievements have always been inclined to stress the lifeless rigidity of forms, the stagnation of East Asian culture and the monotony which results from lack of individualism.

But whoever feels himself drawn to those contrasts in East Asian culture which exercise such a liberating effect on us, must ask himself what lies behind this attitude to life and the world which seems to offer us new and hitherto unknown perspectives.

In China, conditions have radically changed in most recent times. A new, brutal régime has come into power; and it remains to be seen whether it will succeed in completely altering the racial character and in eliminating the traditional mood of the Chinese. We shall concern ourselves for the present only with pre-communist China; for, not until one has to some extent assessed the old China, can one gauge the significance of the communist bouleversement for that country and its culture.

*

As we conceive it, the East Asian *Weltanschauung* is compounded of philosophy and religion. The mystical 'circle' thinker cannot differentiate between these two things; his 'total' and organic thinking causes him to regard all dualisms in our sense as of only secondary importance.

The Chinese says: 'There are three religions, but there is only one faculty: reason.' (He refers to Taoism, Confucianism and Buddhism.) In this context reason is not to be interpreted as something intellectual, nor as reason in the Hegelian sense, but simply and solely as the 'total' and mythical concept of reason, which here can be equated to truth or cognition. The Chinese saying intends not only to emphasize that there is only *one* reason, in contrast to *several* religions, but also to express that this one reason stands *above* the religions. It is this reason, product of the 'total' highest vision, which has created the East Asian world-image. The basic East Asian attitude to life has in fact only tolerated the religions in so far as they have adapted themselves to it. Marcel Granet[2] actually holds the view that a book on Chinese culture should not contain a section on religion at all, as such a chapter would necessarily be quite misleading.

We shall, in the main, regard the world-image of the Chinese as the basic type. As the Japanese have been most strongly influenced by it, a brief outline of the Japanese variant at the end should not present any difficulties.

Let us take as our starting point the I Ching, the *Book of Changes*, for in it, as de Groot[3] says: 'the basic tenets of the whole (Chinese) system are to be found'. This work has in fact had a great influence on practically all Chinese philosophers, beginning with Confucius, and its ideas have also penetrated in all sorts of ways into East Asian Buddhism. Ever since Japan was permeated by Chinese culture, the book has played an almost equally important rôle in that country. There it is called *Eki*, which means both 'divination' and 'change'.

*

In the I Ching the Non-Changeable or All-Highest is called Taiki: literally, 'the Great Limit'.[4] This Taiki produced the two polar basic forces, the creative and the receptive, which correspond to the later concepts Yang (the light) and Yin (the dark). These two basic forces together form the 'Tao'.

Tao, which probably originally meant the course of the stars,[5] means literally, 'Way'. We can interpret it as meaning the principle of order, or the law of the cosmos with all its manifestations. If one bears in mind the organic character of the Chinese concepts it does not matter whether changes are understood as emanations, as the creation of the Tao, or whether the latter is only to be regarded as a principle of order. Richard Wilhelm[6] says: 'For Taoism, Tao (Way, meaning, cosmic law) is the primary thing from which, in its polar separation, heaven and earth proceed. For Confucianism God (heaven) is the primary thing. The Way (Tao) is the means whereby order in nature and mankind is achieved.' This interpretation is however not wholly valid, as there are Confucianists who, like the Taoists, regard the Tao as a kind of highest and ultimate cosmic principle.

To return to the idea of changes, on which the I Ching is based. According to Richard Wilhelm, the I Ching distinguishes three different types of change: the non-change, the cyclical change (*Umwandlung*) and the non-cyclical continuous change (*Verwandeln*). Of the non-change he says:

> The non-change is so to speak the background against which every kind of change is first of all possible. In the case of change there must be a point of comparison to which this change can be related, otherwise a definite arrangement is impossible and everything will dissolve into chaotic movement. This point of reference must be fixed, and must always be selected and determined. It provides the system of co-ordination into which everything else can be fitted. Thus the choice, the fixing of the point of reference stands at the beginning of the world, as at the beginning of thought. Actually any point of reference is possible, only experience proves that already at the awakening of consciousness we find ourselves

subject to a certain paramount relationship structure. The problem is, then, so to select our own point of reference that it coincides with that of cosmic events. For only in this way will the world created by our choice be spared the fate of being dashed to pieces against the paramount structure of relationships with which it would otherwise come into conflict. Of course the pre-condition for this choice is the belief that the world is basically a structure of homogeneous relationships, that it is a cosmos and not a chaos. This belief is the basis of Chinese philosophy—as indeed of all philosophies. This point of reference of the highest order is the very Non-Changeable which forms the point of reference for everything that is changing.

Here, with the help of logical arguments, a not altogether satisfactory attempt has been made to prove why one's own point of reference must coincide with that of the cosmic happening. This could give rise to the wrong impression that the Chinese also had indulged in such reflections. The concept of the non-changing rests just as little on such or similar arguments as does any other important Chinese thought. The emergence, the comprehension and the becoming conscious of such concepts can on the other hand always be traced back to the 'total' vision, to the mystical experience of unity. The coincidence of the points of reference is perceived and experienced, not thought out intellectually, and it has moreover nothing to do with 'intellectual intuitions'.

This 'point of reference', the non-changing, can be understood, according to the different philosophic-religious schools of thought, as the 'Tao', and also as the non-being, the immutable basic law, the 'heaven', the 'mysterious mother of the world' or similar circumlocutions.

'Cyclical change' (*Umwandlung*) refers to the movement and the change in phenomena which always return in a cyclical manner to the same starting conditions as, for example, the seasons, the change of day and night and everything, whether in the life of the human being or in nature, which is connected with these things.

6

'Continuous change' (*Verwandeln*), on the other hand, is concerned with the continuous change in phenomena which do not
keep to an obvious cyclical course, but repeat themselves in a
different form. As Wilhelm rightly points out, we Westerners
would contrast the organic cyclical process of change with the
inorganic causally conditioned process of continuous change.
Not so the Chinese. He does not even consider that which is
causally conditioned, and even continuous change is for him
something organic, inasmuch as he sees it, for example, as a
succession of generations. Finally, too, the idea of continuous
change is really a ring-shaped thought, even if we have to think
of this circle as being sufficiently big to include the whole history
of mankind and of the cosmos.

According to the I Ching's basic idea the 'Ultimate Being',
the Non-Changeable, realizes itself through the two polar basic
forces, the Yang and the Yin, which in turn produce the changing conditions, so that these latter—man, nature, the world—
are a form of expression, indeed part of the ultimate being. This
ultimate being is apart from, or beyond the changing conditions,
but also finds expression in them through its effect. This paradox, which cannot be understood in logical terms, is found in
many East Asian teachings: something is a component, but that
of which it is a component is not contained in the component.
What it actually amounts to here is that, as a result of 'total'
thinking, one and the same thing can be viewed from two or
more angles.

From the Chinese *Weltanschauung* and philosophy only quite
limited views on a beginning or, indeed, on the creation of the
world have emerged, and there have been none at all about the
end of the world. Speculation about the beginning in so far, for
example, as the development of Yin and Yang can be included,
refer not to something which is past but rather to something
which is present and will continue to be effective for all time.
The Chinese are, in general, antipathetic to myths concerning
the Creation and to theories about how the world began;
according to Granet,[7] the aphorism 'Rien ne se crée dans le

Monde, et le Monde n'a pas été créé' is aptly applicable to them.

There is almost a complete absence of eschatological theories and hopes, in characteristic contrast to Christian thought in the West. Doctrines concerning millennia and the end of the world did of course penetrate along with Buddhism; indeed, here and there in Japan chiliastic notions cropped up, but they never gained general currency and never predominated.

*

Chinese philosophy, the bases of which we already find in the ancient *Book of Changes*, has been termed Universism, a designation first used, to my knowledge, by de Groot. According to the universistic approach the universe is a living organism, the components of which influence each other. It is not only the cosmic happening which influences the life of man; but, conversely, the activity of man, his mistakes and his virtues exercise an influence on events within the universe. It is this which represents the world-image of the 'total' thinker in its purest form: a system of cycles which by deduction are all brought into contact with one another. Marcel Granet[8] expresses it as follows: 'Les idées jointes d'Ordre, de Total, d'Efficace dominent la pensée des Chinois. Ils ne se sont pas souciés de distinguer des règnes dans la Nature. Toute réalité est en soi totale. Tout dans l'Univers est comme l'Univers.' On this basic idea a grandiose system was erected which embraces every sphere of life (e.g. patterning one's life on the calendar, the worship of the forces of nature, the magic of the universe, the institution of the 'Son of Heaven', etc.).

In this world-image every animate creature, every thing has its special place and the corresponding special path which it has to follow.

*

In the case of the two basic forces, Yang and Yin, which by their combined activity produce all phenomena, and man himself comes into being, we are dealing not, as was formerly assumed, with a dualistic principle, but with polar, one might almost say, complementary forces. In this case, too, the misunderstanding arose mainly because the things were unintentionally viewed from the customary Western standpoint. Granet[9], on the other hand, says: 'Loin de concevoir une contradiction entre deux aspects yin et yang, on admet qu'ils se complètent et se parfont l'un l'autre—dans la réalité comme dans la pensée.'

Yang and Yin, the light and the dark principle, have likewise nothing to do with the contrast between good and evil. The organic and 'total' concept was far from applying an ethical yardstick to these basic principles.

The concepts 'good' and 'evil' by no means occupy a prominent place in East Asian philosophy and ethics, in the same way as there is no concept for 'Man's Fall'. Ethics are based on the integration of man into the cosmic happening and not, as in Christianity, on the concept of sin, linked up with eschatological images. Added to this is the peculiar 'total' way of thinking which never sees irreconcilable opposites but always just polar and complementary forces which belong and operate together. It is significant that in the case of the Western mystics, too, we never find the concept of sin emphasized in the same way as in Christian dogma. The mystics, like the East Asians, do not deny the existence of sin and responsibility, but their attention is, if one may so put it, optimistically directed towards the overcoming of them. It may be said of the East Asians that they regard the problem of sin in a natural and sensible manner. As 'total' human beings they reject excessive feelings of guilt and remorse because they involve only feeling, i.e. a single psychic function, and not the reaction of the whole being. The over-emphasis of this feeling is regarded as an obstacle on the path towards maturity and the salvation of man. C. G. Jung[10] says: 'The Pauline triumph over the Law is only possible for him who knows how to replace conscience by the soul.' He adds, however: 'only very few are capable of this ("Many are called, but few are chosen").' The East Asian concepts apply in an idealistic and optimistic manner to these 'Few'. In the majority of Indian doctrines also, sinfulness has no metaphysical meaning; only the positive attitude is regarded as conducive to salvation. Buddhism aims at release from the sorrows of the world, not from the sinfulness of man.

The concept of the 'Fall of Man' is not necessarily to be taken dualistically—and the Roman Church does not do so—but it has on the whole had this effect. Good and Evil were not, generally speaking, regarded by Christianity as polar forces; on the contrary, Evil, according to Christian interpretation, is based on a falling away, a cleavage, and is inimical and not complementary to Good. Hence, today it is pointed out in many quarters that the concepts of the Fall of Man and Original Sin (chiefly as interpreted in Protestant teachings) can only retain their validity as long as one thinks dualistically, in other words, rationally.

From time immemorial all who have visited East Asia have been struck by the fact that there the concept of absolute Evil patently does not exist. Granet[11] maintains that even 'les missionnaires reconnaissent aujourd'hui volontiers qu'on ne peut relever en Chine aucun vestige de l'idée de chute ou de faute originelle'. And Sansom[12] says of the Japanese:

> The conception of sin, as distinct from uncleanness, is wanting, or rudimentary, and throughout their history the Japanese seem to have retained in some measure this incapacity to discern, or this reluctance to grapple with, a problem of Evil.

Sometimes, of course, one comes across Buddhist illustrations of the terrible torments of hell which resemble Christian pictures of 'The Last Judgment', but this is a case of foreign ideas which for a time had an influence in China and Japan, but never gained the upper hand. The general tenor of life is natural, philosophical and conciliatory. It is superfluous to underline that the spirits, too, in China are not absolutely good or absolutely evil; 'Sen' and 'Kwei' are emanations of Yang and Yin and are, accordingly, typically 'complementary' spirits.

The East Asians mostly show a complete lack of understanding of the Christian conception of Sin, even if they do not all express themselves in such an offhand way as Lin Yutang:[13] 'You can't make a man a Christian unless you first make him believe that he is a sinner.' It is difficult properly to understand and feel the deep gulf which exists in this respect between East Asia and the West if one restricts oneself solely to literary works, learned philosophical or religious treatises. One must also have seen how the average man in East Asia reacts, how he is apt to feel our attitudes to be unpleasant, embarrassing, un-aesthetic and hence also unethical. In the last few years plays have been produced in China as well as in Japan which bur-lesqued Christians beseeching forgiveness of their sins and God's help. In this way the authors deliberately sought to provoke hilarity among the audiences. From his youth onwards the East Asian is taught self-control as one of the highest virtues; unin-hibited suppliants or contrite sinners he consequently regards as ill-bred and uneducated.

*

Particularly since the time of Confucius the Chinese have prescribed certain formulae and rules for the Tao of man which is co-ordinated with the Tao of the universe but is at the same time a part of it. These relate to the behaviour of man within the family and the community, and also regulate his relationship to the cosmic forces. Whoever offends against these rules makes a mistake and commits a breach of morals, but he does not commit sin in the deeper sense. For his mistake, which has destroyed the harmony of the cosmos, he will suffer misfortune or he will be punished by the laws of man which were drawn up to protect the community, and hence also the cosmic order, from such hazards. According to popular belief it is the Kwei (the dark, the 'evil' spirits) which bring misfortune upon wrong-doers; thus it is important on the one hand not to annoy the Kwei, and on the other, by means of good deeds to gain the support of the Sen (the light, the 'good' spirits). The belief that evil spirits acting at heaven's behest can punish, and good spirits reward, was also fostered by the Confucianist school.

From this, as we shall see, a downright mercantilist popular ethic has developed which involves keeping clear of misfortune and living in peace by means of suitable negotiations and agreements with the spirits. In the words of de Groot,[14] it is a 'morality based on demonism'.

Just as East Asia does not know the dualism of Good and Evil, so it does not know dualisms of any other kind; it does not know 'Here and Beyond', 'Matter and Spirit', or 'Body and Soul'. Of course one can say, for example, that Confucianism and Shintoism stress the Here, whereas Buddhism rather accentuates the Beyond, but only rarely do we find in the East Asian *Weltanschauung* or philosophy a fundamental differentiation, a wrenching apart of these concepts. We should, however, like to draw attention to one point: almost all East Asian teachings speak of the ephemerality or vanity of things, of the non-being of being and of the illusion of phenomena. From this it is adduced that the East Asian attitude is 'directed towards the Beyond', a view which was strengthened by an all too one-sided study based on Buddhist writings. But we should not overlook the fact that in their view the Beyond already lies in the Here, that the ultimate reality (or non-reality) is bound up with this very ephemerality, these very illusions. In East Asia there are many different formulations and many divergent views on this question, but one thing there is not—nor can there be because of the mystical experience of uniformity—namely, that wrenching apart of the Inexplicable, which in the long run will always be felt and seen as 'the One'.

*

In the West, also, a widespread anti-dualistic mood or even an anti-dualistic point of view is now becoming noticeable, and it has its origins principally in the natural sciences. Sir James Jeans[15] speaks of the new dualism in modern physics, which expresses itself in the twofold aspect of the particles and waves of 'matter'. The new members of this dualism are, however,

'no longer hostile and mutually exclusive, but rather complementary'. According to Jeans, furthermore, 'the real world lies
for ever outside our range of vision', and physics hitherto, 'from
the Newtonian mechanics down to the old quantum theory,
fell into the old error of identifying appearance and reality'.
He continues his strictures by saying: 'All earlier systems of
physics were not even conscious of a deeper reality beyond'. In
other words: phenomena are the outer form or the form of
expression of true reality, and are not opposed to it, say, in the
sense of matter and spirit. Phenomena and reality are therefore
only 'identical' in so far as phenomena are a component part of
reality. This reality is, however, different from that with which
classical physics thought it was dealing—it is inexplicable, and
will always remain so.

We must bear in mind, however, that Jeans,[16] like Eddington,
Bernhard Bavink[17] and others, is not satisfied with an acknow-
ledgement and philosophical interpretation of the polar state of
affairs, but tends rather to a spiritualistic solution of the
'dualistic' problem. It seems to us that in this need to arrive at
some conclusion in either a materialistic or spiritual direction,
is revealed the great power of tradition; the old way of thinking
is still alive, it is impossible to break loose from it in one bound.

How closely have the views represented by the modern
natural sciences approximated to those of the East Asian? More
keenly than ever before it is recognized that true reality is
incomprehensible and inexplicable (I do not know its name,
said Lao Tse, it is written as 'Tao'); that the inorganic is not
basically different from the organic (according to the I Ching
the same laws governing changes are valid for all phenomena).
It is also recognized that instead of dualistic contrasts one should
speak of polar relationships, as the Chinese have always done,
and that, finally, matter is no less incomprehensible than the
spirit—again long since realized in East Asia.

All these viewpoints have emerged from the natural sciences
themselves, without any outside influence. But it is quite a
different thing when philosophers, writers and other scholars

express similar thoughts, for in the case of many of them it is abundantly clear that they have occupied themselves with East Asian thought. Three well-known names immediately come to mind: Bertrand Russell, C. G. Jung, and Aldous Huxley. The works of Hermann Hesse, Ernst Jünger and many others, too, reveal that Buddhist, and especially Zen-Buddhist writings are not unknown to them. The remarkable thing, too, is that just in these days East Asian views should fall on such fruitful ground.

*

We should like here to single out a concept of Chinese ethics which is pivotal for the life of the community and of the individual. It is the concept 'Wu-Wei'. Translated literally it means 'Do-nothing', which means, more or less, 'Be effective through your being', or 'Be effective without exertion', or, to use a sophistry: 'Inaction—not Inertia'. This slogan is based on the natural and cosmic happening in which no 'work' is done, but everything happens in an unconstrained, spontaneous manner.

In the *Tao Te Ching* the well-known sentence is to be found:

> The Lord of men is the earth, the Lord of the earth is heaven, the Lord of the heaven is the Tao, and the Lord of the Tao is spontaneity.

De Groot[18] says of this concept of the spontaneous:

> Consideration of the universe led inevitably to the general recognition of the fact that Nature carries out her bountiful task of creation and preservation calmly, that her mighty achievement takes place leisurely and quietly, without exertion, friction or noise, and she does not proclaim it abroad. Tao is hence not a driving force, which initiates all movements and phenomena of the universe, but the totality of these movements and phenomena themselves; it is not that which motivates, but the course of Nature obeying its laws.

In the same way the nature of man must express itself in a natural way without effort—that is the Tao of man. Good is to be unfolded and dispensed calmly, leisurely and without striving, just as in Nature. The I Ching says the same:

> The creative recognizes by means of what is easy . . . the receptive achieves by means of what is simple . . . What is easy is easily recognized; what is simple is easily followed. If one is easy to recognize, one gains followers. If one is easy to follow, one acquires works . . .
> By easiness and simplicity one comprehends the laws of the whole world . . .

This emphasis of the simple and spontaneous and, linked with it, the rejection of the premeditated and purposive, is one of the main fundamentals of Chinese moral teaching. It is also the basis of the 'magic thinking' of Confucius and of his emphasis on the 'magic' of the personality (cf. p. 20).

By living in harmony with the laws of heaven and earth— that is, virtuously—saints and noble-hearted men exert a magic influence which has a salutary and educative power. Hence by 'magic' is to be understood the irradiation and effect of personality, the innate essence of which is difficult to understand and difficult to explain.

This postulate 'Be effective without exertion' was formulated with special reference to government by the Emperor. The two big characters 'Wu-Wei', written in gold are still to be seen in the Forbidden City of Peking on a lacquered wooden panel over the Emperor's throne. Confucius[19] once said of the ruler Sün: 'May not Sün be instanced as one who governed by Wu-Wei? What did he do? He inspired reverence and looked straight towards the south. That was all.' In addition the Master said: 'Whoever governs by the magic of his personality may be compared to the polar star; it remains immovable, and all the other stars bow before it.'

The famous philosopher Chu Hsi (or Dschu Hi) explained to his Emperor, at a time when already half China had been overrun by the Tartars, that the sole cause of his misfortune lay in the fact that he, the Emperor, had failed to adjust his mind and

spirit properly.[21] By not bringing his character into harmony
with the cosmic order, he had disturbed the latter; he had,
moreover, not shown that magic influence which was necessary
if state affairs were to run satisfactorily and the enemy to be
held off.

This conception has always rendered difficult, if not impossible, social, economic or legal reforms in China. For the magic
influence radiating from the ruler, rather than any laws and
regulations, were regarded as of the highest importance for the
government of the country.

*

Together with the belief in the interblending of man with
the cosmic happening, the worship of ancestors unquestionably
constitutes one of the oldest elements in the Chinese *Weltanschauung*. Why, we must ask ourselves, have the Chinese considered human life less in its manifestation as an individual life
than as an endless succession of generations—a long chain
consisting of ancestors, the living and descendants? This also
is in the long run due to the fact that the 'totally' thinking
human being, as has already been said, directs his attention first
of all to the whole, and only later to the parts or individual
members. The 'whole' is the eternal cosmos and eternal human
life which, in their essence, are made up of constant changes.
Hence the succession of generations must be important, and not
the individual human being; the latter is only of importance
insofar as he forms one link in the whole chain. A Chinese is
primarily son and father, and only secondarily just a human
being. The extinction of a family thus means final rupture and
death; the laws of changes have been interrupted, the cycle is
incomplete. It is on such thoughts that ancestor-worship is based.
If there is no heir in a Chinese family, it is usually regarded as a
misfortune, since there will then be no one to offer sacrifices to
the ancestors; even in the poorest families this is regarded as
being a more grievous matter than the fact that there will now
be no one to look after the parents when they are old.

In China, as in Japan, ancestor-worship was originally practised by the ruling families only, and not by the mass of the
people, which in the earliest times did not possess any family
names. The 'democratization' of ancestor-worship only took
place gradually. On the other hand, already in feudal times the
rulers and the nobility erected communal altars in their areas
for the ancestors of their subjects.

Of the greatest significance for the universistic world-image,
and hence for the Chinese social order, was the direct linking of
ancestor-worship with the cosmic forces. This goes back to the
time when the Emperor was proclaimed 'The Son of Heaven',
and his ancestors and he himself were recognized accordingly
as having the same rights and privileges as heaven. This must
have taken place at a very early date, as the title 'Son of
Heaven' was already in use in the earliest times known to us.

In the primeval era the Chinese rulers, or rather tribal
chieftains, were priestly kings who functioned as intermediaries
between the deity and man. The odour of sanctity has always
surrounded the ruler, and with the change in primeval religious
and philosophical ideas it was hence not a very big step to
establish the closest connection between him and 'heaven'. The
political reasons are not far to seek, for by proclaiming the ruler
to be the son of the highest deity—of heaven—his rank was
fixed once and for all as the highest among the kings and princes
ruling on earth. Naturally the promulgation of this doctrine was
linked with endeavours to unite and found an empire; for this
reason it was later supported by the teachings of Confucius,
which were directed towards producing a reasonable and satisfying human order. The same thing repeated itself later in Japan
in a much clearer and unambiguous manner, so to say in the full
light of history. In this connection the Japanese had, however,
at that time (in the sixth and seventh centuries A.D.) the
advantage that they could make use of a perfected prototype,
namely the Chinese system of the Son of Heaven. This system
was introduced quite deliberately and for political reasons into
Japan in order to establish for all time the precedence of the

leading family of the Yamato, which had then come to power. The attempt was, moreover, completely successful, as that still nameless line remains today the imperial house of Japan.

We need not at this point go into the question whether, and to what extent the Chinese originally had a kind of monotheistic religion, and how the concept of Shang-Ti, the supreme God, which was still alive in Confucius' time, came to be superseded by the concept of Heaven. But it is almost certainly connected with the fusion of the concept of the Emperor with the basic universistic cosmic ideas. Once the Emperor had been proclaimed the Son of Heaven and not that of some most exalted god, for political and state reasons the worship of heaven had to come into the foreground. In point of fact already in feudal times the worship of heaven had gained precedence over all other rites as a kind of 'official religion'.

*

But how is it to be explained that heaven was worshipped as a kind of deity? As we have seen, heaven and earth were created by Tao or, according to the way one interprets it, by Taiki or by some other primal cause. The concepts heaven and earth correspond, however, to the two polar primal forces of the creative and receptive; hence they also correspond to the principle of Yang and Yin. But the Yang principle is the more honoured and exalted of the two, although we are not here concerned with a moral evaluation. We do not completely agree with de Groot's[22] opinion that there is a 'heaven-wide difference' between the two, for both principles have always been observed, as was symbolically expressed in the imperial worship of heaven *and* earth. Nevertheless, the fact remains that the Yang principle, the 'light', the creative, heaven, was regarded as the higher of the two. Accordingly the Emperor could rank only as the Son of Heaven.

In this world-image there was no proper place for another 'God'. There was only the ultimate impersonal primal cause, the Tao or the Taiki and the two forces of Yang and Yin which created everything.

Thus, by linking the Emperor and the imperial ancestors with heaven, ancestor-worship and the cosmic world-image were directly connected. Though without this connection this cult was of the highest importance, by interlinking the imperial house with the cosmos its status was enormously enhanced. If the worship of heaven and his ancestors was the foremost duty of the Emperor, by analogy the same must hold good for his subjects, with the difference that, since they were not, of course, sons of heaven, their duty was restricted to the worship of their ancestors.

Apart from affairs of government, the Emperor, in his capacity as Son of Heaven, was responsible for maintaining regulated and satisfactory relations between mankind and the cosmic forces. Unusual celestial phenomena, natural catastrophes, invasion by foreign barbaric hordes, etc. were regarded as warnings and punishments from heaven. The Emperor, in his dual rôle of representative of mankind and of heaven, was responsible for seeing that such afflictions did not occur. If, however, misfortune were not averted, then in accordance with ancient Chinese views he was to go into himself and do penance, in order to expiate the sins of the world, which were his own sins.

The Emperor was holy; he recognized no one above him except heaven, his father, and earth, his mother. Thus, in rank he was superior to all other holy beings, and he was even called the 'Lord of the gods'. As such, he could promote the gods and give them titles of honour, or he could also demote them and have their shrines and images destroyed.

As the High Priest of universism he could also permit or suppress religious teachings, according to whether in his view they strengthened or endangered the universistic system. The Emperor was the only one who might offer sacrifice to his father, heaven, and to his mother, the earth, on the magnificent altars in Peking, which are still preserved. At one time in the dome-like building on the site of the Altar of Heaven in Peking 'tablets of the souls' of heaven actually stood in the place of honour; that is, on the north-south axis facing south. The tablet bore the inscription 'Imperial Heaven, Supreme Emperor'. In the same room, and ranged around it, were the tablets of the souls of the imperial ancestors, whereas, characteristically enough, tablets for the 'retinue of heaven' were in the neighbouring buildings. This retinue included the sun, moon, constellations and the so-called 'celestial gods', namely clouds, rain, wind and thunder.

Observing the heavens and interpreting celestial phenomena were the Emperor's most important duties. Connected with this, and since time immemorial one of the main tasks and at the same time one of the main privileges of the Son of Heaven, has been the making of the calendar. Since he had to see that mankind lived in harmony with Nature, he also had to provide it with the means, that is the calendar. A calendar from the third millennium B.C. is extant, orientating the life of man, even to details, according to the change of the seasons. Originally, in true universistic manner, the office of calendar publisher was held by the imperial chroniclers, so that astrology, chronology and historiography were dealt with by the same officials.

These calendars not only fixed the days for the beginning of work in the fields, the harvest and so forth, but also recommended favourable times for marriages, burials, the building of houses, journeys and important business dealings.

Of the political importance of the calendar de Groot[23] says:

Absolute obedience which man must render to the Tao of heaven manifests itself by the strict carrying out of the instructions contained in the calendar, and hence means absolute submission to the guidance of the author of this book, that is, to the Son and Viceroy of heaven on earth; for the latter, on the other hand, the calendar was the instrument whereby he maintained this subservience to his universal authority. The book has the same purpose in the lands held in fief; there, any refusal to accept the calendar and follow its instructions would have been tantamount to open rebellion against Heaven and his Son.

The Emperor was in addition, so to speak, the supreme magician, the 'most exalted exorcist' of the Chinese. When necessary he had the mandarins take measures to combat the 'Kwei', the evil spirits. Sometimes, too, sacrifices were made to these spirits when, in the 'name of the Emperor', they were requested to cease their malevolent actions.

According to the universistic view, gods and spirits, as well as men, have a special place in the universe, and by the same token they also have their special duties. Thus it happens that Chinese gods are sometimes treated in what strikes us as a strange manner. One must not allow oneself to be misled by the fact that on certain occasions images of gods are carried around, or sacrifices are made to certain gods, Taoist gods or even Buddhist Bodhisattvas, so that, for example, in a drought they will produce rain clouds. It is not a question of these gods being 'implored'. Since by virtue of their office they are there to provide rain, they are simply being called upon to carry out that duty which is allotted to them in the universistic system. Even today the images of these gods are occasionally smashed and their temples are actually destroyed if they fail. Frequently such incompetent gods or Bodhisattvas are simply ignored; their statues and temples are just left to crumble away.

*

Before we finish our outline of the most important basic characteristics of Chinese philosophy a few remarks are necessary on the significance of astrology and the consulting of oracles. For thousands of years, in addition to astrology, another system of interpreting fate and of prophecy has been used, namely the consulting of oracles on the basis of the I Ching.

For the Chinese, the history of man and that of nature have always been identical. Moreover, they have never torn apart the concepts of time and space the way we have. For them there is no space *per se*, but all events are viewed simultaneously also in time. 'Les Chinois n'avaient aucune disposition à concevoir, comme deux milieux indépendants et neutres, un Temps abstrait, un Espace abstrait.' (M. Granet)[24] Here, once again, we notice how closely the ancient Chinese way of thinking approximates to the modern teachings of the natural sciences concerning the unity of time and space.

In astrology and the consulting of oracles we are concerned with this 'concrete' time. The point at issue is to determine the character of the time under consideration, since conclusions, important for the life of man, can be drawn from it.

Since, according to the Chinese organic viewpoint, the three factors, man, nature and the cosmos, are constantly influencing one another, nothing can happen anywhere without also having a bearing on all the other parts. We must now try to understand this idea in a somewhat deeper sense. It is not the case that, say, a comet *directly* influences the life of man, but that the comet is only a sign of something unusual which inheres in time itself. The character of 'concrete' time is the important thing, which likewise influences everything else. Celestial phenomena, bad weather or war are thus only symptoms of the state of time at a particular moment.

This 'total' view of the concept of time brings into focus the *one* fate which forces all things and all living creatures into its orbit. This fate operates everywhere simultaneously, so that from contemporary events man can attempt to draw conclusions which are important for him.

Thus astrology is important in two ways; on the one hand, it offers the possibility of interpreting the character of time on the basis of particular phenomena, and on the other, which is more important in its more exact form as astronomy, it provides a means of fixing time with precision. C. G. Jung[25] says of this:

The possibility which actually exists of delineating character by casting a person's horoscope, proves the relative validity of astrology. The casting of a horoscope, however, is by no means dependent on the actual position of the stars but on an arbitrary and purely conceptual time-system, since, as a result of the precession of the equinoxes, the point of contact has long since moved

7

astronomically out of the o degree Aries. In so far as there are correct astrological forecasts they are based not on the effect of the stars but on the hypothetical qualities we give to time, which means in other words, *whatever is born or created at a given moment of time, has the qualities of that moment of time.*

The use of the I Ching as a book of oracles is based on the same synchronistic principle; but with the difference that the connection with the unknown moment of time is established magically. One can indeed speak of manual magic. The runic rods, either whole or broken stalks, are sorted out according to a rather tedious procedure until only six remain, which then produce one of the diagrams of the I Ching. The book is then consulted for the meaning and interpretation of this diagram which has come about in what is for us a purely arbitrary manner. By means of arbitrary or subconscious manual movements the 'qualitas occulta of the moment of time, expressed by the hexagram in the I Ching, can be deciphered', as C. G. Jung puts it.[26] He adds: 'It is a question of the context of the happening, which is not only analogous to astrology but is even intrinsically related to it. Birth corresponds to the scattered runic rods, the birth constellation to the hexagram, and the astrological interpretation of the constellation to the text which accompanies the hexagram (in the I Ching).'

Every foreigner who goes to East Asia is at first astonished at the enormous influence of astrology, fortune-telling and oracles on daily and practical life there. Thus, at the beginning of the war, stories were being told in Tokyo that the day for the attack on Pearl Harbour had been fixed on the basis of an ancient moon oracle, whereas according to others it had been based on the 'Eki'—the I Ching. Towards the end of the war, by the way, 'Eki' fortune-tellers and other soothsayers were banned from the streets by the police, as their prophecies did not sufficiently coincide with government propaganda. In point of fact, as I was able to see for myself, these soothsayers, however hard they tried to be good Japanese patriots, were unable to do otherwise than prophesy catastrophies.

As yet we have said nothing about the Chinese mystical cult of figures, although this, as the principle of order which permeates everything, plays an outstanding rôle in the Chinese conceptions of things. We should be digressing too far were we to go into the details of this play with figures, so we shall confine ourselves to indicating the fundamentals. Numbers do not mean for the Chinese, or for the East Asian in general, 'sizes' or quantitative measures for computing something else; they are used as controlling symbols. Granet[27] says: 'Les nombres ne sont que des Emblèmes: les Chinois se gardent de voir en eux les signes abstraits et contraignants de la quantité.' That is to say the Chinese treats figures in the same way as he treats written characters or 'concepts'. Numbers are used in order to find conformities and analogies everywhere within the macrocosm and the microcosm. In this connection reference may be made to the extract from the *Book of Morals* quoted on p. 54; the principle of the controlling numbers which it gives, lies in the fact that they correspond to special sequences in the cosmic order. The number of tones in the scale, architectural measures, the enumeration of human virtues and vices, the classification of food and victuals—all this and very much more is fixed by magic-cosmic play with figures. It corresponds to the Chinese neglect of the concept of quantity that these figure-games are frequently completely inaccurate arithmetically; it is never important that the calculation should come out right, but only that it should somehow be symbolically correct. (If, for example, 7×7 is of importance in some connection, the answer will be assumed to be not 49 but 50, if this fits better into the other combinations.) To quote Granet once again: 'On employait les nombres à ajuster aux proportions cosmiques des choses et les mesures propres à chaque chose, de façon à montrer que toutes s'intègrent dans l'Univers.' The Chinese *could*, of course, count in our way; indeed, they did so as far as was necessary for trade and commerce. But this ranked only as the 'ordinary' practical form of counting, which was rejected in all metaphysical and philosophically important cases, just as in the sphere of thought, logic was looked down upon as an inferior method of thinking.

*

Only by considering the universistic world-image in which the Empire played such an important part, does it really become clear how extremely serious were the consequences of the 1911 revolution for the Chinese people. What took place at that time, and what was regarded by the outside world as a political revolution, was very much more—it was a metaphysical collapse. The resulting disorders would be incomprehensible had it only been a matter of replacing the monarchy by the republic. What actually happened was that the ancient universistic system, which was almost 3,000 years old, was shaken to its very foundations. As a result, the ethical bases were shattered, and the bad, negative sides of the Chinese character forced themselves more strongly than ever to the surface. Of course, to a certain extent there has always been corruption, nepotism, greed for money and family egotism in China, but hitherto these tendencies have been balanced by Chinese virtues.

Since the Son of Heaven no longer resided in Peking, the universistic system had neither apex, centre, nor heart. Sacrifices were no longer made to heaven and earth. No one was responsible for seeing that the Tao of man coincided with that of the cosmos. All the official places of worship, including the Confucian temples, were falling into decay. There was no longer any imperial calendar to which to conform. Whilst universism was thus robbed of its leadership and cohesive function, many of its views and institutions lived on in a half-hearted way—according to the law of persistence and because no kind of substitute was available. Ancestor-worship, the family system and national 'universistic' superstition are still very much alive—despite the Communists; for, however hard people try, a 3,000-year-old tradition cannot be eradicated in a few years, even if force is resorted to.

The decades of civil war and disturbance which, more than at any other time, followed the revolution of 1911, are temporarily at an end. Communism appears to be firmly in the saddle, and is ruthlessly pursuing a policy of completely revolutionizing the Chinese way of life and the Chinese outlook. That is something that had never before happened in the whole long and eventful course of Chinese history; true, China had been conquered, but the basic Chinese conception of life had never before been challenged in such a radical and dangerous manner. The conquering nomads did not do so, for they were inferior culturally and intellectually to the Chinese and preferred to adapt themselves to the higher Chinese culture; nor did the only foreign religion really to take root in China, namely Buddhism, which, as everywhere else, carried on its proselytizing in a mild manner, adjusting itself to local conditions. But now Communism arrives on the scene with its wholly rational ideology which originated in the West, and which is as different from the established Chinese method of thinking as fire is from water.

We liberal foreigners were in East Asia always prepared to make allowances; we saw the path towards progress and prosperity in reforms and in a gradual process of adaptation—a similar way to the one which Japan tried to follow. The Communists, on the other hand, want to jettison 'all the old junk' overnight; they want the Chinese people to start again from the bottom, to go to school again, where they will be indoctrinated with something completely different and novel—the 'infallible' Communist ideology.

The Chinese people have never before been subjected to such a crucial test, and everything will now depend on how—in Arnold Toynbee's phrase—'challenge and response' will in this instance work out; that is to say, on whether the Chinese people will succeed in injecting into the new régime enough of their traditionally sensible and carefree disposition, to bring about a reasonably acceptable outcome.

*

Our discussion of the Chinese *Weltanschauung* would be incomplete if we did not briefly mention the great attention which in East Asia has from time immemorial been paid to psychological matters, though of course not in the Western scientific sense. One cannot separate from the East Asian 'world'-image the East Asian image of man, that is, of the human psyche. The human consciousness of itself and of the cosmos, these two things here belong together.

The interest of the mystical thinker who meditates upon the self so as to build the whole world into a synthesis from within this self, must of course be largely directed towards his own psychic processes. It can perhaps be said that the East Asian psychology owes its success to the very fact that it has never been a science in our sense. It is easier for the 'total' thinker to comprehend the essence, effect and significance of rationally incomprehensible elements in the human psyche, than for one who strains every nerve to make headway by using the methods of the natural sciences. Nevertheless and strangely enough, probably in no East Asian sphere of knowledge has there been so much analysing as in psychology, though analysis has always remained a secondary method, a second expedient. This analysing went back in the main to Indian-Buddhist influences, to which in general East Asian psychology owes its development and also its penetration.

It is significant that interest in psychology in East Asia is of ancient origin, whereas the extraverted Westerner has developed psychology only as the youngest and latest science. Nor is it surprising that it was our psychologists who first recognized the great importance of, and deep meaning behind many of the religious writings of East Asia with which people had long been familiar.

A 'Theory of the Unconscious' was already to be found in the I Ching; subsequently every guide to meditation took the unconscious psychic phenomena into account. There are innumerable such instructions, Taoist as well as Buddhist. Perhaps the greatest development—greatest also from the intellectual point of view—consists in those Buddhist theories of consciousness which were likewise taken over and developed by the East Asians. This is a sphere in which a great deal of work still remains to be done by Western research; it is one, moreover, which promises to provide the greatest interest and stimulus.

*

What is it that differentiates the Japanese conception of things from that of the Chinese, and what is it that is typically East Asian and common to them both?

In the Chinese character the emphasis is on reason; in the Japanese, on feeling and sensibility, although these characteristics remain 'totally' conditioned. It is often said of Japanese culture, indeed frequently by the Japanese themselves, that it is a 'culture of feeling', a description which is completely wrong and misleading, as the Japanese are conditioned at one and the same time by feeling and sensibility; and one might well doubt whether it is not the latter that plays the more important part.[28] It is not only the heart (in our sense) but also the nerves and senses which have helped to mould Japanese life, Japanese art and indeed religion. Pure feeling as it is expressed, say, in Western music is hardly known to the Japanese; it is almost always blended with sensations. That is why the Japanese have never achieved anything outstanding in the sphere of 'pure' art. They have, on the other hand, achieved all the more in the field of applied art, so that one might almost call them the people in which artistic craftsmanship has found its classic expression.

These elements of feeling and sensibility in the Japanese character find their purest expression in Shintoism. For the Shintoist belief is of purely Japanese origin, and even today it contains many features which recall ancient times. In that far-off time before Japan had had any contact with China, Shintoism was a truly primitive 'Red-Indian religion'; it was only later under Chinese and Buddhist influence that it took on its present-day forms.

The main elements of Shintoism in its original form were, according to Gundert:[29] firstly, a primitive, unhistorical worship of Nature and spirits; secondly, ancestor- and hero-worship associated with history; and thirdly—of far less practical significance as a cult—the idea of original fathers and original parents, which arose out of the primitive urge to speculate on the origins of things. From the fourth century B.C. onwards this primeval religion was extended with the aid of Chinese-universistic doctrines, that is to say, the foreign conception was grafted on to the indigenous religion. (In this way through the Yang and Yin principle, etc. the 'original parents' were given a philosophical background.)

The primitive, 'total' Japanese were thus raised by the Chinese on to a higher, but equally 'total' plane. No break with the past occurred, no unbearable tensions such as, for instance, made themselves felt following the adoption of Christian-classical culture by the Germanic tribes. There are, admittedly, certain tensions running through the whole of Japanese history, but they cannot be ascribed entirely to the adoption of alien thought and culture; these conflicts were always resolved and a synthesis achieved. At any rate these tensions never led to outright psychic cleavages.

Although 'universistic' ideas became dominant in Japan, this dominance was not absolute. The obstacle to this was the Japanese character, which is conditioned by feeling and sensibility, and which could not break loose from traditional Shintoism. Thus, although the Japanese is influenced to a very great extent by Universism, he has no complete universistic system. In the Chinese system everything from the Emperor down to the smallest soothsayer can be elucidated by 'total' reason. In Japan, however, the decisive factor remains irrational and inexplicable; this is Shintoism, the living belief in the exalted meaning of the ancient myths and in the sacred and divine descent of the imperial house—in a way, of the whole Japanese nation. The Japanese, indeed, also call their Emperor the 'Son of Heaven', but this is due solely to their copying the Chinese imperial system with all its expressions, for in actual fact the Japanese Emperor is neither a son nor any other sort of descendant of heaven, but the offspring of the Sun-goddess. The divinity of the Tenno (the Japanese name for the Son of Heaven) is quite different from that of the Chinese Emperor; it is based on faith rather than on reason.

The Japanese *Weltanschauung* cannot be understood unless one first knows that of the Chinese. In addition to this it is also necessary to understand the spirit of Shintoism. For these reasons it is difficult for the majority of foreigners to have a sympathetic understanding for what is essentially Japanese.

The crucial factor is its 'irrationality': the belief that the Emperor is descended from the Sun-goddess simply does not fit in with the universistic lines of thought. They cannot quite be reduced to a common denominator, and the Japanese have never succeeded in doing this convincingly. However, as they are not particularly philosophically minded they are not unduly upset by this contradiction. Their feelings and sensations are more important to them. The Sun-goddess, the wisdom of the I Ching, the whole of Chinese philosophy and a very devout Buddhism exist in Japan in more or less harmonious juxtaposition.

Although the Japanese imperial system was taken over from China, it is nevertheless rooted in Shintoism; the position of the Emperor in relation to the gods is therefore different from the position he enjoys in China. Tenno is, of course, himself a god, but he is not superior to all other gods. The Japanese Emperor cannot lightly interfere with the hierarchy of the gods, or depose them.

The Japanese in fact took over everything from Universism, including the Confucian moral code, the Taoist spirit world and Taoist practices for prolonging life. They even borrowed gods, the so-called 'Han-gods' (named after the Han dynasty) from the Taoist heaven. There is no Chinese astrological calendar, no book on soothsaying which one will not also find in Japan.

Of the concepts taken over by the Japanese that of 'Tao' is undoubtedly the most important. But it is interpreted by them more in the sense of 'way' and 'law'. The written character for 'Tao' (which the Japanese pronounce as 'do' or 'to'; in pure Japanese it is 'michi') is found in many well-known Japanese expressions, such as Shinto, the way of the gods; Kodo, the way of the Emperor; Bushido, the way of the knights, and so on.

*

Apart from the emphasis on feeling and sensibility, the Japanese further differs from the Chinese by a stronger development of the will. It seems to us as though the emphasis on the will is connected with that of the other two functions, as if a one-sidedness were being compensated by the automatic strengthening of another corresponding characteristic. One might here compare the Chinese and Japanese ink-drawings of Bodhidharma, who founded the Chang sects in China (Zen in Japanese). The features of the Chinese Bodhidharma reveal, not always but in the majority of cases, a superior understanding of the world, and a great, wise matter-of-factness and naturalness. One might say that he has something of the Chinese 'Wu-Wei' about him. The Japanese picture, in contrast, always portrays a pretty fierce gentleman of determined, almost demoniacal energy.

The Japanese will springs, however, from the 'total' psyche; it is not a detached function or, if one prefers the expression, it is not an independent propensity which has gained the upper hand. It is rather what C. G. Jung[30] understands by 'will', namely 'that sum of psychic energy which is disposable to consciousness'. The main aim of Japanese will is 'totality', to find the central point of heart and consciousness, in order then to act rightly as prompted by this centre. Hence one can speak of a will directed towards experiencing unity, and of a will to act rightly.

It is completely misleading, however, at least for the foreigner,

to speak for example of Zen-Buddhism as a 'religion of the will'.[31]
The Japanese never thinks of will *per se*, but of a 'correct' will,
that is to say, a will harmoniously embedded in the 'total'
psyche which should serve neither to disrupt this 'totality', nor
to expose it to one-sided danger, but rather to bring about its
realization.

The Japanese is, of course, also familiar with the Chinese
concept 'Wu-Wei'. If this is translated by 'inactivity—not
inertia', it can perhaps be said that with the Chinese the emphasis is more on the 'inactivity', whereas with the Japanese it
is on the 'not inertia'. The same can be said about the differing
kinds of meditation; if the *leitmotif* of meditation is 'not-willing
—not the absence of willing', then with the Japanese, and
particularly with Zen-Buddhism, the accent is again on the
second part. The important point, however, is that both parts
of these two watchwords are in themselves valid as applied to
both the Chinese and the Japanese.

In Japan the concept 'Wu-Wei' finds its purest expression in
the way the Emperor's rule is regarded. He rules by virtue of
his innate sanctity and divinity, in other words by reason of
the virtue and magic of Emperordom. These attributes belong
less to the person of the Emperor at any given time than to the
whole dynasty; since all is rooted in Shintoism—that is to say,
owing to their divine origin—the Emperors *must*, as a matter
of course, be endowed with a virtuous and magic power.

Despite the decisive impact of Chinese and Buddhist influences, the Japanese have never abandoned their boundless love
—as expressed in Shintoism—of their island home. Seeking
always the best for their fatherland, they sought centuries ago
to assimilate Chinese culture completely, in order to enrich
themselves intellectually. Again, in the nineteenth century they
tried to take over the culture of the West, which once again
called for a prodigious effort. Seen from the psychological angle,
this expenditure of energy springs from their love of their homeland. It also accounts for the extreme ambitiousness the Japanese
evinced up till their defeat in 1945.

This display of energy on the part of these people since their country was opened up again in the last century had another cause. The early tendency towards introversion had been fostered and cultivated beyond all measure by long isolation, so that ultimately—and almost as a psychological necessity—there had to be a reaction. In actual fact the change which came about in Japan at that time was not so sudden as it appeared to the outside world; the country had long been ripe for it, and had been in a state of ferment ever since the eighteenth century.

*

In conclusion, and proceeding from the foregoing analysis, mention should be made of the far-reaching identification of concepts in East Asia; these, with slight differences in meaning, apply equally to all East Asians. Politics, ethics and religion are for them *one*. Politics, for which there is no precisely corresponding expression in East Asia, is really a Western invention which, in the last resort, is connected with the differentiation of psychic functions. In East Asia there was in earlier times no separation of Church and State, and hence the conception of pure politics could not arise. Regular attendance at the Shinto rites at the imperial court in Tokyo remains even today one of the main duties of the Japanese Emperor (despite his recent loss of divine status).

'Power-theories', too, could not develop in East Asia, as there is no place in the organic system for 'power *per se*'. Only in the closest conjunction with all other factors is power allotted its place there; hence it is always religiously and ethically conditioned. Even religion itself is not something independent, but must adapt itself to the exalted laws of heaven and earth. In practice this means, in our language, that it must accommodate itself to political and moral considerations.

In the Li Chi, the *Book of Rites*, we read: 'Music and morals, punishments and commandments are ultimately the same; they are the means of turning the hearts of the people to community and of establishing the way of order.' These views accord well with those of Confucius, who also regarded music as a very important means of education.

In general, emphasis in China has been more on the ethical; in Japan, more on the aesthetic and the natural. On the other hand, certainly not all Japanese would agree with the one-sided view of Suzuki,[32] who says of Zen-Buddhism: 'Zen is indissolubly linked with art, but not with ethical teaching; Zen can exist without morals, but not without art.'

Hermann Bohner,[33] writing recently of Japan, says: 'Soil, kinship and calling are here linked together in a mysterious manner', a mystical homogeneity which is still felt to some extent even at the present day. The feeling of identity between Nature and the homeland, on the one hand, and the social, historical and religious life, on the other, is developed to quite an unusually high degree in Japan.

In the East Asians' outlook and approach to the world, then, we find again and again the same feature: integration and cohesion.

NOTES

[1] Lafcadio Hearn, *Izumo*.
[2] Marcel Granet, *La Pensée Chinoise*.
[3] J. J. M. de Groot, *Universismus*.
[4] Ibid. This theory of the Taiki does not appear in the primal text proper of the I Ching, but in the third supplement thereto, which is widely attributed to Confucius.
[5] According to O. Francke, and quoted by Glasenapp in his *Der Buddhismus*.
[6] Li Chi, *The Book of Manners*.
[7] Op. cit.
[8] Op. cit.
[9] Op. cit.
[10] C. G. Jung, *Die Beziehungen zwischen dem Ich und dem Unbewussten*.
[11] Op. cit.
[12] G. B. Sansom, *Japan: A Short Cultural History*.
[13] Lin Yutang, *The Importance of Living*.
[14] Op. cit.
[15] Sir James Jeans, *Physics and Philosophy*.
[16] Ibid.
[17] Bernhard Bavink, *Die Naturwissenschaft auf dem Wege zur Religion*.
[18] Op. cit.
[19] *Analects*, Book XV, 4.
[20] Ibid, Book II, 1.
[21] According to Hu Shih, *The Development of the Logical Method in Ancient China*.

[22] Op. cit.
[23] Ibid.
[24] Op. cit.
[25] Richard Wilhelm and C. G. Jung, *Das Geheimnis der Goldenen Blüte*.
[26] Ibid.
[27] Op. cit. Granet's book contains a detailed account of Chinese figure symbolism.
[28] We here abide by Jung's definitions of 'feeling' (*Gefühl*) and 'perception' (*Empfinden*). Cf. C. G. Jung, *Psychologische Typen*.
[29] Wilhelm Gundert, *Japanische Religionsgeschichte*.
[30] C. G. Jung, *Psychologische Typen*.
[31] Daisetz Suzuki, *Zen und die Kultur Japans*.
[32] Ibid.
[33] Hermann Bohner, 'Shotoku Taishi' (Mitteilungen der Deutschen Gesellschaft für Natur- und Völkerkunde Ostasiens).

Chapter 4

RELATIVE ASPECT OF RELIGIONS

THE Chinese were united not by a religion, but by a *Weltanschauung* which called for definite conduct in every aspect of living. There were two conceptions of Chinese Universism, a higher and a lower; it is the latter which embraces everything which is commonly called Chinese 'people's religion'.

Universism is made up of two complementary doctrines, the Confucian and the Taoist, both of which came into being and developed on Chinese soil. It would be wrong, however, to maintain that these two doctrines alone made up its essentials, as it is older than they are, and every Chinese was a Universist without necessarily being a conscious Confucianist or a Taoist. On the other hand, Confucianism and Taoism existed quite independently as 'religions', and frequently engaged in criticism of, and hostility towards one another. The confusion increased when ultimately Buddhism was added as a third religion; basically the latter remained independent, but it also became to a large extent interwoven with Universism. Let us imagine three springs which never quite ceased to well forth, and whose waters could not but flow into the same big lake. At the bottom of the lake is another spring, which represents the ancient pre-Confucian and pre-Taoist tradition. How can we now clarify this picture, in which all waters seem to intermingle? It is perhaps best to proceed historically and look at Confucianism, Taoism and Buddhism in turn, and finally to consider the so-called popular religion.

*

The Chinese themselves regard Confucianism as one of the 'three religions', although in the strict sense we should hardly consider it as such, despite the fact that since the Han period it has been the official church and the official religion—to use Western terms. The state official, the learned man, the Confucian and the priest of the official church have since then been one and the same. Confucianism, which was always defending itself against other schools of thought and trying to curb their influence, formed in the main the ethical and social backbone of the Chinese people.

It is not our intention to describe here the teachings of Confucius; numerous translations and appreciations of these are available. What we are here concerned with is the definition of their position within Chinese cultural and social life with its orientation towards the universistic and 'total'.

Is the whole Chinese people, as is sometimes maintained, really permeated with Confucianism? This question can only be affirmed if the necessary explanations and qualifications are added. In the first place, it should not be overlooked that some of the essentials of Confucianism such as ancestor-worship, the family system and many manners and customs flourished among the people before Confucius' day, so that it would be misleading if all these things were labelled 'Confucianist'. It is, however, correct that Confucius gave these institutions a new content and that they were strengthened and fostered by his teachings. Thus, if one says the people were permeated with Confucianism, the statement refers in the main to these ancient pre-Confucian traditions.

Moreover, Confucius' teachings, particularly his moral doctrines, have never had a direct, but only an indirect influence on the people, i.e. through the opinions and example of the state officials and learned men. The illiterate mass of the people had no opportunity of getting to know the classical works. The people were Confucianist in so far as this means universistic, yet even the validity of this view is reduced when we think of Confucius' high level of ethics and of his views concerning the essence of the saints and the noble-hearted. According to the universistic conception of society, it was not really the task of the people to think about such things. The people, mainly the peasants, were to get on with their work in a natural and customary manner and were to follow the regulations laid down by heaven and earth (and the government). Responsibility for the prosperity of the whole, a responsibility which also carried with it the rights and duty to occupy themselves with spiritual matters, rested according to this view with the Emperor and his officials, or at an earlier period with the Emperor and the feudal lords. Apart from the fact that it endeavoured to keep the life of the community and the state on the right lines, Confucianism bothered little about the people. It never aspired to popularity nor did it become popular. It recognized the religious needs of the people but did little to minister to them. Thus it came about that the people turned to magic and later to the popular Taoism and Buddhism.

So far as ritual was concerned, the main activity of Confucianism, as the official church, was the observance of the multifarious imperial sacrificial customs. These were, however, exclusively the affair of the Son of Heaven and his court and not that of the people. The same was true of the state sacrificial altars and the temples in the main provincial centres. To the imperial and official sacrificial service for heaven and earth, for the imperial ancestors, for the stars, for numerous gods and for deceased state officials who had deserved well of their country, one was added for Confucius and the most famous Confucianists. In his capacity as founder of his school he was revered as a 'state-god', and in the official view was more saintly than all the other saints.

The temples of Confucius were probably the most important of all the state places of worship, with the exception of the local altars for agriculture, etc. For, as de Groot[1] says:

A temple in which his soul and the souls of the leading lights of his school dwell was built in every administrative centre or in every walled town of the Empire, so that from these sanctuaries inspiration should emanate which was to arouse a boundless love of classical studies in the people; in this way every province,

8

district and borough was to produce many learned men, and so provide the State with many capable officials.

What are these temples like? These buildings, some of them architecturally magnificent—one has only to think of the famous temple of Confucius in Peking[2]—actually consist only of huge empty halls containing wooden plaques on which are inscribed the names of Confucius, his disciples and his successors. There are no statues of gods, images, golden lotus flowers, candlesticks or anything like that. A puritan spirit prevails there. These shrines in which one could neither invoke the gods or Bodhisattvas nor consult an oracle had no attraction for the people. They were the churches for the state officials or for those who wanted to become such.

There are two basic types among the educated Chinese: those who can be called Confucianist and those who can be called Taoist. Lin Yutang[3] says the Chinese are Confucianists when successful, and Taoists when they have been unsuccessful in life. There is certainly some truth in this, and it is probably linked with the fact that in earlier times youth, still cherishing its ambitions, preferred to honour Confucius, whereas old age preferred to immerse itself in the mystical wisdom of Lao Tse. China was also the land in which young men liked to try their hand at composing learned tracts, which would in any case have been their task if they were going to be officials, whereas old gentlemen composed lyrics. When after the first World War a widespread enthusiasm for Lao Tse developed in Europe and some believed they had now discovered the soul of China, many Chinese could not suppress a smile.[4] For an understanding of the real China both Confucianism *and* Lao Tse are necessary. And in addition the knowledge of certain Buddhist doctrines is indispensable.

*

A strict line must be drawn between Taoism as an attitude to life and a philosophy, and the Taoism which manifests itself as a popular religion. But this does not mean that the upper ranks of the priesthood in the Taoist church do not also include some highly educated Taoists.

As the most important aspects of the Taoist attitude to life were raised in the discussion of Universism, we can confine ourselves here to considering Taoism as a popular religion.

Universism is ancient but Taoism, as a religion, only came into being—and this is significant in the Chinese context—at the beginning of the new era. In the times of Confucius and Lao Tse there was no religion in the form of a Church, sect or any other organization with priests, monks or followers. At that time the rites in the places of sacrifice or in the temples were conducted by the princes and their officials, but not by priests. Nor did the subsequent Confucianist official Church have any priests, and the rites were performed by the Son of Heaven himself, by the imperial princes and the state officials. Prior to the founding of the Taoist Church the magicians, moreover, in so far as they were not astrologers, soothsayers, exorcists, etc., employed by the princes, had no common religious organization but practised their arts as private individuals in accordance with general universistic ideas.

The Taoist Church was founded in the second century B.C. by Chang Ling (usually called Chang Taoling), and from that time onwards his followers have lived as the high priests of Taoism in a monastery in the mountains of Kiangsi. But there was no priestly hierarchy subordinated to the High Priest, as for example is the case in the Catholic Church, nor did he ever exercise more than a moral authority over the faithful.

Thus the foundation took place at the beginning of the Han era when, in consequence of the disorders and distress at the time, the general need for spiritual support was particularly strong. The spread of Buddhism later in China was due to similar causes. Basically, Taoism contained the ancient universistic traditions as well as the teachings of Lao Tse, but right from the outset it embraced that wide field of magic and popular beliefs which had hitherto flourished in a natural and quite unsystematic fashion. Taoism crystallized all those universistic traditions which up to then had not been cared for either by Church or State. But that was not all; simultaneously, new myths were engendered and new gods appeared, and these, rejected by orthodox Confucianism, were incorporated into the new Taoist Church.

Extremely few myths have been handed down from the primeval and early days of China. But whether China was as poor in myths as would appear to us today, it is difficult to say. It is generally assumed that Confucius, along with others, opposed the collection and writing down of many of the ancient myths in order to push more into the foreground the teachings concerning the divine and exemplary Emperors, which were important for State and society. It is certain that in revising and bringing out a new edition of these ancient writings he selected those which seemed to him most suitable for his purpose.

When in the Han period new myths spread, particularly from the southern frontier areas of China, and later also came in with Mahayana-Buddhism, they found ready acceptance. It was primarily the magicians who laid hold of this world of the imagination. Richard Wilhelm[5] describes this development as follows:

> The magicians seized upon the ancient Chinese religion of Nature and interpreted it. In the same way they laid hold of Taoism, for the similes and personifications of Chuang Tse yielded many points of contact in this connection. It is obvious that Taoism underwent a complete reformation and mythologization. But the link-up proved permanent. Taoist philosophers from Lao Tse to Chuang Tse became the founders and saints of this popular religion, and the magic sorcery of the Fang Shi (magicians) became mixed up with their teachings. In this way the first beginnings of the Taoist religion came to be laid; by taking over the Buddhist forms of organization, they were subsequently given that stability which is necessary for a religious community.

According to de Groot,[6] many new gods, too, 'had appeared or had been invented' shortly before the Han era. These were mainly deified mortals, such as holy hermits and ascetics. But Taoism had also embraced the worship of animals and the deification of mountains, trees, rocks and rivers. Thus it came about that there was no end to the number of gods, which was later increased by the addition of the Bodhisattvas; it can only be compared with the myriads of gods who made up the Japanese heaven.

It is almost impossible to discuss all these myths, gods and demons, as to do so would fill volumes, and it is in any case unimportant for our purpose. For this reason only a few of the chief gods and myths will be mentioned.

The Taoist primal god is Pan-ku who existed even before Yang and Yin separated. When this happened he created the 'holy mother of creation' (the earth) and took her as his spouse. In this way the 'great Tao' arose. The union of this divine couple produced thirteen heavenly emperors who reigned for 36,000 years. These in their turn produced eleven earthly emperors, each of whom likewise reigned for 36,000 years. Their descendants are the oldest pre-historic Chinese emperors. Because of this legend, which only arose in the fourth century A.D., the original universistic teaching was given a fresh interpretation in the shape of anthropomorphous gods.

A trinity of gods are usually revered as the head of the Taoist heaven, and the second of these is the deified Lao Tse himself. But the most important and the most popular of the three is Yu Ti (Yu Kwang Ti), to whom temples (Yu Kwang Miao) are dedicated in almost every part of China. The paradise of Taoism is ruled by this Yu Ti, the Pearly King, and to a considerable degree it is equipped in accordance with earthly and human standards. It is also significant that the majority of Taoist gods were gradually married off. Among the very popular gods are Kwan Yu, a faithful and brave general of the Han era who is honoured as the god of war in many temples; Lung Wang, the Dragon King; Tung Yueh, the god of Taishan, the famous mountain in Shantung, and many more. The opposition of orthodox Confucianism was unable to prevent Confucius himself from being raised into this heaven of gods.

According to Taoism as a religion, the existence of a virtuous human being does not end with his death, as in the Beyond he is given eternal life and abiding youth; but, at the same time, he is not obliged to remain permanently in paradise, but as a spirit he can visit the earth and his relations. Thus one can say that the complete renunciation of the Here is intolerable to Chinese popular feeling. In the same way hell, too, which Taoism took over from Buddhism, is not a place of eternal damnation; after he has undergone several metamorphoses as an animal or human being, a man can escape from it and enter paradise. (This is a very popular doctrine and idea which has not, as one might think, to do with a metempsychosis, but after all with a palingenesis related to Buddhist views.)

Ideally, however, perfection and immortality were to be acquired in *this* world. This accounted for the very ancient practices for prolonging life, indeed for acquiring immortality if possible. The chief methods of achieving this were correct breathing, indulging in a certain form of gymnastics, a frugal diet and general asceticism. In the popular form of Taoism this developed, however, into the search for the elixir of life, the draught which was said to give immortality. Chang Ling, the founder of Taoism, was already famous for the elixirs of life which he brewed.

On the whole, Taoism is a definitely materialistic religion with the emphasis on this world, which has been adapted to the practical needs of Chinese life. In addition, as de Groot[7] explains, 'despite its lofty universistic basis it could not outgrow polytheism, demonism, anthropotheism, idolatry and fetishism; on the contrary, it fostered these sub-forms of all heathen religions and helped considerably in their development'.

Details of Taoist practices will be discussed in connection with the so-called Chinese people's religion, as the latter substantially contains the elements of popular Taoism. But as the popular form of Buddhism also helped to make up the people's religion, it is necessary first of all to give a brief description of the development of Buddhism in China.

*

It is difficult to say whether there are more Taoist or Buddhist temples in China, since existing sources of information provide conflicting evidence. The situation probably differs also in the various regions. So far as monasteries are concerned, it is at any rate certain that the Buddhist are more numerous. The temples of both religions, in sharp contrast to those in Japan, are frequently in a very bad state of repair and often lack artistic fitments. Again, in contrast to Japan, their priests and monks are poorly and shabbily dressed. Many are so poor, so badly fed and so badly disciplined that they beg quite unashamedly. It is, for example, hardly possible to enter the Lama temple in Peking unaccompanied.

Buddhism, which came to China shortly after the beginning of the new era, although news of it had probably reached there earlier, finally acquired a firm foothold in the fifth century. The receptivity to religion among the Chinese was particularly marked in the centuries round about the Birth of Christ. Some scholars, however, believe that but for the energetic support of certain Sons of Heaven, mainly of foreign descent, Buddhism would not have established itself.[8] In contrast to this, only scant attention is paid to the suppressive measures taken against Buddhism by other rulers. Richard Wilhelm, however, is of the opinion that the changing measures taken by the different Emperors had little effect on the great and genuine interest shown by educated Chinese in the Indian doctrine.[9]

Chinese Buddhism, which reached its zenith between the fifth and eighth centuries, later declined rather rapidly. It has, of course, exerted an influence on Chinese spiritual life and on art, which is not to be underestimated; but as a religious belief it has never been for the Chinese more than just one of the 'three religions'. The majority of writers who have concerned themselves with this question attribute this not only to the power of resistance of the deep-rooted Chinese *Weltanschauung*, but also to the lack of religious feeling among the Chinese. Bertrand Russell[10] says: 'China is practically destitute of religion, not only in the upper classes, but throughout the population'.

Glasenapp[11] considers the Chinese are 'slightly', but the Japanese 'deeply religious'.

Thus it came about that not China, but Japan which did not take over Buddhism direct from India but from the Chinese, gradually became the leading Buddhist nation, a position it has retained until the present day.

This is thrown into relief by comparing the behaviour of the Chinese and Japanese soldiers in the Buddhist temples during the Sino-Japanese conflict. The Chinese behaved as if they were in a covered market or a railway station. They set up their quarters in the halls of the temples, hung their rifles on the statues of Buddha and swept aside everything, such as bowls of incense, candlesticks, lotus flowers, images, etc., if they happened to be in their way. They even stabled their horses in the temples. The Japanese, on the other hand, in sharp contrast to the disgraceful way they behaved towards Chinese universities and academies, showed the greatest respect for these shrines. They never slept within the temple itself, but in the precincts or forecourts. Every Japanese soldier entered the temple with bared head, and bowed before the holy images as if he were at home in Japan; he never dared touch anything. But even the Japanese met with difficulties from time to time in the very orthodox countries of southern Buddhism, as the Siamese and Burmese occasionally objected when the Japanese troops wanted to bivouac in the courtyards of the temples.

*

All the Buddhist sects in China were founded between the fifth and eighth centuries. Of the original ten sects there are only about five left today. Again, that is different in Japan: the majority of the Buddhist schools in that country are descended from the Chinese sects, but they are all still active today. The Chang sect (Zen in Japanese) had the greatest influence on the spiritual life of China. Even today the vast majority of Buddhist monks in China, of whom there were said to be between 400,000 and 800,000 before the second World War, belong to the Chang sect.

According to Suzuki,[12] Zen-Buddhism can be interpreted as 'the Chinese reaction to the Indian world of thought as represented by Buddhism'. Buddhism and Confucian philosophy influenced one another strongly at the time of the Sung dynasty. Suzuki says of this:

> Zen took its practical attitude from Confucianism, whereas Confucianism as a result of Zen teachings, even if to a certain degree only indirectly, incorporated the Indian school of abstract philosophy, so that it finally succeeded in giving the teachings of Confucius and his disciples a metaphysical basis.

Suzuki also goes on to say:

> Hence it lay in the nature of things that the Zen priests became the propagators of Confucianism, without being any the less Buddhists. At bottom, Zen has no philosophy of its own. The culminating point of its doctrine is intuitive experience, and the conceptual content of this experience can be provided by a system of thought which need not necessarily be Buddhist . . . Zen Buddhists are sometimes Confucians, sometimes Taoists and even Shintoists.

Here we have it clearly expressed that Zen is actually not a religion or a philosophy, but a method. Zen, as a method, was something which completely answered the purpose of the 'total' and organically thinking East Asian. It is hardly possible to understand the Chinese culture of the Tang or Sung periods, without taking the influence of the Chang school into account. It is the spirit of Chang which is reflected in the drawings and poems of those periods.

Most of the other sects, in contra-distinction to the Chang sect, represent a Buddhism which accentuates belief in salvation. This religion of salvation which made a lasting impression particularly in Japan, is in its essence different from original Buddhism. For the latter, belief was only a preliminary stage via meditation towards perception; the goal being illumination and entry into Nirvana. Only very few are capable of treading this very difficult path. Consequently, the idea of salvation came more and more into the foreground of Mahayana Buddhism, and awakened in man the hope that by faith alone he would achieve his goal. For anyone who cannot follow the more difficult path, the experience of 'emptiness' of Nirvana must seem incomprehensible and consequently not very attractive. Thus, in Mahayana Buddhism the idea of Paradise came more and more to take the place of Nirvana. Prayer, faith and mercy took the place of meditation, the striving after perception and illumination.

This form of Buddhism which mainly spread among the people, lost its pure and deep significance very rapidly in China. The possibility of going either to paradise or to hell was pretty quickly recognized by the Chinese as a business speculation. According to their interpretation of Buddhism one could by all kinds of measures, such as influencing the good and evil spirits, services for the dead, the clever calculation of good and bad deeds, avoid the danger of a sojourn in hell in a quite sensible, purely universistic-taoistic manner. As a result, just the salvationist form of Buddhism has in China become a part of what is called the 'Chinese people's religion'.

In general, Chinese Buddhism made very great concessions to existing views and conditions. The Emperor was recognized as the 'living Buddha', and thus his pre-eminence was assured. Ancestor-worship, of course, was also tolerated.

Thus it came about that Buddhist bonzes conduct the rites of ancestor-worship; when they die, their souls are also provided with tablets. That is also the reason why in China one never quite knows in what kind of temple one is, since in Buddhist temples one can find Taoist and Confucian gods, and in Taoist temples, Buddhas and Bodhisattvas. Despite the many concessions, Chinese Buddhism, in partial contrast to the Japanese version, has remained consistent on one very important point, namely the celibacy of the monks, although just this important violation of Chinese family feeling made the advance of Buddhism in China extremely difficult. But the practically-minded Chinese have nevertheless found a way round the difficulty which this presents for ancestor-worship. Boys are often dedicated (or sold) at a very early age to a monastery; in such cases an older monk usually adopts the novice, so that when the former dies the latter can make the offerings due to him as an ancestor.

*

It is perhaps clear from the above why the East Asians have hardly ever belonged to one single religion, as is the case with Westerners and the majority of other nations. The different religions are for the Chinese only alternative ways to salvation; consequently he does not see why he should not make use now of one, and now of another doctrine. The people choose their priests according to the latter's capabilities, the success of their measures and their gods' readiness to help. The choice also depends on whether there happens to be a more famous Buddhist, or Taoist shrine in the neighbourhood. There are also in China, of course, adherents of sects who prefer to attend their own temples or monasteries and who, if wealthy, give financial support only to these. But even adherents of sects, when the opportunity arises, have no objection to taking part in the practices of other religions. The majority of Chinese do not regard the question of membership of a religion or sect as more significant, or worthy of more consideration than an enquiry as to the size of collar they take or their favourite dish.

For these reasons the faithful in China cannot be split up according to the different religions, nor can their number be ascertained. Accordingly, there are no statistics as to how many Buddhists, Taoists, etc. there are. The Mohammedans are the only exception; and, although they are less fanatical than in other countries of Islam, they have kept their religion fairly pure. They number about 20,000,000; most of them are not of pure Chinese origin, but come from the north-west and western territories of the Empire.

On the other hand, in all international statistics dealing with religion mention is made of the 'Chinese people's religion'. Usually the followers of this so-called religion are estimated at 350,000,000, though occasionally it is even higher, depending on the estimate of the total population of the Chinese Empire. Thus the figure given for the faithful of the people's religion corresponds to the figure of the total population less 20,000,000 Moslems.

It is no easy matter to give a person who knows nothing of Chinese conditions an idea of what is understood by this people's religion. In order to do this it is necessary to consider in the first place, as we have done, the ancient universistic basis and then to trace the emergence and effect of the three religions, since it is from the interplay of these elements that the present day people's religion has evolved and crystallized.

The ultimate goal of the Chinese people's religion is happiness, wealth and the prospering of man on earth. To achieve this it is first of all necessary to observe the rites and customs. Whoever does not abide by the customs which are laid down, in particular those concerned with family life, the duties of children, marriage, deaths, the choice of burial places, etc., or does not abide by all the other customs, such as those for the celebration of the New Year, the buildings of houses, the chasing away of evil spirits and for a hundred and one other things, disturbs the harmonious course of events and brings misfortune on himself and his fellow men.

The observance of customs forms the inflexible basis of the people's religion. Some of these regulations have gradually changed in the course of centuries, but others go back direct to the times of Confucius. Confucius himself was the chief follower of the injunction that the rites and customs should be rigidly adhered to.

Chinese life, even today, is largely restricted by regulations and customs which we, from our standpoint, can only regard as unnecessary ballast. In making their plans the Chinese always have to take favourable and unfavourable days into account, so that they can never carry them out according to rational and objective standards—in our sense. Furthermore, marriage and funeral celebrations are a costly business, and the latter in particular occasionally result in the financial ruin of a family.

Today, when a person dies, Buddhist bonzes are always summoned to exorcize the evil spirits and to foster the salvation of the departed, for Buddhism is, so to speak, the most sound of undertakings where all matters pertaining to the next world are concerned.

The Buddhist priests are able to provide the most details concerning heaven, hell and reincarnation, and they also know what methods the relatives should adopt in order to shorten the deceased's painful sojourn in hell. In Mahayana Buddhism the view prevails that the merits of one person can also benefit others; especially in China the original Indian doctrine of sin and atonement has never really caught on.

Thus the bonzes conduct services for the dead, which can last from three days to a month, depending on the financial resources of the family. It also happens in the case of rich people that Buddhist and Taoist services for the dead are held in rotation (in the same way as Buddhist and Shintoist services in Japan).

*

From what has been said it is clear that everything must take place at the right time, in order not to destroy the Tao of the universe. In consequence, one must adhere strictly to the instruction contained in the calendar. (The old imperial calendar has today been replaced by a variety of others.) De Groot's summary of these instructions may suffice for our purpose.[13] Days and hours were appointed for: marriages and the day on which the bride was to be taken to her husband's home; moving house; building new ones; starting repairs to houses, temples and ships; earthworks; felling trees; cleaning the house; putting the warp into the loom; beginning embroidery work; cutting out a new garment; sowing and harvesting; the first day of school; hunting; grazing cattle; bathing; shaving; opening a shop and starting a business; receiving money; exchanging goods; written agreements; journeys; meetings with friends or relations; submitting applications to the authorities; burying the dead; healing the sick; making offerings, and so on. Perhaps this list suffices to illustrate the range of these instructions.

Here, then, we find astrology and chronological divination developed to a point where they completely control a calendar-based existence. But the calendar itself is by no means the only determining factor; in addition gods, astrologers, soothsayers and magicians must frequently be consulted. Superficial misinterpretations and mistaken applications of the basic principles of universism have caused the people's religion to go to absurd lengths. What originally should have had, or actually did have a meaning, appears now as mere foolish superstition.

Oracles are consulted in the temples according to a great variety of methods: by paper cuttings, rods, etc. You can often get a written answer from a god for a few cents. You can also buy elixirs of life, lucky quotations, amulets, etc. It is not without reason that many Chinese temples are called simply 'Institutes for telling the future'.

The priests of all persuasions have, however, not only to observe the harmony between heaven and earth, and interpret the future; they have also to take the proper measures for influencing gods, spirits and demons. Keyserling[14] for that reason called the Chinese temples kinds of 'advisory centres on economic matters, or offices of culture where experts regulate communication with the spirits'. Many a Chinese priest actually sets himself up as a kind of 'specialist' in the exorcizing of demons, the summoning of rain clouds, in geomancy or in soothsaying. It is for this reason, as Granet[15] points out, that the people have so little respect for the priests, for 'l'exorcisme fini, qu'importe l'exorciste?' They are just experts who are paid for the work they do. For the rest, it is assumed as axiomatic that all bonzes and Taoist priests are poor, money-grabbing, and in general completely useless fellows who mainly steal and lie and are gluttonous into the bargain.

Of the 'Sen' and the 'Kwei', the latter—the evil spirits—have in practice the more important rôle in the people's religion. That is why we so frequently find the 'spirits' wall', be it in the old imperial palace in Peking, in the temples or in front of private houses. These walls are erected directly in front of the entrances, as it is assumed that the evil spirits cannot find their way in 'round the corner'.

One great obstacle to the modernization of transport and the economic system in China in geomancy. By 'geomancy' we here mean to imply that the choice of a place or locality is of great importance in connection with all manner of activities and occurrences, since every place is subject to different kinds of good and evil influences. The term, however, does not quite meet the case, as these influences emanate not only from the earth, but also from heaven. In geomancy wind, clouds, rain and thunder operate as heavenly gods, and rivers and the sea, as earthly ones. In addition, mountains, hills, rocks, trees, bushes and even houses are to be taken into account, since symbolic animals can be seen in their shapes. The dragon is the most important animal and its proximity is usually sufficient to create favourable local conditions. This 'luck of place' is mostly called 'Feng Shui' in China, and means 'wind and water'.

Feng Shui not only determines where houses are to be built, but also and in particular, the spot where gravestones are to be fixed. But as every newly built house or newly felled tree can change the Feng Shui, quarrels between neighbouring farms or even village communities are frequent. Sometimes, however, the unfavourable influences affecting the 'luck of place' can be counteracted by little tricks, such as, for example, making a tiny heap of soil, removing the tip of a rock, planting a tree and so forth.

Government and private enterprise for this reason frequently encountered difficulties in building roads and factories or in making an airfield, although the government, of course, tried, by enlightening the people, to shake the ancient belief. Communism will, in all probability, go ahead in this connection—as in countless other instances—more ruthlessly than did the former government of Chiang Kai-shek, which will not exactly conduce towards its popularity. In recent years, when a road was being built, it could happen, particularly if it involved the removal of graves, that the people became convinced that terrible misfortune would overtake the district or the country. If this was then followed by a large-scale Japanese air attack or by floods, then they felt confirmed in their beliefs. Mysterious rumours, prophesying disaster, circulated for example in 1939 in the Province of Szechwan when the motor road to Tatsienlu (East Tibet) was being made.

It is for this reason that the Chinese sometimes erect buildings on what we should consider totally unsuitable sites. For example, in Canton a factory was once built at great expense in a marshy hollow although the adjoining land was higher and drier: Feng Shui happened to be more favourable in the hollow.

Oddly enough it is above all the Buddhist priests who have adopted geomancy. Many Buddhist monasteries were founded for no other reason than to exert a favourable influence on a particular district. One of the chief duties of the monks is to influence the dragons in such a way that they bring neither too much nor too little rain. According to de Groot,[16] 'Buddhist monasticism may with good reason be termed a universistic priesthood of Feng Shui.'

*

The behaviour of the Chinese people is based less on strictly moral principles than on a set of rules which have been devised for communal living and to facilitate men's relationships with the spirits and the cosmos. In the course of time a scale of values has evolved whereby violations of the rules are assessed, enabling the gravity of each offence to be more or less determined. Consequently, good and bad deeds can be balanced against each other, and the constant aim is to ensure that the good spirits and the good influences have a slight ascendancy.

Thoroughly Machiavellian dodges are sometimes employed in this connection; for instance the demands of Feng Shui can be met by putting up a hedge or rolling a large stone into another place. The Chinese believe that spirits and magic forces are bound to particular rules, and it is possible to outwit them if one knows these rules. It is roughly the same as in *Faust*, where the poodle can get in by the door but cannot get out again.

There is in existence an ancient, extremely popular Taoist book, the *Kung Kuo Ko*, which translated means roughly, 'Manual of creditable actions and misdeeds'.[17] There are 1,230 good and bad deeds listed in this 'work of reference', and every deed is given a definite number of points. Thus if, for example, an individual helps his parents in doing a good deed, then he is given three points. If, however, he succeeds in preventing his parents from carrying out some wicked design, he gets as many as fifty points. For using unfriendly or hard words to his parents, ten points are chalked up against him. An official who locks up a suspicious character without interrogating him, loses three points for every day the interrogation is delayed. In this way every one can keep an account of his good and bad deeds. The result is usually totted up before the beginning of the New Year, so that a person whose good deeds outnumber his bad ones can appear before the shrine of his ancestors with a good conscience. On the basis of this method, and with the aid of accounting machines, it would be possible to compute the morality of a whole province!

The government and the Confucian intelligentsia were under no illusions as to the people's powers of comprehension, and they viewed the 'religious' conditions mainly from the pragmatic angle. Moreover, all sections of the people were fundamentally united by the same *Weltanschauung*, namely that of universism, even though the degree of understanding differed enormously. These cultural differences, however, are not to be identified with social classes; in China there are extremely superstitious people at all income levels.

9

Frequently, superstition appears as the obverse side of very sensible people who have little religion. It is the backdoor through which uninvited guests, who are not admitted through the front entrance, try to slip in. Glasenapp[18] says: 'In few countries are so many efforts made to banish the baleful influences of demonic forces as in sober-minded China.' A like predominance of superstition is to be found in all nations which are either ethnologically related to the Chinese or have been culturally influenced by them, as for example the Siamese and the Indo-Chinese. Whereas the Japanese, who are regarded as less rational than the Chinese, are also superstitious, their lives are by no means governed to the same extent by such practices.

*

In the past few decades a kind of controversy has developed over the question of the tolerance of the Chinese; this is probably due to the fact that the customary Western concepts and ideas do not fit Chinese conditions. In purely religious matters the Chinese were mostly pretty tolerant, but they became grossly intolerant as soon as the fundamental principle of their universistic attitude to life was at stake. Universism is composed of philosophy, religion and politics; it has only to be attacked from one of these quarters, to produce a bellicose attitude in the Chinese. According to universistic views one could belong to any religion one liked, provided one recognized the pivotal position of the Son of Heaven, took part in ancestor-worship and, for the rest, observed the traditional customs in civilized fashion. Buddhism was the only alien religion which spread in China because, after initial hesitancy and many battles, it finally subscribed to this attitude.

If, however, Christianity, which spread far and wide in the sixteenth century owing to the missionary zeal of the Jesuits, was later unable to maintain its position, then this was due not least to its reluctance to adapt itself to Chinese conditions.[19]

De Groot[20] was probably the first to point out the complete intolerance which seized the Chinese as soon as they suspected that their universistic system was being jeopardized. Richard Wilhelm[21] also confirms this view, when he says: 'In general, the Chinese government has shown itself to be pretty tolerant in religious matters as long as actual political conclusions were not drawn from such religious beliefs.'

We have evidence from a very early date, of the universistic basis of Chinese intolerance. In primeval days, whoever 'kept to the time fixed by the priest-king belonged to the cosmos, whoever wanted to introduce a new time was not only a rebel in the political sense, but also a blasphemer of the cosmic order'.[22] In the early period the downfall of the ruling house was also connected with the making of the calendar for, as the oldest calendars were often very inexact owing to inadequate knowledge, it frequently happened that official chronology agreed less and less with reality. It was then assumed that this was due to the Emperor's lack of virtue, and he was accordingly deposed.

The burning of books, the bloody persecutions of certain Taoist sects and of the Mohammedans, the coercive measures adopted against Buddhism in the early days and other incidents are evidence that one cannot speak of a general tolerance on the part of the Chinese.

There are reports of five large-scale burnings of books in China, of which the biggest was that in the year 213 B.C. under Huang Ti, the famous unifier of the Empire and founder of the short-lived Chin dynasty; at that time also numbers of scholars were locked up or killed. These measures were connected with the creation of the unified state, and with the criticism to which the Emperor's policy was being subjected by Confucian scholars. Thus it was not only a matter of power but also of a conflict between two schools of thought, both of which could cite Confucius as their authority. Richard Wilhelm says of this:[23]

One must bear in mind that the school represented by the all-powerful minister Li Si (Huang Ti's chancellor) also went back ultimately to Confucius. Li Si was a direct disciple of Sün Kuang. But this was a different school from that of Mongtse (Mencius). Nevertheless, some of the unifications which the Chin dynasty effected in cultural matters go back to Confucius. Confucius laid it down that only men who combined genius with authority should be entrusted with such cultural organization. Genius was necessary to ensure that the arrangements were good, and authority, to ensure that they were uniformly established. Confucius laid great store by uniformity in cultural matters, for only on such a basis could a firm moral code develop.

Here, then, we have an example of two universistic schools of thought clashing, in which the one with power behind it was by no means averse to using violence.

A further example of Chinese intolerance is that of the struggle against the 'Yellow Turbans', at the time of the rise and consolidation of the Taoist church. The Yellow Turbans were supporters of a Taoist school of thought, who were accused of being hostile to the ruling dynasty. The struggles raged for years, practically the whole of China became involved and much blood was shed before this sect was finally exterminated.

It was not necessary to engage in warlike hostilities against the Buddhists, primarily because they did not defend themselves; although they, too, in their early days, suffered some severe blows. For example, in the first half of the eight century 12,000 monks were forcibly compelled to return to the secular life, and the building of monasteries was forbidden. A government order in the year 845 almost proved fatal to the Buddhists; over 250,000 monks were cleared out of the monasteries, these, together with the temples, were destroyed (some 45,000 holy places in all) and the monastic lands were confiscated.

The same Taoist Emperor who issued this order had also prohibited Mohammedanism in China; despite this, a Mohammedan minority has always maintained itself there. In general, the same methods were used against Islam as against the other religions which came to China along with immigrants, as, for example, Christian Nestorianism, Manicheism and others. They were, so to speak, 'sealed off'; that is to say the foreigners were allowed to keep their religions, but one saw to it that the virtuous Chinese people were not led astray by too close contact with them.

In general, the attitude of Universism coincided basically with that of Confucius. The Master, while tolerant in religious matters, nevertheless expressly enjoined that false doctrines should be opposed; by these he could only mean such as conflicted with his teachings, and hence with universistic views. While there were no actual Wars of Religion in China, the country was nevertheless engaged in extremely bloody struggles not unlike those of the Thirty Years' War. These wars in China were waged to maintain the authority of the divine Son of Heaven and the philosophical, political and religious system which he represented.

*

Conditions in Japan are similar. Sansom[24] is right when he says: 'The Japanese as a people have displayed in matters of belief a tolerance amounting almost to indifferentism which has been rare in Europe', but it would be misleading to conclude from this leniency in religious matters that they are tolerant in general. No Japanese régime has ever been tolerant when the survival of the race and the state, and when the fundamentals of Shintoism have been at stake. No Japanese usurper has ever challenged the authority of the Emperor, however much he might have treated it in practice as a *quantité négligeable*. On the contrary, every person wielding power has been at great pains to point out that he is only exercising this power on behalf of the Emperor. It has practically never occurred to a Japanese to make himself the 'Tenno'. For the Japanese, too, religion was never something independent; it always had to conform to all the other general interests. For that reason Christians who went to Japan in the sixteenth century were at first treated courteously, as it was thought that they were bringing nothing more than a new religion. It was only when the Japanese government, as a result of mutual denunciations by the Spanish, Portuguese and Dutch who were engaged in economic rivalry, became convinced that the Spanish wanted to conquer Japan from Manila, did they adopt an intolerant attitude; and they had the Christians, both foreign and Japanese, tortured and crucified. That the persecutions of the Christians in Japan arose solely from political considerations is revealed by the fact that certain Japanese rulers at the beginning actually rejoiced at the thought that the Jesuits would involve the 'conceited' Buddhist bonzes in violent intellectual controversy.

When the imperial authority was again restored in the last century, the situation was similar to that in China as long as the Sons of Heaven reigned there. To put it briefly, in the last decades everything was permitted in Japan so long as it did not tend to undermine the divinity and the supreme authority of the Tenno.

Thus in Japan, too, we never find an intolerance deriving purely from religious sources; it is always bound up with political considerations. Like the universistic Chinese, the Japanese in other respects always endeavoured to be tolerant and indulgent. The good-hearted naïvety which wanted to recognize every religious faith, but which nevertheless adhered firmly to the view that 'the gods of our country and of the imperial house (i.e. Shintoist gods) are pre-eminently helpers and protectors', is expressed for example in *Jinno Shoto-ki*, one of the most famous Japanese histories (fourteenth century). It says:[25]

> While the Emperor shows understanding for religious belief of whatsoever kind and does not cast it aside, it must be imperial policy to ward off evil from both country and government. That is the religious belief in which the Bodhisattvas hold sway. Again, there is the doctrine which lays down that the gods of our country and of our imperial house are pre-eminently helpers and protectors. Whoever thinks only of one belief and despises and abolishes others, is guilty of a great mistake. The natures of men are varied and their powers of comprehension are different; therefore there is no end to the different kinds of teaching. If I do

not properly fathom the faith which I actually hold, and want to despise a belief with which I am neither acquainted nor do I understand, what a highly evil enterprise that would be!

Kitabatake Chikafusa, the author of these lines, was a convinced protagonist of the genuine imperialist cause, and hence of the Shintoist cause, at a time when grave disorders rent Japan, and the imperial house had split into a northern and southern dynasty. As an adherent of Zen-Buddhism, the existence of a divine Japanese Emperor was as much a matter of course to him as the desire to honour and respect all the doctrines of Buddhism. One can say that Chikafusa's words convey the East Asian spirit in its genuine and purest form.

*

As we have seen, whereas every Japanese is a Shintoist at heart, the nation as a whole can be regarded as Buddhist. But what in fact is Shintoism? This faith has no canon, no proper dogma and *Weltanschauung*, no ethic and no moral code, so that some maintain that it is not a religion at all. Nevertheless it has a whole heaven full of gods, numerous holy shrines, a priesthood and many kinds of ritual.

Shintoism can be defined in the first place as an innate feeling, compounded of love of the homeland and of Nature, a consciousness of history and the belief in the special quality, indeed in the divinity of the Japanese race. It might be said that the mystical feeling of identity between Nature in the homeland and the history of the people, makes up the bottom layer of the Japanese soul. Even if it has no writings of its own, holy books nevertheless exist; these are the ancient historical works in which the chronicles of the gods merge into the actual writing of history. Shintoism was born amid charming islands and bays, valleys and hills, with the sun rising over the ocean. Some years ago at the big annual art exhibition in Tokyo an enormous pictorial roll was on view. Its title, when translated, meant roughly 'The radiant, sublime Eight-Islands'. (Oyashima,

'Sublime Eight-Islands' is an ancient name for Japan.) On it Japan's history was depicted in the form of landscapes. Every Japanese, just by looking at a particular area, knows what once took place there, so that to him looking at a landscape is like turning over the pages of a Japanese history book. In the district of Yoshino in the sacred and ancient land of Yamato (the area round Nara) enormous placards are to be found everywhere, covered with detailed descriptions, mainly taken from school text-books, of events which once took place there. From time immemorial the cherry blossom of Yoshino has been famous for its beauty, but what would that amount to if one did not know that once Jimmu-Tenno, the first and almost half-legendary Emperor, crossed these hills to found the Empire, and that later the unhappy Emperor Godaigo and the hero Masashige Kusunoki, the faithful imperial servant, and many other heroes sojourned there?

The feelings and perceptions which form the basis of Shinto-ism are not easy to describe; one might also call this religion a missionary belief rooted in the mysticism of Nature. Basically, the soul of every Japanese is influenced by this Shintoism, even if he does not belong to any particular Shintoist sect.

For this religion is twofold, comprising official or national Shintoism and sectarian Shintoism. The former was revived in the last century, when with the reopening of the country the Emperor once again became the real ruler; some people actually maintain that in the interests of the dynasty and the unification of the Empire this type of Shintoism was entirely re-constituted.[26]

In official Shintoism the worship of the sublime ancestress of the Emperor, the Sun-goddess, together with that of the Emperor himself, and of the heroes who gave their lives for Japan, are of paramount importance. The big imperial shrines and those of the national heroes, as also the priesthood, were maintained out of public funds. The most important rites, like those in the palace, are conducted by the Emperor himself, who at the same time can be called the High Priest of Shintoism. The chief priests in the most sacred and important shrines of Ise, the sanctuary of the Sun-goddess, are of imperial blood. It is boasted that these are the only shrines in Japan in which a Buddhist priest has never set foot. In the national shrines of the heroes the rites are in the main conducted by retired admirals or generals, who appear in the beautiful ancient robes of the Shintoist priests instead of in uniform. Once again we come across the link between the Emperor and the senior priesthood, between the state officials and the ordinary priesthood.

Some years ago the Japanese government announced that official Shintoism was not a religion, but a state service. This step was necessary, as respect for official Shintoism was incumbent on every Japanese subject, and this had produced a conflict of conscience, particularly in the Japanese Christians. Once the deep obeisances and the clapping of hands before the imperial shrines had ceased to be regarded as religious acts, those of other faiths had no longer any reason for avoiding such duties.

After the Japanese defeat, this official Shintoism was robbed of its official character, and now no one can be compelled to hold it in honour. The great national shrines, together with those of sectarian Shintoism, the Buddhist temples and monasteries must as a consequence now be maintained by private donations. One can, however, be certain that the Japanese people will not allow these places to fall into decay. Of course the Emperor carries out the most important of his ritual duties as hitherto, but now they are regarded as his own private affair.

The majority of Shintoist sects came into being only in the last few centuries to satisfy a need for self-affirmation and inner composure in the face of omnipotent Buddhism and of the influence of Chinese philosophy. Today there are thirteen such sects, of which the largest, Tenrikyo, has over 4,000,000 members and followers. Compared with a total of 16,000,000 members of Shintoist sects, there are, however, 42,000,000 members of Buddhist sects, so that the majority of the people, despite its 'basically Shintoist soul', is Buddhist. According to the last census, taken in 1940, the total population of Japan, excluding

Formosa, was 73,000,000; hence 15,000,000 adhere to no sect in particular. Typical of the difference between China and Japan is the fact that in the latter country the number of adherents of the different persuasions, including the exact figures for each sect and sub-sect, can be determined.

All the same, every Japanese takes part, as opportunity offers, now in Shintoist rites, now in a Buddhist ceremony. (We refer to the ordinary Shintoist rites, not the official observances which were formerly compulsory.) In the building of houses, laying the keels of ships, naming aircraft, or planting the young rice, it is always Shintoist priests who are present; in services for the dead, usually Buddhist ones. On the other hand, as in China, on certain occasions such as weddings, deaths, memorial services, etc., both rites may be observed in succession. In such cases the official and social position of those taking part, the family tradition and the religious convictions of the principal persons, or of the deceased, are taken into account. Indeed, in Japanese houses the Shintoist ancestral shrine and the Buddhist domestic altar are to be found side by side.

In the majority of Shintoist sects the Sun-goddess is not the focal point, but reverence is done chiefly to other gods who occupy a more prominent place in the hierarchy of heaven. She only acquired her importance by becoming the ancestress of the imperial house; she is by no means the highest deity or the ruler of the heavenly hosts.

Shintoism has no images of its gods. These first came in from China along with Buddhism and Taoism. Primitive popular Shintoism is still today animistic belief in spirits, but it is not idolatry. The Shintoist shrines, the habitations of the ancient indigenous gods, are quite simple and empty. They are fashioned from wood in a simple style which is nevertheless impressive by virtue of its purity and harmony; their most beautiful adornment is the landscape against which they are set. They are made from natural wood, and are never painted. (In the whole of Japan there is, to my knowledge, only one exception to this.) The chief room of the shrine—mostly they consist of one room only and the shrines can be extremely tiny—is covered with mats. At the back there is usually a rather small metal mirror, (originally a sacrificial offering, but later regarded as the lodging of the deity) framed by two 'Gohei', which are strips of paper cut in zig-zag form and fastened on to sticks; these are symbolic relics of original sacrificial gifts of paper, hemp and fabric which later also came to be regarded as the lodging of the deity. In front are stacks of food, mainly rice cake and fruit, symbolizing sacrificial gifts. There is no room in which the congregation can assemble; it stands in the open in front of the shrine.

To the present day Shintoism has preserved something of its primal naïve and unproblematical character. Its basic note is devout, optimistic and attuned to the world, though this world is permeated by divinity and interwoven with mysteries. The Shintoists have no monasteries; it would not be in keeping with their views to be separated from Nature by monastery walls while at their devotions.

During the past few centuries, until the imperial restoration, Shintoism existed in a mixed, rather than in a pure form. In Japan, as in China, Buddhism carried to its ultimate conclusion its principle of adapting itself to local conditions. As it was unable to prevail against the indigenous gods, it incorporated them into its system. Thus Buddhism and Shintoism gradually merged into one another, and the so-called 'Ryobu-Shinto' resulted. An attempt was made to identify everything, ranging from the equating of the most holy deities of the Ise shrine with Buddhist concepts, to the admission of Shintoist tutelary gods into Buddhist temples; from the Buddhist veneration of Hachiman, the god of war to the images of Buddha, which represented the original stock of the ancient gods of Japan. In many Shintoist shrines Shintoist priests were replaced by Buddhist bonzes. Nichiren, the prophet and famous founder of a Buddhist sect, said: 'All 3,132 Shintoist shrines in Japan serve the protection of the Lotos-Sutra', and all the Japanese are the 'children of Hachiman', who in turn is the shadow of Sakyamuni (Buddha).[27]

The imperial-Shintoist restoration in the last century, however, made a clean sweep of this fusion. Since that time no
Shintoist god may bear a Buddhist title, and no bonze may enter
a Shintoist shrine. All statues, pictures and other Buddhist
paraphernalia had to be removed from Shintoist shrines. But
in many cases a certain confusion persisted; it sometimes happens
that the Japanese themselves do not know whether a particular
deity is a genuine Japanese god, Indian or Taoist, or even a
Buddha or Bodhisattva.

In the Shintoist sects one frequently finds a completely
genuine and deep piety which degenerates occasionally into
downright religious fanaticism. The East Asians otherwise
seldom pray; the ancient Shintoist 'Norito' are in fact hardly
personal prayers in our meaning of the word, but rather
petitions to the gods which are read by the priests. On the other
hand, in the Shinto sects spontaneous prayers are sometimes
offered not only in front of the shrines, but also on the tops of
the sacred mountains, such as Fuji, the 'Incomparable', on
Ontake and others. Shintoist fanaticism need not always, as is
sometimes assumed, be linked up with hyper-nationalism, it
can just as easily refer to the ethical and personal sphere.

Japanese Shintoism, which was nothing but a basic religious
feeling linked to a primitive religion of Nature and ancestor-
worship, was unable to satisfy the ambitious and intelligent
members of the island race. For this reason Buddhism, with its
philosophically well-grounded *Weltanschauung* and its matured
dogmas, found when it penetrated to Japan a receptive people,
ready to believe. Unlike the Chinese, who at that time already
had an ancient culture and the perfected system of Universism,
the Japanese had nothing of the same intellectual calibre to set
against it. Hence the success of Buddhism in Japan was more
widespread and more permanent. Despite the simultaneous
infiltration of Confucianism and of the whole of Chinese culture,
it was Buddhism which was chiefly instrumental in helping
Japan to acquire the status of a leading cultural nation.

*

When Japan first came to grips with Chinese culture, Buddhism was just at its peak period in China (fifth to eighth centuries). Although this religion was introduced mainly by
Chinese and Koreans and only very few Indians reached
Japan, it nevertheless retained far more of its Indian elements
there than it did in China. Glasenapp says[28]:

> Far more significant than all this (namely the preservation of
> Sanskrit grammars and the like in Japanese monasteries) is the
> fact that the Japanese continued the study of the philosophical
> teachings of the great Indian masters, so that today they represent
> the legitimate guardians of an ancient tradition, which has long
> since died out in India.

The great promotor and protector of Buddhism was Shotoku
Taishi (572–621), the crown prince and regent of the Empire,
who is regarded by many as the greatest Japanese who has
ever lived. His memory is still thoroughly green among the
Japanese. Everyone quotes him, Buddhists, Nipponists, pacifists
and militarists. He was at one and the same time a pious
Buddhist and a statesman. He it was who first attempted to
create a State of officials according to the Chinese-Confucian
pattern; he introduced the Chinese calendar, promoted the
arts and crafts, and sent monks and students to China. One can
also call him the first thoroughly nationally-minded Japanese,
for in a speech to the Chinese Emperor he set up the Japanese
Emperor against the latter for the first time as an equal in rank
and privilege. But despite all the services he rendered to politics,
economics and culture he was primarily a Buddhist. He had the
Sutras copied, prepared commentaries on them and read them
aloud at court. All his pronouncements were inspired by the
Buddhist spirit and were interspersed with Buddhist quotations.
Numerous monasteries and temples were built at his instigation.
Yet at the same time it was he who in a special instruction
recommended the worship of the indigenous gods and the
carrying out of the traditional rites. In him one has further
evidence of the conciliatory nature of the East Asian. Shotoku
Taishi can, to a certain extent, be compared to Charlemagne,

although in the course of Buddhist proselytization of Japan no one was compelled to adopt the new religion, and, far from felling the old and sacred trees in which the Shinto spirits dwelt, the Buddhist bonzes blessed them. At a later date Dengyo, the founder of the great and important Tendai sect, preached Buddhist sermons to the ancient Shintoist national gods in order to edify and please them.

The deliberately stronger emphasis laid on Shintoist traditions did not, however, take place until some time after Shotoku Taishi's death when, following Chinese example, it seemed advisable to underpin the prestige of the ruling house and the consolidation of the country with the help of the ancient myths. It was during this time that there appeared the two ancient 'histories', the *Nihongi* and the *Kojiki*, which can be regarded as the sacred books of Shintoism. Despite the unbelievable absurdities which they contain, the Japanese state in the last two decades wanted these books to become the 'official history of Japan'.

Shotoku Taishi did not value Buddhism so much for its esoteric leanings or its monastic orders; rather, as a belief for the laity and as a national religion. 'With this genuine Mahayanistic approach,' says Gundert,[29] 'he determined right at the outset the direction of the whole further development of Japanese Buddhism.' Thus we find that in Japan much store has been set by true piety among the people right from the earliest times.

The oldest Buddhist schools no longer play an important rôle nowadays. Of the larger sects today the Tendai (with over 2,000,000 adherents) and the Shingon (with almost 3,000,000) are the oldest. But numerically they lag far behind the Nembutsu sects, with a following of between 16,000,000 and 17,000,000. Nichiren has over 3,000,000 followers and the Zen sects somewhat fewer.

The Tendai and Shingon sects, both of which sprang up in Japan towards A.D. 800, are later foundations of the important Chinese sects, the Tien-tai and the Mi. The teachings of the

Tendai sect, which has also many adherents in China, is in general regarded as the perfect example of Mahayanistic dogma. The teachings of the Shingon sect occupy a special position inasmuch as they are very strongly influenced by Indian non-Buddhist ideas and rites. What is of the greatest interest in our context is the fact that at first the mystical experience of unity and the practice of meditation formed the core of both sects. But these sects were also at that time familiar with prayer, even if it was not prayer in our sense; rather were they short formulae connected with magic rites. Writing of this, Gundert says:[30] 'Thus in the fundamentally prayerless Buddhism, prayer also found a place, albeit an inferior one.' Both schools have developed an enormous system of magic ritual linked to their dogmatic teachings, according to which in general terms all living creatures are suffused with the spirit of Buddha or are themselves Buddha.

In both schools we find, on the one hand an earnest striving after perfection and illumination and the strict practice of meditation (according to legend Kobo Daishi, the founder of the Shingon sect, went to Nirvana), and on the other, the conducting of magic ceremonies and exorcisms which border on hocus-pocus; in addition, they worship many Buddhas, Bodhisattvas and numerous Indian gods. Even today the Shingon priests rank in Japan as the ablest specialists in magic and sorcery; amongst other things they can provide a good rice harvest, disperse bad weather, exorcise demons and cure sickness and maladies.

Both doctrines split into a philosophical *Weltanschauung* and into a popular religion, so that here, too, in principle we find conditions similar to those in China. In contrast to China, however, a religious revival based on faith soon took place in Japan, and affected large sections of the nation. A very large part of the Japanese population which was unable to follow the difficult and superior path towards illumination, but which on the other hand rejected the senselessness and superficiality of a formalistic common religion, now embarked on the path of faith.

The change was gradually brought about by the Nembutsu sects, in whose religion of redemption a merciful and benign Buddha and the idea of a pure paradise were the most important elements. Belief and the invocation of Buddha, and not meditation, were regarded as the proper way to salvation. To quote Gundert[31] once again: 'In this way, there came about in the depths of religious life the significant changeover from meditation to faith, from perception to simplicity, from subjective redemption by one's own efforts to objective redemption through the efforts of another.'

The most consistent of these sects is the Shin, which draws hardly any distinction between the priests and the laity, since it holds the view that salvation does not lie in having special knowledge, nor in asceticism and meditation, but exclusively in the trusting belief in Buddha which finds expression in the repeated invocation of his name. 'Only through the power of Buddha does salvation come about.'

These schools reject most sharply every kind of magic art, exorcism, geomancy (introduced from China), also soothsaying and the regulation of one's life according to the calendar. Originally, however, their teachings, too, went back to Chinese and Indian traditions.

It is characteristic of the complexity of the Japanese character that Zen mysticism came into existence at the same time as these efforts towards a renewal were under way, and that these two diametrically opposed schools of thought are today still extremely active. We have mentioned Zen teachings so often that we need not go into them again. As the influence of the Zen school has been generally of a spiritual kind, it cannot be judged by the number of its adherents. The spiritual leaders of Japan in recent centuries have been influenced mainly by Zen and only to a smaller extent by other Buddhist schools.

The most original Buddhist sect in Japan, if one may so term it, and at the same time the only one which was a purely Japanese creation, is that of Nichiren. Nichiren, who lived in the thirteenth century, wanted to create a kind of Japanese national Buddhism. It is for that reason that in modern times there has been such a particularly lively interest in his teachings. In the past few years the otherwise so self-controlled Japanese could be seen at their most fanatical at meetings addressed by priests from the Nichiren sect or at plays in which Nichiren himself was portrayed.

Nichiren began as a member of the Tendai sect, but after a long search he found salvation in a doctrine which is similar in essence to that of the Nembutsu sects. Meanwhile the Sutra of the 'lotus of the good law' was for him the sole basis of Buddhism, and he was, moreover, so possessed by belief in his mission—he felt himself to be the reincarnation of an early Buddhist saint—that he was intolerant of any other opinion.

When he had become convinced that the pious invocation of the Lotus Sutra was the one and only true way to salvation, he turned one morning upon the mountain top towards the sun rising over the Pacific, and repeatedly invoking the Sutra, proclaimed his new discovery to heaven and earth. In that hour the Nichiren sect was born.

Nichiren was a zealot and behaved quite differently from the way in which the Japanese usually behave. For example, he preached in the streets and squares to the assembled multitudes. Whenever he was banished by the government, or some other injury was inflicted on him, he looked upon it only as retribution for his own sins. He was neither reserved, nor very balanced, neither kindly nor wise, nor typically East Asian, but fiery, fanatical, filled with deep emotions, and also aggressive, enthusiastic and haughty. He believed in salvation through Buddha, and in the wonderful mission of his fatherland, Japan. But he did not interfere with the ancient gods of Japan. It was not a Shintoist but Nichiren, one of the most pious Buddhists, who as far back as the thirteenth century first spoke of the great world mission of Japan.

*

Somehow or other the Japanese will always remain Shintoists, regardless of whether they profess Shintoism as a religion. After their defeat in the second World War one might have expected, by the way, that there would be a Buddhist renaissance, but instead—the opposite of what one expects usually happens in East Asia—it was reported as early as the autumn of 1946 that the number of Japanese Christians had risen to 2,000,000; in other words in eighteen months one and a half million Japanese had been converted. For the present, however, one does not need to take this mass conversion very seriously, for except in a few genuine cases it was the fashionable thing to do. The Christian faith is the religion of the victors, and that is the main reason why it seems advisable to go into it a little more thoroughly. Bearing in mind earlier conditions, the christianization of Japan would not make such a big difference, as the Japanese would Japanize Christianity in exactly the same way as they did in the case of Buddhism. Should Christianity, however, prove intolerant and unwilling to make concessions to the East Asian psyche and to the East Asian *Weltanschauung*, then it could become quite a dangerous religion for Japan. Even the pacific-minded Buddhism was unable to prevent the emergence of the quarrelsome Nichiren and the modern Shintoist national fanatics. To a certain extent Japan has always harboured dangerous and explosive forces and men who from blind faith have been prepared to sacrifice themselves. Might it not be that an intolerant Christianity, whose history in any case is filled with crusades, inquisitions and wars of religion, would arouse and incite quite unnecessarily these elements in the Japanese people? In any case these are questions which can be approached from very different points of view.

In this connection I would draw attention to the very informative book entitled *The Meeting of East and West*,[32] by F. S. C. Northrop, Professor of Philosophy at Yale University. Northrop, too, seeks to get to the bottom of the West–East dichotomy, but attacks the problem rather from a philosophical than a pyschological angle. In broad outline he comes to the same conclusions as those arrived at in this study, but, by and large, I feel that the psychological approach to the subject is the more rewarding.

The fundamental difference between East and West consists, in Northrop's view, in that East Asia (by which he understands India and the countries to the east) fostered and represented the aesthetic component of living, the Occident the theoretic. These two components exist, according to him, independently of one another, but are nevertheless complementary. Each can be understood only from out of itself and not with the help of the other: Eastern perceptions can no more be understood by means of logical thought than the atomic theory could be evolved solely by virtue of the intuitions.

Everywhere in the Western world Northrop finds the same leading trait, namely an urge to seek out and explain the theoretical elements in existence. The truth which was thereby uncovered in the course of centuries was in general designated reason or Logos, and implicated the Western idea of the Good. For this reason, too, the divine was, in all Western religions, equated with the rational—what Northrop regards as the manly principle. In the West theism prevails, with the conception of a personal God.

Now, in this theoretical and at the same time theistic orientation, Northrop sees one of the principal causes of the many wars which have been visited upon the Occident. Not only the personal God—let alone the tribal God—is by virtue of his very nature intolerant and can evoke fanatical missionary zeal, but so are the theories themselves. A theory counts as the absolute truth up to the moment when irrefutable evidence to the contrary is produced, whereupon it is replaced for the time being by another theory which is in its turn regarded as absolute. The succession of differing philosophical systems is based on the way of thinking, and so also on the scientific *modus operandi* of the West. The East hardly knows these changes in philosophical outlook; each generation endeavours to rediscover the truths that have once been apprehended.

The different nature of the religious life in East Asia is thus to be deduced also from Northrop's train of ideas.

In point of fact we find that actual religions clearly occupy a secondary place in China, whereas in Japan they pulsate more strongly in the national life. But even in Japan the religions were always embedded in a search after a higher wisdom, so that no religious belief was able to acquire a dominant place in the national and spiritual life. The Japanese, like the Chinese, is also at heart a sceptic in religious matters. He is not a sceptic, however, in matters concerning the ethical and philosophical bases of human society and its adaption to the great harmony of the cosmos.

NOTES

[1] J. J. M. de Groot, *Universismus*.

[2] Whereas the majority of the Confucius-temples are today in an uncared-for and derelict state, the Chinese National Government—chiefly thanks to foreign encouragement—began on the restoration of the beautiful Confucius-temple in Peking during 1935 or 1936; this work was continued under the Japanese occupation. The whole of the Altar of Heaven and the Temple of Heaven, together with a few other old constructions were restored already before the occupation.

[3] Lin Yutang, *My Country and My People* (1932).

[4] Cf. Chang Hsin-hai, 'The Intellectual Situation in Modern China' (Comptes Rendus des Séances de la Société des Sciences et des Lettres de Varsovie).

[5] Richard Wilhelm, *Geschichte der Chinesischen Kultur*.

[6] Op. cit.

[7] Ibid.

[8] Cf. Marcel Granet, *La Religion des Chinois*.

[9] Richard Wilhelm, *Chinesische Philosophie*.

[10] Bertrand Russell, *The Problem of China*.

[11] H. v. Glasenapp, *Der Buddhismus*.

[12] Daisetz Suzuki, *Zen und die Kultur Japans*.

[13] Op. cit.

[14] Hermann Graf Keyserling, *Das Reisetagebuch eines Philosophen*.

[15] Op. cit.

[16] Op. cit.

[17] Mimpei Miyahara, 'Taoism, The Popular Religion of China' (Contemporary Japan, 1940).

[18] Op. cit.

[19] The Jesuits had accepted the Chinese term 'Tien' (Heaven) for the Christian God, while they acknowledged also ancestor-worship as a non-religious and traditional memorial celebration for the dead. This did not, however, satisfy the post-Jesuit Orders, who required a more precise interpretation of the Word 'God' and proscribed the heathen practice of ancestor-worship. This gave rise (1634–35) to the 'Battle of Rites' of nearly 100 years' duration, which further prejudiced the situation of the missionaries who were already facing heavy odds. In 1700 the Emperor Chang Hi sanctioned the Jesuits' viewpoint, but Pope Benedict XIV came out in favour of their opponents in 1742. Thereby Christendom was dealt a decisive blow, particularly in that a power outside China, namely the Pope, had

allowed itself to meddle with the religious affairs of the Middle Empire which in the Chinese view was entirely the province of the emperor. From then on, the persecution of the Christians grew worse.

[20] Cf. in particular J. J. M. de Groot, 'Sectarianism and Religious Persecution in China' (Royal Academy of Science, Amsterdam, 1903–4).

[21] *Geschichte der Chinesischen Kultur*.

[22] Ibid.

[23] Op. cit.

[24] G. B. Sansom, *Japan: A Short Cultural History* (1936).

[25] Kitabatake Chikafusa, *Jinno Shoto-ki* (Book of the true God-Emperor lineage). Translated and annotated by Hermann Bohner.

[26] Cf. in particular B. H. Chamberlain, *The Invention of a New Religion*.

[27] W. Gundert, *Japans Religionsgeschichte*.

[28] Op. cit.

[29] Op. cit.

[30] Ibid.

[31] Ibid.

[32] F. S. C. Northrop, *The Meeting of East and West: An Enquiry concerning World Understanding* (1947).

Chapter V

COMMUNITY WITHOUT COLLECTIVISM

THE peculiar characteristics of the East Asian world concept tend to produce, as far as society is concerned, an emphasis on the communal as opposed to the individual, and the idea that human beings fall into natural and organic groups within the community, the latter consisting of an organic hierarchy in which all parts, the upper as well as the lower, have definite duties and rights.

Our modern concepts of 'individualism' and 'collectivism' cannot do justice to the East Asian ideas of community, nation and State. East Asian collectivism is entirely different from that which is understood as such in the West today; it might be described as synthetic collectivism, as a concentration of natural communities, whereas modern Western collectivism could be called an analytical one, that is to say the concentration in a purely conceptual way of a society which is split up into individuals. Basically the East Asian is neither a collectivist nor an individualist. It all depends from which angle we view him. If we remember that he puts the whole before the parts, then we might call him a collectivist; if, however, we consider the way in which he defends the place allotted to him in his conception of the organic society and which can be taken from him neither by a Son of Heaven nor by the gods, then again he must appear to us as the defender of individual rights.

The deeper reason behind the East Asian's unawareness of the individualist-collectivist, or any other dualism, lies in the 'total' mystical experience of Oneness. If I hold the view that there is a basic unity in all earthly phenomena, if accordingly I have a strong feeling of identity with all existing things, then the fact that, in the process of coming about and realizing itself, this unity apparently split up into small parts, can only be of subsidiary importance to me. The whole and the parts belong together, they are complementary, none of them can exist alone and independently of the others. This splitting up is only the method whereby 'Oneness', the Absolute or the Tao is realized.

We have already touched on the problem of dualism (see p. 79) but we must return to it, as the views on which the East Asian social forms are based would otherwise be incomprehensible. Besides the conception of its organic structure, it is these basic views which produce a certain impersonal and anonymous element in East Asian society.

*

In this context, therefore, we must also consider the East Asian attitude to the concept of Subject and Object. In East Asia, Subject and Object belong together; they are ultimately the same. It never occurred to the East Asian to separate these concepts, as he really 'experienced' the opposite; namely the unity which is at the basis of all things, and also the relationship of all things to each other. These relationships are regarded as real, or at least apparently real, but the Subject has no reality apart from the Object, and vice versa.

Once again, as was to be expected from the foregoing, we note agreement with the findings of modern natural sciences. Of the many remarks on the matter we quote only two. Sir James Jeans[1] states:

> The division between subject and object is no longer definite or precise; complete precision can only be regained by uniting subject and object into a single whole.

Weizsäcker[2] says:

> The split between Subject and Object lies not in Nature but in our thinking—or rather, in Nature only in so far as we and our thinking have been created by her. Nature is not of two different kinds, but it is we who see the same thing in two different ways.

Our view that these philosophical ideas of the modern natural sciences lead to similar, indeed in part to the same results as those of East Asian mystical thinking, has also been put forward by others. In the last few decades many authors, particularly as a result of the study of Buddhism, have been led to surmise that the validity of many East Asian views would probably be strengthened by modern science. Recently Aldous Huxley,[3] amongst others, pointed out how modern science had confirmed mystical thought which for so long has been at a discount. Huxley's remarks refer more to the Western mystics than to those of East Asia, but as both thought forms are identical, it does not affect our argument. He says:

> Separate, individual existents are illusions of common sense. Scientific investigation reveals—and these findings, as we shall see later on, are confirmed by the direct intuition of the trained mystic and contemplative—that concrete reality consists of the interdependent parts of a totality and that independent existents are merely abstractions from that reality.

We follow this with a second quotation from Huxley, as this, to a certain extent, forms a bridge to our discussion of the concept of a personal God.

> More recently investigators, trained in the discipline of mathematical physics and equipped with instruments of precision, have made observations from which it could be inferred that all the apparently independent existents in the world were built up of a limited number of patterns of identical units of energy. An ultimate physical identity underlies the apparent physical diversity of the world. Moreover, all apparently independent existents are in fact interdependent. Meanwhile the mystics had shown that investigators, trained in the discipline of recollection and meditation, could obtain direct experience of a spiritual unity underlying the apparent diversity of independent consciousness. They made it clear that what seemed to be the ultimate fact of personality was in reality not an ultimate fact, and that it was possible for individuals to transcend the limitations of personality and to merge their private consciousness into a greater, impersonal consciousness underlying the personal mind.

The impersonal, or even supra-personal consciousness to which Huxley refers, is precisely that which conditions the views and actions of the East Asian. This consciousness, which experiences everything in one and one in everything, cannot envisage the concept of a personal God any more than it can individualism in the Western sense. It leads to a feeling of identity which is at the root of the East Asian 'total' organic conception of the community.

Northrop,[4] too, draws attention to this feeling of identity. According to him truths which we cannot comprehend with our logical-intellectual process, are arrived at 'intuitively' by the East Asian. They are inexpressible, yet not fortuitous and beyond our control, and the practice of meditation, which has already been tried out by numerous Occidentals, Northrop regards as scientifically unexceptionable. That which men discover through the technique of meditation, which cannot be expressed in words or at most can only be negatively paraphrased, is not just a 'nothingness'; it could just as legitimately be termed an ineffable 'something'. Northrop designates it an aesthetic continuum, which, as he sees it, disintegrates into an undifferentiated and a differentiated continuum. On this basis every existing thing would subsist in the self-realization of the undifferentiated aesthetic continuum by a process of differentiation. This is the basis of the identity feeling which binds the East Asian with all existing things, both organic and inorganic.

*

In general nothing is stranger to the East Asian than the Christian concept of a personal God; and a Japanese, Kakuzo Okakura[5] gives suitable, if polemical, expression to this attitude when, leaving aside Christian mysticism for obvious reasons, he says:

> In Christianity they never ascended above the human godhead to the vision of the ultimate universal. Eastern polytheism is a conscious symbolism, not a remnant of primitive personification.

Our philosophy in its eternal search for unity in variety has long ago scaled heights which modern Europe vainly tries to discern.

The same basic experience has led genuine mysticism within Christianity to emphasize the impersonal Absolute at the expense of the personal God; likewise it has not recognized the metaphysical reality of the individual.

Recently in the West the concept of God has also been discussed in the light of the results of the modern natural sciences; as a consequence these tend to support such views of the Christian concept of God as either represent pure Pantheism in Goethe's sense, or so-called Panentheism. In the latter we have an attempt to preserve at least in some form the shaken belief in a personal God. Without going any further into this pivotal question it can be said that mystical and East Asian thought in respect of the ultimate Divine have arrived at an unequivocal result. For this kind of thinking, when it reaches the plane of supra-personal consciousness, the Godhead, the Absolute, the last Unity—or Nothingness also—is something definitely impersonal. If a personal God is discussed at all, then he is not the Ultimate but, in the same way as man, he has been created by this Ultimate. A personal God would thus be something secondary, inasmuch as he is only a creation of the Absolute; his existence corresponds to thought on the plane of personal consciousness.

It will have become clear from the foregoing that the East Asian attitude not only differs from our modern, but also from our medieval attitude. At first sight it might seem as if the organic community of the Western Middle Ages, which likewise was barely acquainted with the distinct concept of the individual, were very similar to the social order of East Asia. Without doubt there were formerly more points of contact than in the modern age, but particularly on the most important questions (the concept of God, attitude to the Hereafter, the problem of the Emperor and the Pope) divergent views appeared at a very early stage. For our part, we did not foster the genuinely organic origins, did not broaden them or hold fast to them; what we did, rather, was to 'go on developing'. The differing philosophical and psychical foundations of our medieval community precluded the evolution of a 'universistic system'. What for us was a transitional state which did not fully develop, was brought to full maturity by the Chinese and became a permanent state. The aforesaid applies not only to the community, but also to the concept of personality. Many things which we can still observe today in East Asia have also influenced our development antithetically as reciprocal factors, but they have never become predominant in the West.

*

Part of the cosmic-organic concept of things is the view of the naturalness, unconstraint and spontaneity of happenings within human society (cf. p. 81 ff.). The Son of Heaven does not actually 'govern', but he fulfils certain functions at the centre, in the same way as the people have certain other important functions on the periphery. Indeed, the old 'universistic' Chinese system might even give one the impression at times that these functions ran on parallel lines, never cutting across one another. That was, of course, the ideal; everything was to run smoothly and harmoniously along the prescribed lines; there was to be no need for the Emperor to issue regulations, or to interfere in any other way. The observance of customs and the faithful fulfilment of duties by all members of the nation extended their beneficent influence in a miraculous fashion over the whole. Not only the virtue of the Emperor was important, but that of the people equally so. To quote Granet:[6] 'L'empereur enseigne le peuple et le peuple enseigne l'empereur.' Mencius, in a well-known saying, even went so far as to maintain, 'of the greatest importance is the people, then follow the altars of the national gods; of least importance is the Emperor'. Here we might quote a passage from the writings of the philosopher, Kuan Tse (also called Kuan Tsung or Kuan I Wu):

When the first Emperors under Heaven were alive the people were guided by the latter's divine and shining virtues; that they were excellent rulers lay, then, with the people. O, had they listened to alien advice they would have ruled unwisely; but they listened to advice which came from the spirit of the people and so they were holy. They had the noble virtues of a Tang and a Wu (famous Emperors of old), nevertheless they adapted themselves to what the people in the street said. Hence the wise Emperor yields to the mood of men; he suppresses his passionate nature and proceeds from that which gathers in the souls of the people. The first Emperors were good by nature and therefore formed with their people one body and one soul.

This thoroughly democratic-sounding view was ultimately the cause of the many revolutions and changes of dynasty in China. Japan in ancient days also experienced many revolutions and civil wars, but no change of dynasty. This was due to the Shintoist attitude of mind with its emphasis on faith. Nevertheless, the unquestioning feeling of kinship, indeed the identification of Emperor and people, is continually stressed also in Japan. The enormous devotion to their Emperor which the Japanese showed, particularly after the defeat in 1945, goes back in the main to this attitude. The people have a bad conscience and a consciousness of guilt towards the Emperor, because a war for doubtful causes had been provoked and then lost. The Emperor has rightfully been called the national conscience of Japan.

It is not the law but customs and the moral code which form the basis of the East Asian political organism. Laws as something abstract, theoretical and notional have always played a secondary rôle. All Chiang Kai-shek's speeches, as well as the announcements and propaganda of the Chinese National Government, always contained a moralizing element which sometimes seemed strange to us. Also, anything on lines similar to those of the 'New Life Movement' which, under government patronage, aimed in the pre-war years at the general revival and modernization of the Chinese way of life on a purely moral basis would be almost unthinkable in Europe. It was, however, chiefly the 'Officers' Moral Endeavour Association' which, added to the fact that it was directed by Madame Chiang Kai-shek, made such a strange impression on the foreigner. This association, which *inter alia* was opposed to drinking, smoking and even tea-drinking (Chiang Kai-shek himself drinks practically nothing but hot water), had a large modern club in Nanking where officers from the rank of lieutenant upwards had to listen to fairly unctuous admonitory speeches. One can hardly imagine that officers of any other army would allow themselves to be treated in this way like school-boys, and have their moral attitude and their habits laid down for them.

This tendency is, if anything, even more pronounced in Japan. The patience with which adult Japanese, whether soldiers, factory workers, employees or officials either listen to or read moral lectures is quite unbelievable. Most public and private speeches and addresses consist in fact of moralizing admonitions. Humility and virtuousness always come in for a lot of praise, and the faces of the audience adopt a corresponding expression. The Japanese suicide pilots were not wild, foolhardy fellows like the German S.S. types, for example, but quite mild young men who might almost have been called pious, and who with bowed heads listened to the paternal and pedantic words of their captain before they took off on their last flight.

The attitudes we have just described go back in the main to Confucius. But in China, in more pronounced form since the third century B.C., other views have been expressed, which however never quite managed to catch on. As an example reference may be made to the reforms of the great statesman, Wang An Shih, in the eleventh century; the influence of some of his reforms has extended down to the twentieth century. But the Chinese reformer was denied the complete realization of his plans. As the reasons for this are very typical of Chinese conditions, we cannot do better than quote Richard Wilhelm[7] on the matter:

His success was not a decisive one, and the strangest thing about it was that many of the most important and ablest men of the time were among Wang An Shih's most vigorous opponents. Why was this? Seen from the European standpoint all Wang An Shih's measures were of a thoroughly sensible, one might almost say, modern kind. Moreover, the energetic way in which he set to work on the antiquated system would certainly have earned for him in Europe the name of a great man. He regarded the state as a precisely operating machine. And in creating conditions which would enable the state machine to function precisely by riding roughshod over everyone, he would certainly have been successful in Europe where he would have found understanding collaborators in wide circles of society. It was different in China. He was regarded as an innovator. And that was the end of him. A number of the most important men fearlessly rose against him and remonstrated when he was at the height of his power, without even considering the evil effects this might have for them. The contrast was not only one of methods and aims, but also of the entire emotional approach.

*

The fact that in ancient China one depended on moral laws rather than on constitutional laws, civil codes and police regulations, also offers one explanation for the corruption which to a certain degree has always existed in China. Such a political organism pre-supposes well-intentioned, decent, honourable and incorruptible state officials and, owing to the lack of adequate legal control over those in authority, it gives all too much scope to wrongdoers and egoists. Ku Hung Ming,[8] one of the leading Chinese intellects at the turn of this century, declared: 'Good government in China depends solely on the moral character of the rulers. Thus, when morally inferior men reach high and influential positions the damage they do is enormous.'

The reason why corruption in Japan was, and still is much milder, is that until 1870 Japan was not a State of officials but a feudal State. The ruling caste of the Samurai was forbidden to engage in financial dealings and the moral code of the feudal nobility was rigidly adhered to during the Tokugawa period. Subsequently, modern imperial Japan introduced legislation on the European pattern, so that from then on control was possible, even parliamentary control from time to time.

Though in recent times both were constitutional States in our sense, the effects of this innovation have been completely different in each country. In China we had chaotic conditions, dereliction of duty by judges and officials, corruption and frequently open evasion and even non-observance of the laws; in Japan, on the other hand, we find public order, comparative reliability of judges and officials and adherence to laws and regulations which borders on bureaucratic excess.

If we dwell briefly on the bureaucratic spirit of the Japanese, it is because the latter is also indirectly a result of the old ways of thinking. The Japanese today clings as rigidly to the legal standpoint and to the law as formerly he did to morals and customs. He simply must have something impersonal, of general validity, which shall hold the whole together. In Japan it is not the official but the law which has the final say.

Even in time of war and emergency the laws are always obeyed in Japan; they can, at best, be altered by new legislation or one can somehow skilfully evade them. On one occasion in Southern Japan purely bureaucratic reasons prevented the Emperor from inspecting his troops. According to regulations only second- and third-class coaches were used on the branch line on which the Emperor was to have travelled; the Emperor's special coach, also according to regulations, had to be a first-class one. As no way out of the dilemma could be found the imperial inspection had to be abandoned. The efforts made by the police and the gendarmerie to keep their despotic rule at all costs within the law were just as typically Japanese. In Japan, as in all civilized countries, there is a regulation whereby an arrested person can be kept in prison only for a certain period without being brought before the courts. In consequence hundreds of politically undesirables had to endure the so-called Tarai-mawari (literally: driving about in the wash-trough); that is, for years on end they were moved from one provincial prison to another so that they should not spend longer in one province than the prescribed period after which court proceedings had to take place.

Regulations for putting the law into practice, which play an incomparably more important rôle than in other countries, are a special characteristic of Japanese legislation. The law alone is actually nothing more than a norm, which has no validity in practice. It is as if the Japanese mind cannot grasp the abstract, theoretical provisions of a legal clause and all its implications. He needs very precise regulations—that is the concrete, the practical, before he can make anything of the law. Of course this only increases bureaucratic pettifoggery.

*

In considering the structure of State and society in East Asia one is again impressively reminded that our customary concepts are not quite adequate to explain all the phenomena. If, for example, we ask if ancient imperial China was centrally organized, we cannot answer with a simple yes or no. If we bear the supreme power of the Son of Heaven in mind and the fact that he sent the mandarins and officials into the provinces, then we are inclined to say that this political system was centralized.

On the other hand, if we consider the definitely individual life of the provinces and the independence of the country districts and towns which almost bordered on autonomy, then the impression is that of a decentralized state.

The term 'centralized' has a 'mechanical' rather than an organic connotation and is thus totally inapplicable to East Asian conditions. We can best visualize the ancient Chinese State somewhat as follows: a vast land in which all classes go their own way quite automatically and as a matter of course; above them, a thin layer of officials who, rather like traffic police, only intervene to direct and put things right whenever congestion occurs in this ant-hill. In China, however, there was no *laissez faire*, for that is a condition arising from liberal ideas. China was not liberal, but organic; each person had his place within the family and within his class, and for every class definite rights and duties, manners and customs were pre-scribed. Whoever wanted to take a 'liberal' attitude and dis-regard an ancient custom would in many cases be considered a criminal and be treated as such.

We know that under energetic leaders provinces and classes rose against the central power, and that the supposedly peaceful China has experienced just as many civil wars, revolutions, disorders, revolts and wars as, if not more than any other nation. Frequently the cause of this lay solely in the fact that the imperial court and its staff of officials did not represent a proper central power, so that it was relatively easy for any dissatisfied and adventurously-minded individual to stir up disorder in the State.

The organization of feudal Japan was very complex, owing to the complicated system of vassalage. The Tokugawa princes, in their capacity of shoguns, were the lords of the Empire, whereas the Emperors lived in their somewhat shabby court at Kioto rather like high priests. But the foundations of this State, which had been deliberately underpinned by Chinese teachings, were equally organic; each class—warrior, peasant, craftsman and tradesman—had its proper place and its corresponding traditions, rights and privileges.

Modern imperial Japan represents a mixture of ancient organic traditions and modern Western political ideas. It has retained the ancient traditions mainly in three spheres—in the family system, in the anonymity and impersonal nature of its form of government and in the system of graded responsibility.

*

The most important group within the East Asian community is still that of the family. It is a collective organism; the head of the family, be it father or grandfather, has authoritative power;

at the same time, in all important decisions, he is accustomed to summon the family council in which the women also take part. Hence he is no 'individualist', as he attunes his opinion to that of the family. For the rest, the hierarchy within the family, and the duties of its individual members have been fixed since the time of Confucius. One of the Master's innumerable sayings dealing with the family serves to underline the harshness of this system: 'If a son does not serve and does not obey his father, he shall be put to death.'[9] The five capital offences in ancient China, in order of gravity, were: rebellion against Heaven and Earth, defamation of wise men and heroes, revolt against the social relationships, blasphemy of the gods and spirits, and finally murder.[10] Opposition to established human relationships, above all to those of the family, was thus regarded as a greater crime than blaspheming the gods or murder.

The main results of this system were, firstly the domination of youth by age, secondly the relative dependence of the individual, and thirdly the difficulties which beset the gifted, the able and the ambitious. The great social value of this family system lay, however, in the fact that it ensured the livelihood of every single member.

The domination of youth by age also offers one explanation for the general conservatism of the East Asian; this, together with the lack of freedom of the individual members of the family, today forms one of the most difficult social problems in East Asia. Many young people, including a large number of minors, run away from home, either because they can no longer bear the tight rein of the head of the family or are unwilling to put up with the obligations of family life in general. In recent years a number of them, not so much for political reasons as out of opposition to the family system went over to the Communists, as they are the only group who want to break with all traditions. On the other hand, some who could no longer endure the over-regulated and circumscribed life at home have cleared off into the mountains where, as in olden days, they have become soldiers, bandits or guerillas.

Japan doubtless has the same problem, but in this much smaller country the youngsters who run away often find their way home again, or else succeed in finding some kind of livelihood elsewhere. Conditions there were, of course, quite different from those in China; Japan was an expanding national State on the upward grade. Everyone could make a living if only he wanted to. And the majority did not run away from home out of viciousness but in order to serve some cause. In addition to this in Japan the nation always stands above the family, and thus it is impossible for the head of the family, unless he wants to be ostracized, to forbid his son to become a soldier or an official, or to adopt any other profession which obviously serves the nation's interests. Nevertheless, in the last few decades the number of those who have run away has assumed considerable proportions. In Tokyo alone, in one year just before the war, 25,000 minors ran away. This flight from home has, incidentally, set in once more during the post-war years.

(The East Asian is in the first place a member of the family, in the second, a member of a class or professional group, and only in the third, an individual.) If, for example, a Chinese or a Japanese does not get on with his superior, then this is not a quarrel between two individuals, but between the employee's family and the firm, or the authorities and so forth.

If an East Asian is successful in business or gains a lucrative post or position, he never enjoys the fruits of his endeavours alone. Not only his immediate family, but all his kinsmen too, have a moral right to profit from it. He must maintain the family home, or acquire an estate sufficiently large to accommodate his near relations; he must grant loans to his cousins and nephews of the second and third remove and provide them with recommendations. But the worst aspect of all is that as many of them as possible must either be found posts in his business or in the ministry he represents. That is the main reason for the large number of employees in all the offices in East Asia; roughly two-thirds of them are fairly inefficient idlers, and superfluous into the bargain. Frequently in a group of from ten to twenty people the actual work is done by one efficient man. In view of all this a successful man in East Asia frequently has a heavy cross to bear.

*

Foreigners who criticize these customs as being uneconomic and wasteful overlook the socially valuable side of the system. East Asia has no social insurance and scarcely any unemployment. The family is the permanent life insurance, and so the State does not need to step in.

It might be said that fundamentally one of the cardinal problems of our age is solved by this system, namely the right of every individual to work. The sickly, the cripples, the less gifted and even the weak-minded are employed by the family and are given simple tasks to do either in the home or in some occupation. When we consider East Asian conditions one thing becomes clear: that providing for every member of the nation is only possible at the expense of the able, and only if the view is held that efficiency and talent impose obligations, and must not exclusively serve the well-being of an individual. East Asia is unacquainted with the right to political freedom, but it does know the right to work and to security.

When during the last war over ten million city dwellers in Japan were rendered homeless by air raids the government did not need to provide them with accommodation, as practically all of them 'dispersed' among their relatives in the country. (Only about ten per cent who had no relatives in the country stayed behind and built themselves little huts amid the rubble out of rusty corrugated iron.) The Chinese used to behave in a similar way, with the difference that the catastrophes arising from war, civil war and floods could in their country assume such proportions that the proceeds of family insurance were just as inadequate as any other insurance in the world would be in face of such conditions.

(In the life of the State, too, the basic group, the family, can exercise a decisive influence.) This was until recently especially true of China where, since the disruption of the State following on the collapse of the monarchy, families and clans more than ever before just looked after their own vested interests without giving a thought to the general well-being. The most powerful of the clans had usurped the power of the State; it declared that it was working in the interest of China as a whole, and by no means in its own. This was the Sung clique which made a kind of family business out of the new China.

Chiang Kai-shek was never a completely independent 'Führer', but a representative of the Sung family into which he married in 1927 as a successful, but impecunious general. This does not mean that Chiang Kai-shek is not a brilliant and outstanding personality, but that in his dealings he had to consider the opinions and interests of the family. The Sung family council was of greater importance for the fate of China than the meetings of the Central Committee of the Kuomintang (on which the decisions of the Chinese Government depended). The most prominent representatives of the Sung clique are: Chiang Kai-shek, his brother-in-law T. V. Sung, and his wife's brother-in-law H. H. Kung. Madame Kung and Madame Chiang Kai-shek are T. V. Sung's sisters; at an early age the youngest of the Sung sisters married the much older Sun Yat Sen, the father of the Chinese Revolution. Thus, apart from the prestige of large-scale capitalism, the distinction of revolutionary struggle hovered round this family. Yet, the opposition of the Communists apart, they could never succeed in setting up a completely satisfactory régime; a clan which acquired power by cunning is incapable of combating all those terrible weaknesses and prejudices on which its own importance is based. One cannot abolish nepotism if one prefers to give appointments to one's own relatives, and one cannot attack corruption if the members of one's own family pocket money or speculate at the expense of the State. Still, Chiang Kai-shek's Government had no option but to act in this way.

*

China has thus for years been governed by a group with an outstanding and capable representative. Japan, too, has always been ruled by cliques, but in the last few decades these have lacked any really outstanding personality. Moreover, the Japanese groups are not pure clan combinations, but are to a considerable extent made up of economic, political and military interests. But in Japan, too, in sharp contrast to the West, family connections and clan relationships play an exceedingly important part in the formation of these groups. Here, too, it is quite impossible to understand politics without having at hand a reference book containing the genealogical trees of the leading families. It is impossible to understand the composition of a Japanese cabinet without for example knowing that General X is the son-in-law of the well-known industrialist Y, whose sister is married to the new Finance Minister, and so on. Furthermore, in Japan it is very useful to know the age groups, as it will be found that certain officers had already been together at the military academy, certain officials at the university together, and so on.

The Prime Minister and the other ministers do not rule, for they are usually pushed into the cabinet because they represent certain cliques. It is these anonymous and usually bitterly hostile groups which hold the real power in Japan. Japan has always been governed more or less in an authoritarian manner, but it is a completely impersonal authoritarianism which is not always easy to recognize.

Just as the Sung family council was the decisive authority for Chiang Kai-shek, so for the Japanese Prime Minister it was the counsel of his friends and not the cabinet meeting. In the latter he represents not his own individual view-point, but that approved by his group. This accounts for the fact that in Japanese politics one hears constant talk of the 'men behind the scenes' and the 'real wire-pullers'. When the Prime Minister resigns and his successor belongs to the same circle, then it is only an apparent change of government. A genuine change of government only takes place when a whole group is made to give way to another, as for example in the autumn of 1941 when Prince Konoye was dismissed in favour of the bellicose Tojo and his cabinet. In such a case the whole of the clique which has lost office, together with its clan appendages, falls into disfavour; constantly under suspicion, it is spied on by the police.

(This Japanese system of cliques in which one never knows who is the most important in a group, reminds one of the way the Japanese fishermen are accustomed to drag their nets along the shore, or carry out other communal activities without a chief. Frequently one sees thirty, fifty or even more fishermen hauling in an enormous net without being directed by anyone or even without a single word of command. Such communal labour has become virtually instinctive.)

The East Asians are fond of telling the story of the millepede who, when asked how he arranged all his many feet, stopped to consider the matter. In so doing he became so confused that he was unable to walk again, and died. The Japanese sometimes behave in very much the same way; asked 'just how do you do that?', they easily lose their composure and produce confused and irrelevant arguments which are nothing more than evasions, as they do not know what to say. Suzuki[11] is quite right when he says of his compatriots: 'Our conscious behaviour is in general not a very reliable yardstick with which to judge us.'

These anonymous groups which lack any organization or a chief and do not put things to the vote, etc. somehow always produce results. Frequently they talk at cross purposes for weeks on end, until one day the light suddenly dawns. It is a similar process to that which we have already described in discussing East Asian thought.

*

This rule by more or less anonymous groups is typical of the whole history of East Asia, although from time to time great political leaders have been thrown up. In China, owing to the possibility of a change in dynasty, some of these were identical with the Emperors, but this never happened in Japan. Apart from the half-legendary Emperor Jimmu, who founded the Empire, there have been no very famous Emperors in Japan. Emperor Meiji, who ruled for more than forty years, during which time modern Japan developed, is often called 'great' and he is said to have created modern Japan. Up to the present, however, historical and biographical research has not established just how important in fact was the rôle of this Emperor who was certainly not a complete nonentity; for to investigate the life and personality of any of the sacred rulers is regarded as sacrilege in Japan.

It is significant that ingenuous Westerners frequently focus their attention upon figures other than those the East Asians themselves would single out. Let us take, for example, the assessment of the famous Japanese trio, Oda Nobunaga, Hideyoshi Toyotomi and Iyeyasu Tokugawa (the founder of the Tokugawa shogunate), all of whom were active in the second half of the sixteenth century. Practically every foreigner instinctively turns to Hideyoshi, who is incidentally also the only Japanese statesman of old of whom we have a biography in a foreign language.[12] We feel his spirit is akin to ours, as he was a great individualist, a man of enterprise, great cleverness, energy and vitality. He was a poor, ugly youth and not even a member of a Samurai family, yet despite all the current class distinctions he managed to become the head of the State. While the country was still suffering from the effects of civil wars he conceived the idea of a great and prosperous Japan. He promoted oversea communications, commerce, industry and art, and—for the first time for over a thousand years—sent his troops to Korea and as far as the frontiers of China. But of the three the Japanese respect him least.

With the Japanese, Oda Nobunaga is the most popular. He was the first to restore a certain measure of order in the Empire, but he did not live to enjoy the fruits of his labours, since he fell as the result of a surprise attack by his enemies at the age of 48.

It is the sincerity of his efforts, the straightforward temerity of a bold, if not always very astute warrior, which appeal to the Japanese.

For the politically conscious Japanese, however, Iyeyasu is the greatest. If his achievements have not always been seen in their true light, that has been due to the fact that the imperial restoration in the last century was dependent upon the subjugation of the Tokugawa, the foundations of whose dominion were laid by him. In contrast to Hideyoshi, Iyeyasu was a typical East Asian. He was a man of endless negotiations and councils. In his politics, marriages were just as important as battles. He never pushed himself too much into the foreground and, perhaps for that very reason, again in contrast to the great and ambitious Taiko, he secured his line's rule over Japan for a period of 250 years.

A characteristic story is told about these three famous Japanese. One day they were shown a nightingale which would not sing. Nobunaga cried: 'Nightingale, if you don't sing, I'll kill you.' Hideyoshi remarked: 'Nightingale, if you don't sing, I'll force you to do so.' But Iyeyasu said: 'Nightingale, if you don't sing, I'll wait until you do.'

The English authority on Japan, Murdoch,[13] author of the most comprehensive history of that country, shares the opinion that Iyeyasu is one of the greatest statesmen in world history. For who, apart from Iyeyasu, can boast of providing his people with the foundations for 250 years of peace, both at home and abroad? This is surely an achievement unique in the history of the world. Thus the 'bellicose' Japanese achieved what was impossible for the 'peaceful' Chinese in the whole of their long history.

We find the same conflicting views about individual personalities in Chinese history. An instance is that of Richard Wilhelm on Wang An Shi (cf. p. 149). Wang An Shi never enjoyed a great reputation in China, but in European history he would probably have ranked as one of the greatest statesmen and innovators. Richard Wilhelm[14] also attempts to do justice

to the policy of Huang Ti and his chancellor Li Si by emphasizing the great importance of their centralizing measures,
which had as their aim the creation of order and the strengthening of the authority of the State. The Chinese, however, have
always had only a poor opinion of Li Si, not only because of the
ruthless and cruel way in which he put his plans into effect, but
chiefly because they instinctively rejected the idea of the 'State
as a perfectly functioning machine'; just as later, for the same
reason, Wang An Shi was a thorn in their flesh.

In general the East Asians are definitely sceptical of great
men, and they are less inclined than Westerners to become
enthusiastic followers of a religious, political or military leader.
For them the true concept of human greatness does not lie in
individual distinction, but in adapting oneself to the community,
and in such a capacity as to realize the most perfect form of such
a community.

*

Because of the organic structure of East Asian society the
division of responsibilities is in general different from that in
Europe. To take affairs of State first. Here one might speak of
'graded responsibility'. According to the ancient Chinese viewpoint, as we have already seen, not only the Emperor but also
all classes of the people had certain obligations in the promotion
of the well-being of the whole. Each had to carry a good share
of responsibility himself, either in his official capacity or in his
profession. It was not as though the Son of Heaven could use
centralized methods and issue orders right down to his lowest
officials, as was done, for example, in Germany under the Nazis.
The regulations of the Son of Heaven and his government merely
established the principles and were of a general nature, and
in the first instance did not get beyond the mandarins. The
latter's job was to see to the details of execution and so forth,
and it was not customary to interfere with them once they had
their instructions. The Emperor and the senior ministers were
not interested in how a mandarin organized repairs to an im-

portant canal in his district, or by what methods he collected taxes. In the same way the mandarin could not issue orders to his subordinates or clerks if these orders interfered with their sphere of responsibility. The system of graded responsibility existed throughout.

In principle the same tradition prevailed in the State system of modern China, but owing to a variety of reasons this system was so corrupt that the old concepts had become quite blurred. In Japan, however, we still find this tradition in its pure form. On this subject the American writer, Ruth Benedict, says in her admirable study of the Japanese character:[15]

> The State, moreover, is meticulous in recognizing 'proper place' for the will of the people . . . The State official advocating State-guaranteed farmers' credit associations or farmers' co-operatives for buying and selling must hold long-drawn-out round-tables with the local notables and then abide by their decision. Local affairs require local management. The Japanese way of life allocates proper authority and defines its proper sphere . . . Japan's motto is: Everything in its place.

But apart from this, it is chiefly Japanese politeness which high-lights consideration for subordinates. A Japanese who has been insulted is more prone than a Chinese to threaten suicide and in certain circumstances to carry out his threat. In Japan the power of superiors, including that of the government, always extends only as far as the next lower grade, and it frequently happens that instructions are held up by lesser officials who consider that certain laws, regulations or customs prevent their implementation. It is very difficult for a Japanese minister to carry something through if for personal or material motives his subordinates have made up their minds by hook or by crook to find some legal counter-arguments. Foreigners who believe that only contacts with senior officials can be helpful are sometimes disappointed. For it can happen that, despite solemn assurances from a minister or his deputy, the promised action is not taken.

The obverse side of this system is seen in the quarrels about spheres of responsibility which arise not only horizontally between ministries and other important departments, but also vertically between one grade and the next. Thus, for example, during the last war, despite repeated appeals for national discipline, it actually happened that the whole department of economics in the Japanese Foreign Office staged a strike, as the officials objected to the arrangement whereby some of their work was to be taken over by a new department.

It is where they pertain to everyday economic life, rather than to officialdom, that these old ideas have been more pronounced in China than in Japan. In addition to the division of responsibility, there was a strict delimitation of tasks and respect for the work and the profession of one's fellow man. The strict observance of these traditions is directly connected with the over-population of East Asian countries. It is only mutual respect which enables the different sections of the people to live peacefully together, despite this over-population.

Every foreigner who set up house in China was immediately aware of the importance that is attached to questions of qualification. The cook, indeed the cook's little assistant would, under no circumstances, carry food into the dining-room, or even dust and clean shoes, as that was the man-servant's job. The poorest ricksha coolie looked apprehensively about him if by chance he was carrying a suitcase, as it would have been a serious matter for him if his friend the porter happened to catch him. Even quite poor Chinese had an expert do things for them which they could quite well do themselves; the tacit understanding was, of course, that they could count on being called in when a job of their own line was to be done. To a considerable degree the Chinese identified themselves with their class or profession; only rarely did they change their profession. Despite widespread hatred of the Japanese, the reason why so many young Chinese did not want to do their military service was, at least at the beginning of the second World War, due to this attitude and not only to conditions in the Chinese army, which became more and more scandalous as the war continued. The average Chinese argued to himself roughly as follows: 'I am a cobbler; how can I suddenly become a soldier?' In addition, soldiering was generally regarded as a pretty inferior occupation and no one willingly changes his customary job for one which is not so highly esteemed.

All East Asians in dealing with workmen, peasants, fishermen, factory workers, shop assistants, etc., are extremely polite. The dignity of the other is never forgotten. At one time tips were always handed over in envelopes—in Japan they actually used special ones intended for gifts. It was foreigners who first introduced the crude practice of just pressing money into another's hand.

One of the most famous Japanese actors of the eighteenth century was accustomed, whenever he stopped before a workshop, to bow and ask permission to watch the craftsmen at their work, in order to gain first-hand experience. On leaving, he was equally polite in his thanks. It is said of Confucius that whenever the peasants held their ceremonial processions for the purpose of driving off evil demons, he dressed himself in his ceremonial court dress and stationed himself in front of his house at the point reserved for the reception of guests. Whenever the villagers arranged a carousal in honour of the old men (over sixty), he joined them. The Master never tried to play the part of the affable and familiar gentleman: he remained reserved and polite towards everyone.[16]

Respect for human dignity is even more pronounced in present-day Japan than in China. Chamberlain,[17] in his *Things Japanese*, which was written at the turn of this century, but is still worth reading, says:

> The most fundamental and all-pervading breach of courtesy —from the European standpoint—is displayed in the way servants and other inferiors behave towards their superiors. You tell a jinrikisha-man to set you down, that you may walk a hill. You will probably have to do so four times before he obeys:—he assumes that you surely cannot mean it. You order your cook to buy mutton. He goes straightway and invests in beef:—he knows beef to be cheaper, and thinks to spare your pocket. Disobedience,

in fact, is the rule—not disobedience from malice prepense, but from an ineradicable assumption on the subordinate's part that he can do better for his master than his master can do for himself.

The same writer also emphasizes that the Japanese, with all this politeness, never forgets what is due to his own dignity and sense of responsibility. 'Their courtesy does not go to the length of discarding their methods in favour of those of a social superior.' In no circumstances, in East Asia, must one shout at a person or vigorously upbraid him, not even if he has really done something stupid or wrong. If one does, one quickly realizes that it is pointless and at most it can result in disadvantage to oneself.

The Japanese are not quite so scrupulous as the Chinese in not poaching on the professional preserves of others; nevertheless, even after the big air raids on Tokyo had begun, one could notice that people avoided carrying their own luggage to the station, as this would have meant poaching on the preserve of the transport men. In any case the latter had more work than they could cope with, and in addition to enormously high rates, they usually demanded food and other payment in kind. But the Japanese are too tied to tradition; if a certain thing is 'not done', then it is difficult to disregard the fact. Foreigners living in Japan adapted themselves in the main more quickly to wartime conditions than the Japanese. If there is no alternative, the Westerner does not mind repairing the roof or the electric wiring; he will trundle his luggage to the station on a handcart, fell trees, plant potatoes or think up some device which will make it possible to get hot water for tea or coffee in an air-raid shelter. That was difficult for the Japanese; as this kind of 'individualism' was too alien to them, they constantly suffered from inhibitions.

*

The East Asians' lack of desire for political independence and their limited enthusiasm for the franchise is connected with their view of the organic structure of the classes and the professions. Politics is the occupation of members of the government and of state officials. It is not a good thing to become mixed up in matters of which one understands little because one is engaged in a different occupation. The Japanese were not particularly depressed when in 1940 the franchise was restricted to such an extent that it practically ceased to exist. In passing, it should be pointed out that it was not the wicked military who were responsible for the first step in this direction, but the conservative and pacifist Prince Konoye, with whose politics the people were in general agreement.

If, after their defeat, the Japanese evinced great enthusiasm for the franchise, this should not be taken any more seriously than their mass conversion to Christianity. It, too, is a matter of 'being in the fashion', and part of the tactics of getting on the right side of the victors. 'The Emperor expects that of us now', was roughly the way the people argued. Indeed, it is most unlikely that the Japanese or the Chinese, whose tradition differs basically from our own, will ever set up a democratic state in the Western sense and thereby create a society composed of the sum of many independent individuals.

The East Asian community of old did, however, have strong and genuinely democratic features. In general there is a greater disposition to attribute a certain democratic spirit to the Chinese than to the Japanese; hence, in order to do justice to the Japanese, we will consider their conditions in somewhat greater detail.

In the case of China it is pointed out with some justification that the change of dynasty made it possible to replace incompetent or unpopular Emperors by more energetic ones. China was an authoritarian state and the people had no right to interfere in affairs of government. If, however, in some part of the country the people's grievances became too great, they were accustomed to seek an outlet for their resentment in disturbances and insurrection. If these revolts found suitable leadership and support they were afterwards sanctioned.

The officials in the Chinese Empire were selected according

to democratic methods; that is, on the basis of examinations which were open to all. Only the sons of beggars and prostitutes were excluded. Actually this system worked well on the whole, partly because it did not cost very much to study, so that the sons of rich parents had not too great an advantage. This class of officials, selected on a democratic basis, and which to a considerable extent was identical with the learned men, formed the only class in Chinese society which enjoyed a special position and which had to be treated with particular respect.

Many Chinese—and this was true of ancient times too—endeavour to have as little as possible to do with officials, as they find it unpleasant and irksome to have to indulge in even more polite flowery phrases than are normally called for. There are old people who boast of never in their lives having entered an office of the authorities. Lin Yutang[18] aptly describes the social atmosphere in China:

> In a primitive agricultural society which China always remained, the spirit was essentially democratic. There was no class antagonism, as there was no need. The intercourse between these classes, except, as we have mentioned, the Yamen class (officials), was not marred by 'class feeling' and snobbery. In the best social tradition of China, a rich merchant or a high official may ask a wood-cutter to have a cup of tea and chat quite sociably with him, perhaps with less condescension than the inmates of an English manor-house speak to a farm hand. The farmers, the artisans and the merchants, being all part of the sap of the earth, are humble, quiet, self-respecting citizens.

Since 1867 in Imperial Japan the officials have been trained and employed in the same way as in Western countries; that is, on a democratic basis. Since 1890, apart from the interruption from 1940 to 1945, both government and officials have, moreover, up to a point been subject to criticism by Parliament.

But, as in China, the ancient indigenous democratic traditions in Japan are different. The extract from Lin Yutang, quoted above, also applies to Japan. Chamberlain,[19] referring to Japan, writes of 'the comparative social equality of all ranks and stations'. He continues: 'the Japanese and Far Easterners generally are at bottom more democratic than Anglo-Saxons on either side of the Atlantic'(!). He correctly describes also the complete absence of social snobbery:

A total absence of snobbishness towards the nobility is a commendable feature of the Japanese character. They do not, like us Britishers and Yankees, dearly love a lord—follow him about, imitate him, snap at him with kodaks, egg on their daughters to snap him up in a manner still more daring. They simply do not care. In their eyes, 'a man's a man for a' that!' Very often they do not so much as know whether the man has a title or not, and except in print rarely make use of it, but mention for instance Count Okuma as Okuma-san, 'Monsieur Okuma', as the French, too, would often say.

This indifference is also applied to the richest capitalist, the highest military ranks, and even towards the Imperial princes—but never to the Emperor himself. No one in Japan bothered about a general or an admiral in public; if senior officers were not actually travelling on duty they had to put up with elbowing from the crowd like everyone else, nor were they given precedence over others. Many foreigners, who, at the mention of Japan, thought only of militarism, were extremely surprised at the modest and reserved behaviour of the Japanese officers and at the complete indifference with which they were treated by the people.

In service life this is, of course, different, but we must always remember that it was from us that the Japanese first took over militarism in its full sense, with its drill, strict discipline and a centralized command. It was by no means only the tradition established by the bellicose Samurai rule of the Tokugawa—who gave their country a peace lasting 250 years—which was responsible for the modern militaristic behaviour of Japan, but in the main the influence of the Western spirit. The least of the Samurai or the simplest soldier would not have let himself be ordered about the way modern Japanese officers have treated their men, who were drilled on the European pattern. (The

12

army was first influenced by the French and then by the Germans, whereas the navy was modelled on the British.)

Another Japanese characteristic which ultimately goes back to ancient ideas is the number of strikes by school children and students. They are due to the fact that youth, both at school and at the university, regards itself as a class and hence, like all other classes, is insistent on its own peculiar status and responsibilities.

We find parallels among the Chinese students, but there are fewer strikes in the intermediate schools. There the professors and students regarded themselves as the descendants of the old learned class and to a considerable extent co-responsible for the political developments in their country. This accounted for the many demonstrations or protests on the part of Chinese students.

Lafcadio Hearn quotes many typical stories of Japanese school-boys, but as Hearn occasionally let himself be carried away by his affection for the island people, we prefer to quote Chamberlain, who was a very critical observer. He writes:[20]

> As for the typical Japanese student, he belongs to that class o youths who are the schoolmasters' delight—quiet, intelligent, deferential, studious almost to excess. His only marked fault is a tendency common to all subordinates in Japan—a tendency to wish to steer the ship himself. 'Please, Sir, we don't want to read American history any more. We want to read how balloons are made.' Such is a specimen of the requests which every teacher in Japan must have had to listen to over and over again. Actual insubordination has now become frequent, scarcely a trimester passing without the boys of some important school or other striking work on the plea of disapproval of their teacher's methods or management. Herein lies a grave danger for the future.

Chamberlain thus saw this danger as early as the turn of the century. In actual fact things continued in this way in the Japanese educational system until shortly before the outbreak of the second World War, when youth became seized with the idea of national honour and they came to heel, although some of them very reluctantly. Even before the Americans had landed

in the autumn of 1945, school-boy strikes broke out all over
the country. These were the first clear signs that there was a
change in the régime. Strikes by workers for economic and other
reasons did not take place until later, and they were fewer in
number. This tendency of youth will certainly persist in the
future; it was the older generation which was responsible for,
and lost the war, and youth will now want to do things better.
But one must not confuse such East Asian phenomena with
political democracy in the Western sense.

*

The Japanese were allied with, and have long had certain
leanings towards Germany, but none towards National
Socialism. The reasons for this are perhaps clear from what has
already been said. The very idea of a 'Führer' must be an
abomination to every East Asian; he saw in this idea only an
excess of Western individualism. National Socialist emphasis
on the 'people's community' he did not take seriously, as in his
view all Western nations are quite incapable of understanding
the essence of true collectivism. For him the National Socialists
were only disguised individualists. This is, of course, due to the
fact that so much of the ancient organic structure of the community still remains, and hence the East Asian can hardly
imagine a collectivism built up of individuals. Only Chinese
who have been schooled in Marxist rationalism can do this;
they wish to destroy the last remnant of the old organic community and introduce in its place so to speak a 'mechanistic'
collectivism. Should this new collectivism prove as potent as the
family system, which has lasted close on three thousand years,
then we should be faced in China with the replacement of one
form of collectivization by another. Paradoxically, however, it
is not beyond the bounds of possibility that Communism will,
to a certain extent, contribute towards the development of
individualism there, in so far as it is not the family which is a
member of the Party or a constituent part of the Communist

state, but the single individual. It is, however, still too soon to tell how things will pan out. Quite possibly the family will, despite all theories to the contrary, in practice retain for some time to come a certain significance. Besides, it must not be forgotten that the East Asians have from the beginning shown a better understanding of the communal idea than of the individual. They are never likely—and this goes for the Japanese also—to become pronounced individualists like the Occidentals in recent times.

What no East Asian can, by virtue of his tradition and instinct, abide is assertiveness, pomposity and a patronizing attitude towards subordinates. It makes a painful impression, for example, on a Japanese if a person so far forgets himself as to become conspicuous. Probably in no other country is it so difficult for leading personalities as it is in Japan. Politicians, or political generals, conductors of orchestras, press people, economic leaders and reformers know this to their cost. The better-known personalities in Japan are usually fairly old; it takes many years of arduous routine work and consistent intrigue before one has created a circle or joined up with a clique on whom one can depend.

Many Japanese politicians, on the assumption that it is 'modern' and a democratic sign of the times, have tried to become popular, but mainly to their own disadvantage. When Matsuoka, the Foreign Minister, a man of great intelligence who had studied abroad and who in 1933 created a sensation by announcing Japan's exit from the League of Nations, later began to give popular addresses in the Hibiya Hall in Tokyo, most people turned up their noses and regarded it only as playing to the gallery. Even General Tojo, who in any case was backed by a powerful group, forfeited much of the esteem in which he was held by the people when during the war he also felt it incumbent on himself to become 'popular' by going to the fish market and by allowing the newspapers to publish all kinds of sentimental and pompous anecdotes about his morning ride.

The fate of Seiji Nakano, the only thorough-going Japanese Fascist of whose name people had heard, was significant. A great admirer of Hitler and an enemy of the Anglo-Saxons, he built up an organization of uniformed youngsters and held public meetings at which he thundered in the Nazi manner. He had a certain number of followers, particularly in the country districts, but the broad mass of the people regarded his un-Japanese behaviour as ridiculous. The end of the affair was that the disillusioned Nakano committed suicide in 1943 (an act which met with the full approval of Tojo's Government).

A political leader more to the liking of the Japanese people was Prince Konoye who, unable to endure the ignominy of being suspected by the Americans of being a war criminal, committed suicide the evening before he was to have been imprisoned. (He would most probably have been acquitted.) In the first place, in the eyes of the people the Prince was from the outset justified in interesting himself in the country's affairs, as he came from a family in which for centuries there had been a tradition of service to the Emperor and to politics. In the second place, he had the dignity which was expected of him, that is to say he behaved like a statesman, and not like a tribune of the people.

The authoritarian form of government in Japan in the years preceding the defeat had nothing to do with Fascism or National Socialism. With equal, or even with greater justification Chiang Kai-shek's régime could be termed fascist, for in China there actually was a Führer figure—although, as we have seen, his power was restricted—and a one-party system (the Kuomintang). It may be objected that the statement that Japan was not fascist is quite unimportant, as in any case the Japanese were also an aggressive nation. This, however, would be to oversimplify the historical aspect. If two nations temporarily pursue similar aims, it by no means follows that they have the same character and the same mentality. Roughly from about the end of 1941 Japan was a military dictatorship which was supported mainly by the army and not by any party. In the course of the war this dictatorship became increasingly despotic.

This despotism represented an exceptional state of affairs and had little in common with the previous form of government in Imperial Japan.

*

It is sometimes maintained that it is the element of freedom which characterizes the Western countries whereas despotism characterizes Asian countries, including the East Asian. But here we should recall Hegel's antithesis (mentioned in Chapter I). Even if it is true to say that the element of political freedom in the individualistic sense is characteristic of the West, it is nevertheless doubtful whether in its long history East Asia's sufferings under despotic and arbitrary rule have been greater than ours.

As in Europe, arbitrary rule was always an exceptional state of affairs determined by the times, or a sign of deteriorating conditions. A despotic government which set aside customs and laws and did not respect the rights and duties of the classes always met with just as much hatred on the part of the East Asians as it did with us.

A brief description of the Tokugawa dynasty in Japan may serve to indicate how difficult it is to judge the internal conditions of a country fairly. It was not pure despotic rule, as everything was done bureaucratically and strictly in keeping with the regulations; yet at the same time it was the most strict, the most ruthless and also the most cruel government Japan has ever had to endure. The Tokugawa held the people together with an iron discipline and in accordance with the laws people were cold-bloodedly beheaded and hanged. Cruel punishments were introduced which were a novelty for Japan, whereas in Europe, for example, such methods had been the usual thing for centuries. Murdoch,[21] however, holds the view that this was the most exemplary feudal system the world has ever seen; he calls it a 'marked illustration of the apotheosis of feudalism that in interest and instruction is not surpassed in the feudal history of the world'. He also maintains that the Japanese in the seventeenth and eighteenth centuries lived better and had a better time than the French before the Revolution; in short, the Japanese people at that time were 'one of the happiest, most cultured and most prosperous in the world.' Sansom[22] is less enthusiastic; in particular he emphasizes the misery of the peasants, and the hundreds of regulations which enabled the government to interfere in every aspect of the private lives of all classes.

It is a fact that under the Tokugawa Japan blossomed econmically and culturally. It is fairly unanimously agreed that in a certain sense the country at that time was one of the most civilized in the world. For over 200 years no Japanese tax-payer needed to give a single farthing to meet war expenses. As against this there was the growing misery of the peasants at whose expense the ruling warrior caste lived and the merchants piled up riches, and an increasing dissatisfaction with political suppression. It is in any case extremely difficult to decide whether the Japanese people derived more benefits than dis-advantages from this highly authoritarian régime.

*

Before we conclude our consideration of society, mention should be made of the 'style' of the East Asian peoples, as through it they outwardly expressed their 'total' and organic views. By 'style' we understand the forms which govern the whole of their lives; that is, not only the arts, handicrafts, archi-tecture and costumes, but also social intercourse and the way in which manners and customs manifest themselves. Life in East Asia resembled a cult in which everything was ethically and aesthetically hallowed.

Up to ten years ago Japan could still have the effect of a revelation on an observer from mechanistic Europe; it was the last civilized nation which at least still had the remnants of an organically developed style. These traditions had disappeared in China at an earlier date.

As we have already observed, a strong rational and moralizing element predominates in the Chinese character, and an element of sensibility and aestheticism in the Japanese. For that reason Japanese style really embraced everything from a garden fence down to the last rice bowl; China has never shown such consistency. Greater and more significant works of art were created there, whereas Japan has produced a more uniform style. It would be possible for a Chinese who writes poetry or does thoughtful ink-drawings to live in an inartistic room and eat his meals from rough, inartistic plates. In Japan that would be almost impossible; the Japanese, when doing his ink drawings or Chinese characters, must sit in a well-proportioned, a very simple yet artistically appointed room. The room must be tidy and the straw mats clean; in the niche there will be some flowers or twigs arranged according to some symbolic or aesthetic principle in a vase suitable to its contents and to the time of year; usually a whole section of the sliding doors is pushed back, so that he can look into the open. Only then, when everything—but literally everything—harmonizes, does the Japanese feel in the proper mood. Everything must be 'kirei', which means both beautiful and clean, for the Japanese does not distinguish between what is aesthetically beautiful and hygienically clean. As far as eating utensils are concerned this cult has been developed to such an extent in Japan that the quality of the dishes and bowls and their harmonious combination is more important than the food itself.

In East Asia one still finds something of the charm and grace of movement which the West has completely lost. Even the Chinese, who have forfeited so many of their ancient traditions, are still superior to us in the art of movement. Even the porter, perhaps not in Shanghai but out in the country, involuntarily adopts a rhythmical and graceful way of moving so that his heavy work gives the impression of being almost light and elegant. When barefooted or badly-shod Chinese troops cross mountains they do not march, but step out in lively fashion and with excellent balance. Despite their raggedness they are a beautiful sight, and one could set them, just as they are, on the stage. All educated Chinese, except those who have lived a long time abroad, move with dignity; they detest the hasty, matter-of-fact and 'inartistic' movements of the Westerner, which they regard as an incomprehensible barbarism in otherwise quite intelligent folk. Those acquainted with the Chinese theatre will be able to confirm that it attaches more importance to the movements than to the looks and declamatory technique of the actor, or even to his delineation of character. One has only to think of the famous Mei Langfang and the much admired way in which he used his hands. The movements of the Koreans are the most beautiful of all. Korean peasants of both sexes walk through the rice fields as if they were taking part in an act of dedication.

The Japanese, despite their consciously accentuated cult of movement, are already strongly influenced by the modernization of life. Yet, even during the war, when people were hanging on to the outsides of over-crowded trams and railway coaches, newspaper articles were dealing with the question as to how the undignified impression caused by people hurling themselves on to conveyances could be avoided. They said that a culturally conscious Japanese ought to be ashamed of making such a ridiculous spectacle of himself. Actually it took a great deal, such as half-burned towns and disrupted means of transport before the Japanese began to press, push and get out of breath as Europeans do in such situations. If formerly one had seen a person walking hurriedly and purposefully along a Tokyo street one could have been quite certain that he was a foreigner.

The art of the dance still occupies a central position in Japan, and to a considerable extent influences music, the theatre and entertainment. The artistic dance is still privately cultivated in the same way as, for example, playing the piano is with us. Prominent Japanese statesmen and business men are experts in the 'Noh' dance, which incidentally is very difficult. At evening entertainments the artistic dance of the geishas is more important than the songs and music which accompany it.

*

As a 'total' being, the East Asian does not like living in a town in which romanesque, gothic and baroque churches stand, so to speak, cheek by jowl. He has never developed entirely different styles one after another, his 'styles' are actually nothing more than variations of the same theme. What interests us in the East Asian style is its unity of form and composition, which is in no way mechanical or stereotyped, and never monotonous. Every saucepan, straw mat, folding door, etc. is the same in Japan, but they are not 'mass' produced. In their bearing and behaviour all East Asians follow certain forms, customs and rules of etiquette, but their communities are no mere ant-hills. It is a collectivist style minus all the mass-produced termite-like disadvantages of which we complain in the mechanized collectivism of the West. Being based on symmetry of form, it is also beautiful.

The secret of this style is practical communal sense, with the result that it is just the simplest things in everyday use that are well thought out in an objective and artistically satisfying way. Many wrong judgments of East Asian art are due to picking out individual pieces and judging them in isolation. One cannot look at a Chinese ink-drawing or a Japanese woodcut, and then talk about East Asian 'art'. For these things are only part of an all-embracing communal style. It is pointless to look for, say, depth, for individual or unique greatness, or even for originality in an art which does not even strive after such things, but which in part consciously rejects them. The modern Japanese word for 'pure art' (*geijitsu*) was, by the way, only coined as the result of foreign influence after the country was opened up again. Strictly speaking, ancient East Asia not only had no art, but also no handicrafts; there was only artistic craftsmanship.

In Ancient China the national costume for every class was prescribed. The ranks of the officials were distinguished by different colours and patterns. The colours were chosen in accordance with 'universistic' analogies, so that the colour of his garment already vouchsafed each official his allotted place in the cosmic order. On ceremonial occasions not only the garments of the officials, but sometimes also those of the people, harmonized with the colour of the public buildings. The patterns on the materials consisted mainly of symbols—animals, plants and certain signs. Here everything had to have a meaning; that is, it had to express human relationships in terms of the seasons or the cosmos. Of course costumes in China underwent changes, but often they were not even the 'slow changes of fashion', but resulted from external influences (as for example having Mongol and Manchurian Emperors on the Throne of Heaven). Even today the Chinese still have an aversion to what is fashionable. For decades men and women in the towns have worn the ishang, whereas in the country both sexes still wear trousers and a short jacket (it can also be called a shirt), a style which goes back to olden times. The ishang is a much more practical, a cheaper and also a more social costume than European attire; accessories such as collar, tie, waistcoat and belt are dispensed with. Nor does it require ironing, as it is cut in such a way that after being washed it can be hung up on rods, when the creases fall out.

Unfortunately very little remains of the ancient Chinese arts and crafts. The traditions of the world-famous ceramics have died out, and today the Chinese eat from inartistic and poor quality plates of Western design, which even the poorest Japanese would only produce in an emergency and then with many apologies. The artistic treatment of everyday objects was never so widespread as in Japan, as becomes immediately evident when we compare the ordinary Chinese house or cottage with its Japanese counterpart. As against this the Japanese have never produced anything which even approaches the Forbidden City in Peking. One might describe these differences as follows: Japanese art is 'more democratic', as the Japanese have more feeling for communal style. There are no Japanese 'palaces' as such; even the imperial buildings are only finer and bigger dwelling-houses.

On the whole the Chinese have less feeling for materials,

though it did come out in ceramics and in certain woodwork, bamboo wickerwork, etc. Many Japanese are incapable of appreciating to the full the beauty of the Forbidden City, as they cannot get over the fact that the pillars are not made of stone or trunks of trees but are for the most part hollow, tubular wooden frameworks covered with a kind of clay and then painted. The Japanese regard this as bogus, as a sham display of splendour.

Among the foundations of a national style must be counted more or less uniform dimensions, that is to say a kind of 'standardization' in modern terms. From time immemorial many things were standardized, such as clothing, the dimensions and proportions of buildings, the rims of cart-wheels, the size of fields and that of wineglasses and rice bowls.

Just as people's movements and manners had to be beautiful, so had above all, customs and ceremonies. Art fosters customs, and conversely customs and ethics were there to 'give expression to beauty'. We read in the *Li Chi*: 'To harmonize the feelings and to lend beauty to expression, that is the task of manners and music.' (Cf. p. 100.) Confucius once remarked that when he came to an unknown district he could tell from the behaviour and manners of a water-carrier whom he met by chance, that good music was held in high esteem in that country.[23] The Master said of the classical *Book of Songs*, which up to the Revolution of 1911 was one of the basic texts for the Chinese state examination: 'The 300 songs in the book can be summed up in one word: Think nothing evil.'

Of all the rites the most important was the offering of sacrifice to heaven by the Emperor on the Altar of Heaven in Peking. This must have been one of the most wonderful and most beautiful sights the world has ever seen. A hymn to beauty—not merely an official religious act.

*

There was no other country in the world, China included, in which clothing was so much an integral part of the national style as it was in Japan. The basic shape of the kimono, as it is worn today, was taken over from the Chinese during the Tang dynasty, a thousand years ago; since then it has only undergone relatively minor alterations, whereas in the meantime in China other costumes have come into vogue.

The second World War dealt the old national costumes an unprecedented blow, affecting even the women's kimono which had hitherto remained immune. As one of the air raid precautions the government ordered all women to wear trousers over their kimonos, so that their movements would not be so impeded. In addition the long flowing sleeves of the ancient kimono were banned. Although the number of casualties was thus almost certainly reduced, this was nevertheless one of the most unpopular government regulations. We shall probably never again see the stylish and beautiful sight presented by the streets crowded with people wearing the kimono.

If we were to list the basic rules of Japanese craftsmanship they would be: simplicity, genuine materials, realism, usefulness and beauty; that is to say, the internationally recognized standards of every artistic craft.

In Japan, art and craftsmanship are to the present day concretely anchored in the religious. Many masters of their crafts still have ancient instructions and secret formulae which give particulars as to materials, dimensions and in what order and manner the various steps of the work are to be carried out. For example there are directions giving the number of hammer blows in a certain kind of work, whether one begins at the top or the bottom, and in certain cases, which fingers are to be used in holding the sewing needle, and so on. All these regulations are Buddhist-Shintoist, in part also Chinese-universistic, in origin. The carpenter, the swordsmith, the lacquer-master, none of these could carry out a single movement in their craft without being brought into contact with the laws of heaven and earth. At the very moment of their creation all things were sacred, even if they were only cheap straw sandals or troughs for washing clothes. But only that can be sacred which is at the same time both sensible and attractive, both realistic and aesthetic. That is the basis of Japanese art. A master-craftsman who produces successful work is the perfect human being who has fulfilled his 'way' (Tao).

To work out what is simplest is sometimes very difficult, and to set the right standards is equally difficult. Quite apart from modern industrial products, the following have been standardized in Japan since time immemorial: the size of the straw matting in houses, sliding doors, window shutters, chopsticks, towels, soup bowls, rice bowls, toilet paper and troughs for washing clothes; bed-covers, wooden patterns, brooms, feather dusters, the width of materials, the cut of the kimono, rolls of writing paper and so on. Most of these things can only be bought in one size, though some, such as rice bowls or troughs for washing clothes, can be had in several standard sizes. In the building of houses, too, everything is standardized. The only deviations are usually in the form of half-sizes. In consequence moving house is not a very big problem in Japan, as one can be certain that everything will fit into the new house. The Japanese has only few pieces of furniture, and the cupboards, also standardized, are always built-in. From the social point of view it is an ideal way of living and, moreover, allows of great mobility.

The carpenter has a particularly respected position among Japanese craftsmen, for houses more than anything else determine the character of a town and also of a landscape. Even during the strict feudal period many master-carpenters were permitted to carry two swords like the Samurai. The carpenter is so important that even now he is almost 'one of the family'.

Bertrand Russell[24] maintains that if they were as rich as the Americans, the Japanese even today would build 'towns as beautiful as Venice'. I myself am not entirely convinced of this. The spoiling of the Japanese towns in the last few decades is not solely due to all-too-rapid industrialization. As a result of this development many Japanese have lost all genuine and pure feeling for Nature and beauty, for architecture and craftsmanship. One cannot build houses of reinforced concrete in the spirit of those made of wood, and a certain time must elapse before one has accustomed oneself to the character of the new material and its suitable uses. A steel frame is a very different thing from a wooden one.

The Japanese street decorations for Shintoist festivals or Buddhist celebrations in the temples used to be unbelievably beautiful. Every street had its unity of style with definite colours, bunting, columns, street lights and lanterns, branches and flowers. Local organizations defrayed the expenses, and donations were always forthcoming from the normally frugal Japanese.

The tea ceremony is a characteristic feature of the Japanese way of life. We Westerners can sit quietly and silently together in order to listen to music; the Japanese, however, can sit just as quietly and silently in order to give themselves up to the aesthetic atmosphere of a room in which tea is served, or to that of a garden. They enjoy the cleanness of the straw matting, the veining of the wood, the bubbling of the water for making the tea, the branch of flowers in the vase—and in all these things, quite simple in themselves, the secrets and harmonies of the universe are revealed to them.

The national style which the Japanese once possessed, rested, as did the Chinese, on a 'total' basis; but with the former it has been moulded by the artistic sense of the people down to the very last detail. Hence the ancient East Asian communities formed not only philosophical and religious, political and ethical, but also artistic entities.

NOTES

[1] Sir James Jeans, *Physics and Philosophy*.

[2] C. F. v. Weizsäcker, *Geschichte der Natur*. (Twelve papers read in Göttingen, Summer 1946).

[3] Aldous Huxley, *Ends and Means*.

[4] F. S. C. Northrop, *The Meeting of East and West: An Enquiry concerning World Understanding* (1947).

[5] Kakuzo Okakura, *The Awakening of the East*.

[6] Marcel Granet, *La Religion des Chinois*.

[7] Richard Wilhelm, *Geschichte der Chinesischen Kultur*.

[8] Ku Hung Ming, *Chinas Verteidigung gegen Europäische Ideen*.

[9] Li Chi, *The Book of Manners*.

[10] Ibid.

[11] Daisetz Suzuki, *Zen und die Kultur Japans*.

[12] Walter Dening, *The Life of Toyotomi Hideyoshi* (1930).

[13] James Murdoch, *A History of Japan* (1925). The author characterizes Hideyoshi and Iyeyasu as follows: 'Where the Great Taiko might have ventured on the accomplishment of the impossible, Iyeyasu would never have done so . . . of these two it is Iyeyasu who is really the representative of the Japanese genius at its best . . . Hideyoshi was no representative Japanese; for pitted against even an Alexander, or a Hannibal, or a Caesar, or a Napoleon, he might well have come off on equal terms, chiefly on the ground of his incontestable originality. Against any of these great men Iyeyasu would have made in all probability but a poor appearance. At the same time, Iyeyasu was able to do what none of these great men (except Caesar, who was especially fortunate in so far as his heir and successor, Augustus, was a man of rare ability) were or have been able to accomplish, to transmit his power and his position to his known descendants for more than a dozen generations.' He writes in another place: 'To the broad, tolerant mind of Iyeyasu, centuries in advance of European statesmen in his attitude towards freedom of religious belief and profession, the aggressive, intolerant and persecuting spirit of contemporary European Christianity must at once have seemed loathsome and dangerous in the extreme, to the best interests of any country whose ruler was eagerly bent (as he himself was) on the maintenance of domestic peace and order.' He ends his discussion of Iyeyasu's clear-sightedness and tolerance with the words: 'Therefore, hats off to Iyeyasu—very respectfully.'

[14] Op. cit.

[15] Ruth Benedict, *The Chrysanthemum and the Sword: patterns of Japanese culture* (1947).

[16] Cf. the *Analects*, Book x, 10.

[17] Basil Hall Chamberlain, *Things Japanese* (1902).

[18] Lin Yutang, *My Country and My People* (1932).

[19] Op. cit.

[20] Op. cit.

[21] Op. cit.

[22] G. B. Sansom, *Japan: A Short Cultural History* (1936).

[23] According to L. Adams Beck, *The Story of Oriental Philosophy* (1928).

[24] Bertrand Russell, *The Problem of China*.

Chapter 6

PERSONALITY WITHOUT
INDIVIDUALISM

'FROM the Son of Heaven down to the common man the same applies: for all the moulding of personality is the key.' This saying of Confucius[1] cannot fail to recall Goethe's well-known lines from the 'West-östlicher Divan':

> Peoples, slaves and tyrants too,
> They have always this confessed,
> Of all blessings man can have
> Personality is best.

This concept has at all times underlain the philosophy and *Weltanschauung* of all East Asians, whilst in the West it has either been forced into the background by other tendencies or has sunk into oblivion.

By 'ideal of personality' we mean man's realization of himself, his prime and maturity, as well as his fulfilment in a death that is pregnant with meaning. Self-mastery and self-abnegation are the conditions necessary for the development of an untramelled, independent and mature personality. The concept of personality is an organic one, since it further implies the successful adaptation of man to his immediate environment, and his successful incorporation in it. This concept remains unaffected by individualism and collectivism: it rises above both.

*

Realization of the self is normally referred to in modern psychology as 'individuation'. C. G. Jung[2] points out that it is easy to misinterpret this concept by failing to understand that

185

self-realization and self-abnegation belong together and do not conflict. He says on this point:

This misconception is quite common, and lies in an inadequate distinction between individualism and individuation. Individualism consists in deliberately giving prominence to and emphasizing presumed originality, as opposed to collective considerations and responsibilities. Individuation on the other hand means a better and more complete fulfilment of man's collective responsibilities, in that, by making adequate allowance for what is peculiar to an individual, better fulfilment of his social aptitudes may be expected than when these characteristics are neglected or suppressed. One must by no means interpret the uniqueness of the individual as something unusual in his substance or his composition, but much more as a unique combination of qualities, or a distinction in the degree to which functions and faculties, universal in themselves, have been differentiated.

Every human face has a nose, two eyes, etc., but these universal factors are variable, and it is this variability that makes individual personality possible. Individuation can therefore only represent a process of psychological development leading to the fulfilment of given individual conditions or, in other words, to the evolution of the particular predetermined entity that is man as we know him.

He does not thereby become 'selfish' in the generally accepted sense of the term, but simply fulfils his own specific nature. As we have already noted, there is a world of difference between this and egoism or individualism.

In so far, therefore, as the human being as a living entity is made up of universal attributes, it is collective in the full sense of the term, and consequently, in no sort of antithesis to collectivity. To accentuate that which is peculiar to an individual is therefore to contradict this basic fact of existence. Individuation, on the other hand, seeks to ensure an active co-operation of all factors.

This concept of individuation coincides exactly with the basic outlook of the East Asians. It provides the explanation for the fact that the East Asians are deeply conscious that the point at issue is not so much the realization of an individual being (in our sense!) as of a given human type. Since, according to the organic view of things, every man has his own particular place in society, with which a special 'way' (Tao) is associated, it follows that the process of individuation can only be accomplished in conformity with this 'way'. The East Asian strives to become the perfect type of craftsman or artist, of learned man or soldier, and by achieving this aim he becomes at the same time a perfect being—a 'personality'. The higher and better the stage of development to which a given type can attain within organic society, the more harmonious will be the whole entity. It is for these reasons that the high estimation—indeed cult—of personality is of such prime significance in East Asia.

In this ideal of personality greater weight attaches to universally human characteristics than to individual peculiarities. Individuation, and with it the doctrines of consciousness which were developed particularly in association with the practice of meditation, are based largely on the 'universal factors' referred to in the passage quoted above. Jung's theory that the individual nature of a personality is not determined by 'something unusual in his substance or his composition', but rather that it must be understood as 'a unique combination of qualities, or a distinction in the degree to which functions and faculties, universal in themselves, have been differentiated', corresponds to Buddhist teachings.

The purpose in life of every East Asian is, at least in principle, to achieve an assured unfolding of the Self, a purity—one is almost tempted to say, hygiene—of the soul: this striving runs through the whole of East Asian culture.

These considerations explain, moreover, why it is that the East Asian so easily gets the impression that the present-day Westerner is 'unclean', for he believes that he detects in him a lack of this hygiene of the soul, an ignorance of the workings— the unconscious conflicts, disharmonies and impulses—of his own self.

In this sphere also the Western world is today about to resume contact with ideals it once possessed and later forgot; ideals that had an affinity with those of East Asia. In his most ambitious novel,[3] the action of which takes place *in the future*, Hermann Hesse has this to say:

> It is certainly the case that what we today understand by personality has a quite different meaning from that which it had for the biographers and historians of earlier times. One might almost say that the most significant feature in a personality appeared to them, and notably to the writers of those epochs having a pronounced leaning towards biography, to be anything divergent, at variance with the normal, singular, or often even pathological. We of today, on the other hand, only speak of a man as a significant personality when we encounter some-one who, abjuring all originality and singularity, succeeds in attaining the highest possible degree of conformity with the universal, of service to that which is above personality. If we look into the matter more closely we find that this ideal was already known to antiquity: the ancient Chinese figures of 'the wise man' or 'the perfect man', for example, or the ideal of Socratic moral philosophy, are scarcely distinguishable from our present-day ideal. Many great spiritual organizations, furthermore, such as the Church of Rome at its periods of greatest influence, were familiar with similar principles; and many of its greatest figures appear to us to be classic representatives of types, like the figures of early Greek statuary, rather than individual persons.

Related to this East Asian idealization of personality is the concept of man's immanent divinity, which, in the lower forms of religion, finds expression in the worship of saints and sages, and in the erection of statues representing them. Saints and sages, in the eyes of the ancient Chinese, took precedence over the Gods, for the mysticism of the 'total' outlook does not conceive of anything higher than man, who has achieved the most profound insight into things. The highest human types have achieved identity with the Absolute—with the original divine power. This the Gods cannot do since, in the last resort—not, of course, in popular belief—they are conceived merely as psychic projections. (Cf. the extracts from the rules of meditation on p. 41 et seq.)

In East Asia, therefore, a region of 'anti-individualism', it is man that is accorded the highest reverence.

These highest and perfect human figures are timeless; they first came on the scene thousands of years ago and could live today or tomorrow exactly as they did then. The East Asians fully support Jakob Burckhardt's view:[4]

> Neither the soul nor the brain of man has grown demonstrably in stature in historical times; at all events their capabilities long ago reached full development. For this reason our presumption that we live in an age of moral progress is utterly ludicrous . . .

*

To understand the East Asian's concept of personality it is important, amongst other things, to make allowance for the fact that his attitude to the unconscious differs from our own. The unconscious is for him as natural an element as air and water.

The East Asians have at all times been strongly aware of the unconscious. It was their friend or foe in all phases of life, and they either cultivated or combatted it according to circumstances. On the higher plane one came to terms with the unconscious through the process of individuation, while on the lower plane relevant manifestations (gods and spirits) or even displays of magic served as guides.

The unconscious is to a large extent collectivistic; therefore its influence on human beings must have a generalizing and typifying tendency. And it is precisely this—a stereotyped and completely unindividualistic quality—that strikes the Westerner in East Asia time and time again. The amiability of the East Asian is impersonal, as are his failings also. The phenomenon of these identical, or at any rate similar reactions originates in the same way as the mass suggestion or mass psychosis with which we are familiar in Europe: nevertheless these manifestations may not—in other respects—be equated unreservedly, on account of the differing social structures of Europe and East Asia. In East Asia it is a question of small social units in the framework of a larger society, not of individuals in a mass. Similar reactions need not therefore appear throughout the entire populace; this is more likely to be the case within certain groups. In Japan there is a certain form of laughter appropriate to the geisha, which differs from the giggle of the girls of the tea houses: this, in its turn, naturally differs from the laughter of the schoolgirls.

This tendency is, of course, further strengthened by the deliberate fostering of the spirit of community. That all members of a family respond alike to a given stimulus is something that happens quite unconsciously as a general rule, except that it may to some extent depend on a previous decision of the family council. A Chinese or a Japanese will scarcely ever rely exclusively on his own judgment when taking an important decision: he will always consult his family and his friends beforehand.

It is above all the way the East Asians allow the unconscious to work, coupled with the impersonal nature of their decisions, which—next to their self-mastery—make it so difficult for most Europeans to understand them. We are accustomed to noting the words of a man and also ascribing meaning to them, but less so to 'getting the feel' of what he means. With us the unconscious lies more in the background, more in the distance; when things cannot be expressed in words, we have difficulty in understanding them. Hence the references one hears to the 'inscrutability' of the East Asians, or to their unpredictability and guile. Mostly the reason is that we simply fail to grasp their essential nature, which is something quite unequivocal. Let us recall the words of Suzuki, quoted above, which express the opinion that the conscious behaviour of the Japanese provides no standard for the assessment of his nature (cf. p. 159). The Japanese writer Kitayama[5] explains that 'the true ego of East Asian man eludes any attempt to measure it by application of the well-known standards of measurement based on the theory of cognition'.

It is less true of the East Asian than it is of us that he consists of an 'ego' alone; rather does he constitute a 'we'—something most difficult for us to grasp. We usually look only for the ego, or rather the 'you', and inevitably approach the East Asian on the same assumption. But the East Asian resembles the iceberg, of which only a relatively small part is visible, while the greater portion is below the surface. To complete the picture we should have to imagine the underwater part of all icebergs as being joined together.

One can hardly do justice to the art and culture of the East Asians if one does not bear in mind that their achievements in these fields largely originated in a deliberately impersonal way, namely, through the operation of the unconscious. This approach to the arts was, for example, especially practised in the contemplative rites of the Zen School of Buddhism. Even the Western artist was, and is, conscious that it is not he that is the creator, but rather that he is only the creative medium. In the West, however, we have never consciously or systematically cultivated this approach.

The following reflections of C. G. Jung relate to the positive aspect of the unconscious:[6]

It would be unjust if we were to stress only the unfavourable aspects of the unconscious. In all the usual cases the unconscious is only unfavourable or dangerous when we are not at one with it, and are therefore ranged against our instincts.

If, however, it is given to us to reproduce that function which I term *transcendent*, this disunity is removed and we may take pleasure in the favourable side of the unconscious. For we then receive from the unconscious all that help and encouragement which flow in rich abundance from bountiful nature . . .

The unconscious is ever active and disposes its materials in combinations that serve to determine the future. It creates subliminal prospective combinations just as our conscious mind does also, but the unconscious combinations are considerably superior in subtlety and range to those of the conscious mind. As a guide to mankind, therefore, the unconscious has no equal.

The unconscious has always provided the East Asian with this sort of guidance. This fact enables us to understand why it is that anything which speaks with too great a clarity, not only in words and thought but also in the sphere of art, conveys little to him: it strikes him as hollow, pointless and banal. All Chinese and Japanese have therefore the greatest difficulty in appreciating Greek art of the classic (i.e. as opposed to the archaic) era. Christian art speaks more distinctly to them, our medieval painting having for them suggestions of Buddhist painting. The Japanese philosopher, Nishida,[7] maintains that Greek art lacks depth. 'The Greeks,' he says amongst other things, 'conceive of eternity as something visual; they do not feel it enfolding us from behind.' He makes this significant observation about Goethe: 'Behind the figure of the "promethean" Goethe, in the background, is the gleam of moonlight.' It is this moonlight, this mysterious 'background' quality in Goethe's work, that makes the Chinese and Japanese count him as one of them. Let us, therefore, quote Nishida further on the subject:

> In Goethe one cannot distinguish between the internal and the external. Everything is as it is. It has its point of departure in nothingness, and to nothingness it returns again. And in the very fact that it springs from, and fades away again into nothingness, is a faintly human note . . . Such thought eddies in the depths of the oriental culture that has surrounded us since childhood.

There is a connection between the relative insignificance of the individual and the cult of the unconscious: both derive from mystical 'total' thinking.

We referred earlier in our discussion of East Asian grammar to the remarkable blurring of the subjective principle (cf. p. 63 ff.). There are sentences in Japanese in which there is no certainty whether the speaker is 'I', 'we' or some quite general 'one'. The different attitudes to perspective in East Asian and Western painting can be ascribed, from the psychological viewpoint, to the same causes. Our own approach to perspective, which can be called the 'subjective' one, is to look at things solely from the position, or viewpoint of the single artist, so that the spectator, when he looks at the picture, is translated into the individual position of that artist.

On account of its excessive one-sidedness, this conception of perspective is regarded by the East Asians as the most primitive of all. They themselves seek to represent things from two or even more viewpoints, with the result that their pictures can simultaneously comprise several perspectives. The chief difficulty for the Asian artist lies in the way that this problem is worked out artistically. Here, once again, is the tendency to look at the whole from all sides (enveloping thought).

To this context also belongs the inability of many East Asians to distinguish left from right, because such indications of direction are something purely subjective; they mostly go by the points of the compass. Anywhere he happens to be, the East Asian knows exactly where the points of the compass lie. In present-day China this is carried to the point where, even in rearranging a room, they do not say: 'The cupboard should go farther to the right', but, 'a little farther east'; similarly, the table will be moved to the south or the settee to the north-west. The Japanese have gone further in adapting themselves to the subjective indications of direction, but this does not prevent half the Japanese taxi-drivers from driving, after some hesitation, to the left when told to bear right!

Other standards apply to the East Asian concept of personality than do to our own, because man is seen primarily as a member of a community. Individual characteristics, in so far as they come into conflict with society, matter only in the degree to which they are overcome. For this reason there are, for example, no great love stories in East Asian literature. Moreover the rape of Helen strikes the East Asian as an incomprehensible and highly immoral story, for it is unthinkable to them that nations should be dragged into the misery of war for the sake of a woman. Love as a 'private concern' can arouse sympathy, but nothing lofty or precious is seen in it. Love stories are only appreciated when the action unfolds within the framework of the social ethic; there are stories enough about happily married

couples, but this is principally on account of their correct observance of that ethic. Even a loyal and patient persevering
bride-to-be can become a heroine, but only indeed if she is
'officially' betrothed, or succeeds in winning her family's consent
to the man of her choice. Should by any chance a war have
resulted in China from a case of abduction, then it will not have
been for the sake of the woman, but because of the infringement
of the Chinese social ethic.[8]

The result is that when the East Asians first came into closer
contact with us and made the acquaintance of our literature,
they found our love stories both novel and fascinating. The
youth of East Asia swallowed them wholesale.

*

The true standard of values in East Asia is the attainment of
maturity; this is what all strive for from early youth onwards.
Old age, a wise prudence and a balanced personality are the
things that matter, and not youth with its stormy adventur-
ousness.

The Japanese writer Kitayama[9] says: 'A man incapable of
self-examination will fail to achieve natural maturity; he will
remain a plebeian'. What, then, is this maturity that is the
object of all East Asian endeavour? It is the life 'from the
centre', natural and spontaneous, unconstrained and unsullied
by passion. It is, moreover, the steady certitude of the complementary, homogeneous and indeed, identical nature of life and
death. It is the feeling that man in his later years must once
again lead a life as pure, harmonious and as natural as during
his childhood. A life fulfilled is the most perfect preparation
for death. According to Goethe,[10] 'the happiest of men is he who
is able to link together his life's end with its beginning'. It is in
this sense that the re-attainment of genuine simplicity is a sign
of maturity. How often do we not find Chinese and Japanese
pictures or ink drawings representing saints or philosophers,
woodcutters or peasants, who laugh as simply and naturally as
children?

The East Asians make a sharp distinction between a significant and a meaningless death. They never throw their lives
away. Although, indeed, they spend a lifetime in preparation
for death, they do not court it. They wish only to be ready
against the day when the end can no longer be avoided. In a
certain sense the Chinese and Japanese are more 'cowardly'
than we; they shrink from a death that is frivolous or sense-
lessly precipitated. For this reason they have no fondness for
daring achievements in sport such as motor racing, first ascents
of mountains and the like, for intrepid deeds of life-saving or
of military valour. It is not only that they are too 'sensible' for
such things and have too great a love of life; their training is
in some measure also responsible. The individual has not the
full right of decision, but is a member of a family and has in
consequence no title to absolute authority over his own life.
Confucius goes so far as specifically to forbid sons to endanger
their lives, or to undertake journeys too far afield.

Japanese bravery is different from our own: it is always
related to the end in view. The Japanese is basically as much a
coward as the Chinese. When a Japanese is trained in the idea
that it is his duty to fight for the Emperor, and perhaps die for
him, he will do so. But he never embarks on something dangerous out of inborn valour or recklessness. Long and thorough
training, beginning as far back as in the elementary school, was
necessary to make the Japanese into soldiers of Tenno, ready
to face death. The ethical motive has a strong bearing on all
this. During the second World War articles appeared in the
Japanese press, maintaining that Japanese bravery was of a
higher order than that of the West because it was 'spiritual':
Western courage amounted to nothing more than sudden fury,
it had no more to it than the foolhardiness of a fox-terrier.

Nevertheless Suzuki[11] is right when he asserts: 'The Japanese
has perhaps no basic attitude to life, but in place of it he has a
basic attitude to death'. The same assertion could apply to the
Chinese, for all his realism and joy in living. It is very difficult
to characterize and interpret this fundamental cast of the

oriental mind, that embraces both joyful acceptance of life and constant preparedness for death.

On the whole, perhaps a reference to the natural and organic element in East Asian thought will come closest to the mark. Both death and life are natural and inevitable. Death is no more terrifying than life; for the very reason that it is just as real—or also just as unreal—as life, one must be prepared for it. The worst of all things is death without meaning; it is the consequence of a trivial and superficial life.

The East Asian knows neither the anxiety nor the mechanistic contempt for death. In this connection we may refer to John Hersey's little book *Hiroshima*. After the atom bomb had been dropped, the terribly burned and wounded folk of Hiroshima died without a sound or a complaint—even the children.

Whenever, during recent years, East Asians have died as a result of the impact of war, they met their end in the same noble and exalted fashion. When confronted by death, there is no difference between the Chinese and the Japanese: both are possessed of the same philosophic calm and transfigured expression. Because they make no sound, it does not mean that they are apathetic, nor that they are empty and feelingless because they make no complaint; but merely that life has withdrawn into themselves. They die with their mental powers undiminished, in full consciousness of the fulfilment of their personal destiny and that of their country. To die with a clear conscience in cleanliness and purity: this is their ideal. And it can only be attained if one has striven for it all one's life. In death we are inferior to the East Asians; there is perhaps nothing else in their culture and spiritual life that so undisputedly arouses our highest admiration. And that is no mean achievement.

Questions of maturity and death have always been the central problems of East Asian philosophy. In the West they were for a long time excluded from philosophy altogether and have only recently been held worthy of consideration once more.

*

Our 'conception of work', and in particular the conception of sacrifice for one's work are quite unknown to the East Asians. In their eyes work counts only as an emanation of personality. That a man should sacrifice himself for a thing, and thereby neglect both self-examination and the maturing of his self, they count as immoral and even ridiculous. It is inconceivable to an East Asian that a painter of beautiful pictures should not at the same time be a ripe and harmonious personality. He has not the slightest admiration for an engineer or inventor, however talented, unless such a professional man at the same time fulfils the demands of his ideal of personality. Otherwise he sees in him nothing but a tinker, or somebody of no account.

In East Asia, a philosopher who lacks wisdom and the ability to master both life and himself, is not regarded as a philosopher but as a futile babbler. Goethe is for them one of the greatest philosophers of the Western world, because he moulded his life as a work of art and thus wielded—and still wields—a 'magical' influence by his example. He was a 'master' in the true East Asian sense.

Perfection in an achievement depends on the degree of perfection in the personality behind it, whether it be a work of art, a philosophic doctrine, a piece of craftsmanship, or skill in music or archery. This might well account for the fact that in East Asia mighty individual achievements have seldom occurred. The most important source of instruction for the East Asian is man, the living creature, not the text-book, or indeed any kind of book. This may sound strange at first, in view of the fact that the East Asians are among the most literary peoples of the world and probably surpass even the French in the pleasure they find in reading, and in their habits of writing and versifying.

Books, however, are significant less by virtue of their factual content than because they reflect and illuminate the great personalities of former times. The Chinese classics are only media through which it is possible to comprehend and assimilate the spirit and 'magic' of Confucius, Mencius and wise and holy men of still more ancient times. Books are not only read with the help

of the understanding, but are allowed to exert their influence on
the reader in every possible way. It is, moreover, impossible in
the eyes of an East Asian to withdraw to one's room in order to
'study' the classics, and to hope in that way to absorb something
of their spirit. To do this requires interpretation by a living
master. The teacher, who can be conceived as the latest link in
a chain of practising masters stretching back over the centuries,
provides living contact between the pupil and the great minds
of the past. The teacher-pupil relationship is therefore something that in East Asia has always been consciously fostered.
Teachers are called 'Sensei' in Japan, a term which, literally
translated, means 'one born earlier' or in other words 'elder'.
Hermann Bohner[12] thus describes the state of affairs in East Asia:

> The Sensei institution is part of the basic structure of the East,
> of Japan as well as of China, and it extends into all aspects of
> living . . . It is fundamental to the Chinese world, and in particular
> to Confucius . . . The isolated individual—what a waste of effort!
> Throughout the empire and at all times power has constantly
> been exercised by an unbroken succession of masters and appren-
> tices, related as though by family ties. This Chinese institution
> linking up with its Japanese counterpart, has steadily grown in
> strength during the course of history. Parallel influences from
> Indian Buddhist sources also assert themselves. Here also the
> institution of master and apprentice is well developed. The East
> is not ignorant of the growing power of spiritual life. And do
> not interpret this in too absolute, too theoretic a sense! The
> powerful development of the ego concept in the West is a strong
> inducement for us to overlook the sense of community that exists
> between creative workers, their *unum corpus*.

Here we have a further case of a phenomenon little heeded
and therefore uncultivated in the West, but, by contrast,
systematically developed in East Asia.

*

The East Asian strives after perfection, not originality. His
conception echoes Goethe's dictum:[13] 'The most stupid mistake
of all is for sincere young minds to believe that by acknowledging

truths recognized by others before them, they abandon all claim to originality'. To live great thoughts over again, to attempt the repetition of great achievements and, above all, to turn also oneself into a fully developed being—that is the goal.

This conception can naturally lead to the growth of rigid and lifeless ways and means; for, should these once become cramped by fixed patterns or regulations, it becomes difficult to breathe a new spirit into them. Once a great master in East Asia had discovered a certain style, it became his pupils' preoccupation to imitate this mode of expression, perfect of its kind, and if possible to reproduce it yet more perfectly. When, however, certain styles recur too often, one becomes so accustomed to them that they cease to make a strong or lasting impression.

Neither the Chinese nor the Japanese have avoided this trap; many symbols and artistic devices ceased to have more than a limited meaning for them and became conventionalized. Conversely, they also ran the risk of being blind to new possibilities. Once it has been established, for example, that cherry or plum blossom in the snow is among the most moving and expressive motifs of early spring, this motif will be repeated time and again; nobody will hit on the idea of painting, for once in a while, spring flowers breaking through the snows of a mountain pasture. The fact that maples and chrysanthemums are symbols of autumn, ensures that they too will be reproduced by the thousand in pictures and poems, and on flower vases and fabrics —but there will be not a hint of any other plant. If custom dictates the writing of a short poem on a moonlight occasion, nobody will write a long one; and if it is established that certain motifs should be rendered in ink and not in colour, then every self-respecting artist will prefer ink. The fact that many East Asians are no longer capable of an original sentiment is due to the fact that they see everything, so to say, through the glasses of artistic tradition. When one accompanies them on an outing they will walk past not only lovely views, but beautiful trees, rocks and streams without heeding them, until they encounter some motif familiar to them through painting or poetry; for example a peculiar rock shaped like a tiger, or a particular branch that inclines at a conventional angle. Then they break into conventional expressions of rapture.

In East Asian eyes it is almost impossible, or at best a most rare occurrence, for a young person to achieve anything note-worthy, since he has not yet reached maturity. Again and again one hears it said that only someone of mature years can achieve true master's status. By way of example, we shall cite *The Sequence of the Nine Steps*, a set of injunctions by Seami[14] the celebrated Japanese master of the 'Noh' drama (strictly speaking, a dance-drama). Seami puts forward three main degrees, or steps, of attainment in dancing and acting, each of which is sub-divided into three further subordinate steps. The highest degree, reached only by extremely few, is a thing of wonder; it has 'a fathomless beauty'; it is 'degree without degree'; 'words fail, thought and feeling stand still'. But now follows the remarkable thing: Seami maintains that only he who has reached this high-est degree of attainment is able to master and do full justice to the manner of acting of the lower degrees. The lowest degree is 'coarse and violent', 'crude and leaden'. 'This order can do a wide variety of things, but nothing fully and thoroughly; it is coarse, leaden.'

We see, then, that only the master, who has completed a process of development, can adequately play coarse and simple parts—for example in farce. The younger player who has not yet completed his training cannot do this, although we might have thought that, in the very nature of things this would have come more easily to him than more difficult rôles portraying complex characters. But he is unable to portray simplicity, since he is not experienced and has not reached an advanced stage of human development; he will therefore all too easily fall into the error of playing himself and not his part. The actor must not lose himself in his part, but, on the other hand, it must look as though he had. As was said earlier on, the reconquest of conscious simplicity is a goal that is hard to reach. But the power to do so constitutes one of obligations of the great actor.

The pre-eminent artist is not so much the man who is able to translate a cultured and initiated audience into a higher sphere, as one who can bring something beautiful and noble to even the simplest of men. Precisely the same idea prevails here as in the sphere of artistic craftsmanship; simple things are the most difficult to achieve, but are at the same time the most important.

In China and Japan an actor begins his career at the age of ten or twelve, sometimes even earlier. It is nevertheless rare for an actor to achieve fame before roughly the age of fifty. The most famous are always between fifty and seventy years old. And the principle is the same in all the arts, crafts and branches of learning. Maturity can only come by an organic process; it cannot be forced.

As well as the family system, then, the ideal of personality has contributed to the high esteem enjoyed by old age in East Asia. Even in modern China, old men are still regarded as free from guilt, although citizens' rights on the Western model have been introduced. But respect for old age is so great in China that even the modern reformers could not accommodate themselves to our ideas on this point. In East Asia a man is good because he is old. Should an old person nevertheless commit an act of stupidity or even a crime, popular judgment will show indulgence; it will probably be assumed that the old person must have had some secret motives for his action, which his juniors could only comprehend with difficulty. It is a fact that in China and Japan old people can often commit the biggest follies and eccentricities—in politics also—such as would never be risked by younger people. In Japan the leading fanatical nationalists and ultra-Nipponists were thus always old people; the younger ones constituted only their following. When in Japan young assassins failed to receive the punishment due to them, it was not through any disinclination to shoot young, though misguided, patriots; the principal reason was rather that they were shielded by these elderly fanatics, whose age protected them.

*

One of the most striking peculiarities of East Asia is the practice of self-mastery on which the ideal of personality and the life of the community are largely based. Self-mastery is certainly one of the greatest of the cardinal virtues of East Asia, but even this excellence, like all virtues, has its drawbacks. It would certainly be a most interesting and rewarding task for a psychologist to make a close examination of the effects and consequences of this long-practised—and in our eyes often exaggerated—self-discipline. We are convinced that in it is to be found the key to the understanding of much that is peculiar and strange in East Asia.

Some of the most dangerous outbreaks to which the East Asian is prone may certainly be ascribed to the practice of a self-mastery exaggerated to an almost unnatural degree. Only very rarely do you meet an East Asian who has lost his self-control—but should this happen you would be well advised to make yourself scarce! An East Asian is able to keep control of himself for a long while, but once the fetters are broken he becomes unpredictable and mostly knows nothing of what he is saying or doing. All the grievances, the anger and dissatisfaction he has bottled up over months or perhaps years, are suddenly let loose. A husband can, for example, be consumed with jealousy for three or four years on end without anyone noticing it: then in one single day he will slay the lover, the wife or himself—perhaps even all three. The East Asian never brings his feelings out into the open, he never allows himself to 'let off steam', until one day—unless he is capable of the necessary inner restraint—he bursts, so to speak.

We Westerners have, without always fully realizing it, many different ways of 'letting off steam'. We can always complain, make angry comments, or even display unfriendliness and openly give vent to our displeasure now and again; moreover, we can indulge in a major or minor 'row'. All this is denied the East Asian; such behaviour would strike him as unmannerly, coarse and barbarous.

Another drawback to the exaggerated practice of self-mastery is the suppression of individual qualities and abilities. The life of the East Asian consists for the most part in showing consideration for his fellow men. It would be impossible to enumerate here all the restrictions to which the freedom of action of the individual is subject. Chinese and Japanese students have, for example, the greatest difficulty in concentrating on their studies, because they are constantly being interrupted by family matters and other social obligations. When an elderly relation dies—and this happens fairly often in consequence of the large size of most families—custom requires a three-day-and-night-long vigil at the death-bed, as well as other time-consuming obsequies: should a relation (especially a rich one!) fall ill, the sick-bed must be promptly visited. Should an uncle or some fairly conspicuous gentleman of the circle of their acquaintances depart on a journey, the young people must hurry courteously to the station to see him off (one gains 'face' by having a large following)—and so on and so forth. But this happens not only in the family circle; the business and professional worlds also make their demands. In the latter there is always something that has to be represented or celebrated; gifts and courtesy visits must be exchanged. A young man has neither the time nor the money for what can be very expensive customs. He cannot make his way alone but must be advanced by the efforts of the entire clan.

It was general in China—except with the Communists—to cleave tightly to family traditions, though the old usages and manifestations of courtesy had partially disappeared from the business world. This great country has suffered such disruption in every way as a result of the disturbances of the last decade, that quite uncultured 'nouveaux riches' were able to thrust themselves into prominence. In the seaport towns this was naturally augmented by Western influences. Furthermore, in periods of chaos and social disruption there is always more scope for strong personalities, for 'individuals' in our sense of the term.

The conflict between family interests on the one hand and the demands of the State or business on the other, remained an

everyday problem in Chiang Kai-shek's China. Chinese officers
did not think twice about leaving either the front or their men,
were some family matter to recall them. Many Chinese military
doctors were confronted with a most difficult human problem,
for trained medical men were scarce and each of them had
hundreds, if not thousands, of wounded under his care. What
was such a doctor to do if his father fell ill and there was a
possibility that he might die? In one such case known to me
the doctor, who had studied in America, remained at his
hospital. He was quite clear in his own mind that this was his
duty, yet he resented bitterly that it should result in his being
labelled as someone 'heedless both of custom and morals'. In
another case, however, a doctor for whom there was similarly
no one to deputize, left without hesitation both his hospital and
his wounded in order to take his family to a place of safety—a
family which could equally well have made the journey on its
own. This doctor, so far as I could ascertain, did not 'get talked
about' and his action struck nobody as in any way strange.

In this connection let me instance an oddity of the Japanese,
a cunning method of doing business such as can only occur in a
land where courtesy and manners have at all costs to be observed. When somebody decides to open up a new firm or
business that runs counter to the interests of his competitors,
the latter decide among themselves to inundate him with visits
to such an extent that he is quite unable to get on with his work
or to do anything for his business. These visits go on for days—
indeed for weeks—beginning in his private house between seven
and eight o'clock in the morning (such early visits are permitted
in Japan), and continue in unbroken succession at his office.
In this way the wretched man can be brought to ruin before
he has even begun to think about his work. He is, of course,
unable to throw the visitors out, because he would thereby
offend against propriety and put himself in the wrong. Only by
resorting to the subtlest cunning can he save himself in such
cases.

In China, too, similar types of 'communal action' can be

resorted to if it is necessary to compel a person to do something. Should, for example, a man who has become well-to-do make the exceptional decision to close his ears to the demands of his relatives, it is possible for the entire clan—kith and kin, bag and baggage—to encamp on his very doorstep and not to budge from the spot by day or by night. Passers-by are informed at the tops of enraged or plaintive voices of the reasons for this family encampment. The wealthy man runs the risk of losing 'face'—and as a rule is soon ready to come to a compromise.

*

The training for self-discipline and for adaptation to human society has, however, more directly stultifying consequences. This can be observed, for example, in Chinese and Japanese children. East Asian children are almost unbelievably well brought up and good—perhaps just a little too good. They do not take dolls, watches or gramophones to pieces, nor do they hang around railway stations watching engines, because they know that all this is forbidden. This stifles their natural curiosity, the thirst for knowledge, and, what is more, every tendency to act independently. Modern East Asian boys are no longer as little interested in technical things as were their forefathers; many of them would welcome the opportunity of peeping under the bonnet of a motor car. But they desist because it is forbidden.

In Japan consideration has been given to this problem for some time. Well brought up and obedient children were of course desired, but there was also a need for capable scientists, scholars and engineers. On one occasion, shortly before the last war, the Japanese Ministry of Education released a communiqué which actually stated that Japanese children were 'too good'. Parents and teachers were counselled to be more indulgent when the little darlings smashed things, brought impossible worms and beetles into the house, or insisted on standing at the front end of a tram-car next to the driver. This sort of thing was not necessarily 'naughtiness', it was stated, but was rather a quite natural urge to investigate and to learn. The occasion of these admonitions was an American film about Edison which the Ministry went out of its way to recommend. Edison, so went the Ministry's official explanation, was by no means always well-behaved as a child but nevertheless he became a great scientist, and such scientists—this was naturally the moral of the story—were needed in Greater Japan also.

It is not easy to give a clear idea of East Asian decorum because nowadays we of the West, generally speaking, evince little understanding for such things and have almost entirely discarded our own former traditions respecting such matters. One must learn from actual experience how utterly incomprehensible our 'natural' behaviour can seem to the East Asians. For, far from striking them as natural, it seems to them often as positively animal-like. For a so-called civilized person to be unable to control his feelings and keep his opinions to himself is something they are quite incapable of grasping. To slap someone on the back by way of a greeting or to embrace in full view of everyone strikes them as laughable and absurd. In one of his books Lin Yutang, who has a long-established reputation as an anti-militarist and anti-Fascist, extols the heel-clicking and bowing customary among German officers. This he does purely and simply because in it—at long last—he reckons to have discovered a survival of 'form' in the contemporary Western world. The Japanese, who one might assume had to some extent accustomed themselves to our ways, were horrified anew when, after the arrival of the American occupation troops, the G.I.'s. wanted to walk arm in arm along the street with their Japanese girl friends. General MacArthur, who knows his East Asia of old, thereupon forbade this; and he was absolutely right, for to be exposed to ridicule can only harm the prestige of any army of occupation.

*

The danger in East Asia of habits and customs becoming fixed in a particular mould extends of course also to manners and morals. The normal usages of everyday life freeze into a mask behind which the real and the true life goes on. The dictates of the social code are in many cases no longer complied with, but are merely exploited. In this way an element of insincerity and spuriousness—even of falsity—enters into human relationships. We mentioned earlier that East Asians are at times unjustifiably regarded as insincere by us Occidentals, because we fail to penetrate to their essential being. But besides this supposed falsity a real one exists—which manifests itself in the deliberate misuse of smiling and etiquette.

The demands made on the East Asian by manners and morals are excessive; most people are unable to conform to them in every detail. Only a few contrive to feel genuinely well-disposed towards those at whom they smile, or to feel real respect for those before whom they make their deep bows. The average human endowment of energy is just enough to keep up appearances while illicit desires, impulses and emotions find devious ways of coming to the surface. We stressed this discrepancy between practice and the ideal on an earlier occasion, namely when we discussed the nature of the Chinese State, and saw that the illusion that every Civil Servant is a 'gentleman' brought the most fearful corruption in its wake.

The smoothness of the East Asians' indirect approach is further accentuated by a certain psychological streak, which all of them possess. The introvert who knows his own soul and his own reactions up to a certain point, is not innocent and unsuspecting in his attitude to his fellow men. He studies them and tries to see through them. The East Asians have been able to bring deception and subterfuge to a fine art.

East Asian politicians such as Chiang Kai-shek, or any Japanese statesman, are past-masters at it. Chiang Kai-shek was able to maintain himself in power, 75 per cent through intrigue and all manner of manipulation and manœuvre, and only 25 per cent by force of arms. He has always been careful, and has calculated to a meticulous degree the consequences of his measures. The Battle of Shanghai in 1937, in which some of the best and most modern divisions were sacrificed, was, militarily speaking, quite un-Chinese. To fight right on the coast where Japanese seaborne reinforcements could easily reach the battle area, was quite contrary to normal Chinese strategic thinking. But on this occasion the more important thing to Chiang Kai-shek was the psychological effect on his own people and on world opinion.

When in 1938 General Han Fuchu, Governor of Shantung, was arrested, his guilt as a traitor was most difficult to establish. One day it was announced that his execution had taken place, and it transpired that both public opinion and the press responded well to the announcement. But this was only a *ballon d'essai*: the General had not been executed; Chiang Kai-shek only wanted first of all to see how public opinion would react to the sentencing of Han Fuchu. Had it reacted unfavourably, references to an 'inaccuracy' in the reports would always have been possible. As it was, the actual execution of the General followed shortly afterwards.

It is difficult to decide which of the two nations outbids the other in cunning. It is usual to credit the Chinese with the superiority in this respect because they have the 'longer-standing culture'. But it is idle to go into the refinements of the question. At all events Tokyo was in recent decades probably more riddled with intrigue than any other capital in the world. General Araki, a most notorious Nationalist who was War Minister at the time of the Manchurian incident and later became Minister of Education, declared at the beginning of the second World War that he hoped Tokyo would be levelled to the ground by bombs so that this foul nest of intrigue might disappear from the face of the earth. But the General himself was a corrupt city-dweller and true representative of his race: when, later on, repairs were being done to his house, the workmen discovered, amongst other things, tons of hoarded rice and other foodstuffs underneath his floorboards.

The events leading up to the Treaty of Portsmouth after the Russo-Japanese War of 1904–5 provide a familiar historical example of the Japanese method of approach. The Japanese Government deceived the Russians—and also the Japanese people—into believing that they would insist on enormous reparations. It was only on the strength of this assumption that the Russians participated in the conference at all; they believed that it would certainly founder on account of the unjustifiably large demands of the Japanese, and that the latter would thereby forfeit world sympathy which they possessed in larger measure than the Russians. The whole thing was only a trick, though; for, the Japanese Government had not for a moment thought of demanding reparations on anything like this scale. As a consequence the Russians, who, on the assumption that the negotiations would founder had gone a good way towards meeting the Japanese on other questions, found themselves obliged to sign the treaty. The Japanese people had naturally enough failed to see through this manœuvre, and the Government had to go to some trouble to pacify the outraged spirits who maintained that Japan ought to have received reparations on a larger scale.

The most representative type of sport in Japan is certainly Judo (also called Jujitsu), a form of exercise whose object—to put it briefly—is to exploit your opponent's strength whilst giving way to him. Of Judo you can literally say that the greater the strength of your opponent, the worse and more dangerous it is for him. Lafcadio Hearn has the following to say about Judo:[15]

What is so wonderful about jujitsu is not so much the supreme degree of skill shown by the contestant, as the absolutely unique oriental idea which finds expression in this form of art. What Western brain could have evolved the remarkable doctrine of never opposing force with force but of controlling your opponent's strength and turning it to your own advantage, of bringing about the collapse of your enemy through his own strength and of defeating him entirely by means of his own efforts! No European would ever have hit on such an idea. The Western mind seems to work in straight lines, and the oriental in wonderful curves and circles. But what a magnificent symbol—the outwitting of brutal strength by means of the intellect! Jujitsu is much more than a science of self-defence; it is at the same time a philosophic, an economic, and an ethical system (yes, indeed, I forgot to add that a greater part of jujitsu training is of a purely moral character); most of all, it is the expression of a racial genius not yet clearly recognized as such by those powers who dream of further conquests in the Orient.

Hearn elaborates this by saying that, in fact, all that the Japanese have accomplished in the decades since the reopening of the country—modernization and imitation of foreigners— was not a giving up of old ideas, as many Europeans thought at the time, but mental jujitsu. In this connection it is worth recalling that during initial contact with the outside world various armed encounters took place in which the Japanese, owing to the enemy ships' superior fire-power, got decidedly the worst of it. (Kagoshima, 1862; bombardment of Fort Shimonoseki, 1863.) But this did not lead to reprisals; instead, the Japanese responsible for the incidents (the then still powerful Chosu and Satsuma clans) sought immediately afterwards to make friends with the foreign powers concerned, in order that they might learn from them the secrets of their technical superiority.

Subsequent events have also borne out the truth of Hearn's statement. Was there not something of judo in the recent Japanese reaction to the American occupation? They responded to every American prompting and carried it still further in the execution. Nothing was 'democratic' enough for them; they wanted to be more democratic than the Americans. They wanted to constitute an American buffer against Communism: they told the world that they were fully in the American camp—but why all this? They hoped, of course, thereby to regain their status.

The East Asians have always thought more highly than we of a certain measure of cunning; and they have always taken it very much for granted. Even Confucius, that epitome of everything ideally perfect, used to deceive frontier officials, and once, when an unwanted visitor called, he sent him the message that he was not at home. This he followed up by playing a loud and purposely audible tune on his flute, so that the caller should know of how little account he was to the Master.[16]

*

All East Asians are born spies and have, furthermore, been trained as such since ancient times. The classic Chinese books on strategy and the art of war devote considerable attention to espionage, and some highly dubious methods for practising it are adduced and recommended.[17] Incidentally, it has been repeatedly alleged—no doubt with some degree of justification —that the Communist generals of China in particular are past-masters in applying to present-day warfare certain of the ruses and tactics described in those works. It is said that Mao Tse Tung personally considers these precepts to be quite as import-ant as the modern rules of warfare devised by Soviet Russia. In this field the Japanese, too, have proved apt pupils of the ancient Chinese. Some of the most important battles in Japanese history were decided, not solely by force of arms, but by the considerable assistance derived from espionage, treachery, intrigue and defection. Espionage, moreover, has not been confined merely to the military and political spheres; it has always played a considerable part in industry too. It was thought remarkably clever and cunning—in no way despicable —to insinuate oneself into a certain master's establishment, work with him for a long period, gain his confidence and even manage to be adopted as his apprentice and successor—only to slip back one day to one's own family with some special trade secret!

East Asian heroes are, probably without exception, more akin to Odysseus than to Siegfried, though for the most part they comport themselves with less scruple and more cunning than the Greek hero. Moreover, as Hearn points out in his remarks on jujitsu, there is no question of its not being thoroughly honourable to outwit one's opponent by deceit and cunning. East Asian dragon-killers do not 'fight' with their dragons: they make the creature drunk, then cut off its head, or heads (for it often has several). As for the Chinese, it is generally admitted that they have no special regard for heroism, and that their mythical and legendary figures usually achieve success by means of cunning and magic; whereas quite mistaken ideas are often held regarding the Japanese conception of heroism. If one goes through all ten of the reading manuals commonly used in Japanese schools during the last twenty years, one will not find a single story in which a hero of mythology or of Japanese history achieves success and victory other than through astuteness and fraud. When children read nothing from their sixth year onwards but stories in which enemies are butchered in their sleep, or where princes of the blood disguised as women treacherously slay their hosts, one can imagine what sort of a mentality is the result. Some ten years ago a film about William Tell received great acclamation in Japan. Why? Not on account of the idea of freedom, which the Japanese did not properly understand and in fact left them quite cold, but principally on account of the scene where Gessler asks Tell why he has a second arrow in his quiver. Tell's frank admission to the tyrant that the arrow was meant for him in the event of his child being wounded, struck the Japanese as an astoundingly upright and honourable show of heroism.

The art of judging and handling men has always been considered so important by the East Asians that they are, by and large, much our superiors in this respect. Nevertheless one must here make one important, though really self-evident qualification: for the most part they fail to understand us Western folk and our reactions because our psychic structure is so different from theirs. But this much can be said: they have a higher degree of self-knowledge than we, so understand themselves better. The good qualities of the East Asians are maturity, self-mastery, and *savoir faire*: failings inseparable from, and complementary to these are malice, cunning, falsity, and, in consequence, persistent mistrust and an inclination to suspicion. Innocence is the last thing to expect from East Asians, for these races are shrewd and can therefore be highly dangerous.

We have digressed somewhat from our description of the East Asian ideal of personality, but we thought it necessary in this particular connection to draw attention to the shortcomings which go with these oriental ideals. We started with the premise that the East Asian ideal is 'the individual in the community'. Now, the strange thing is that exactly this has always been—and still is—current in the West also, although the development of East and West has in practice been so dissimilar. Perhaps in the ultimate analysis it is only a question of difference in emphasis: we lay more stress on personality in the individual sense, while the East Asians orient themselves more towards the community. As a consequence we have developed failings which derive from undue emphasis on individualism, while those of the East Asians result from the constant necessity for social and human adaptation.

*

The East Asian has an instinctive aversion as much to the idea of political liberty, as to individualism. He does not regard it as an ideal. By liberty he understands mostly something licentious, uncontrolled and uncivilized. He associates this idea first and foremost with the wild animals of the jungle, or with primitive and barbaric tribes of nomads or hunters. Liberty is for him a kind of barbaric and primordial condition associated with the earliest ages of man. He considers civilization and culture to begin at that moment when men band together in a community and establish a communal legal and moral code. Thus the instincts of the East Asian and the way he interprets things are directly opposed to ours; for it is generally speaking our wont to characterize lack of liberty and collectivism as barbaric and primitive, as a reversion to a condition we have long outgrown. The East Asians relegate freedom to the jungle, and we, collectivism.

These diametrically opposed conceptions, each in its way both right and wrong, may without doubt be ascribed to differences in psychic make-up, which in their turn were determined by the origin and history of the races in question. The East Asians were agricultural peoples at a very early stage in their history; they (and in particular the Chinese) were compelled to live together in the well-watered plains bordering the rivers. Such conditions soon called for a social code which was binding upon everybody. The majority of our ancestors, on the other hand, were forest dwellers, down to historical times. In the eighteenth century Diderot was of the opinion that 'freedom, that wonderful flower, bloomed first in Germany's wild forests'. More recently, Alfred Weber[18] has made the penetratrating observation that the ideas behind the French Revolution were not only of a rationalist character but that 'an outcrop of ancient Western—above all, Germanic—rock' once again came to the surface. This spirit, which almost died out in the land of its origin (if one assumes this to have been Germanic territory), was then disseminated throughout the world by the Anglo-Saxon races, which never quite lost it at any period of their history.

The East Asians, then, strive after freedom of outlook, but not after political liberty; they do not even attach importance to intellectual freedom, which is closely connected with political freedom.

*

The character of the East Asian is of a quite different complexity from our own. Foreigners often say, with particular reference to the Chinese, that they are 'psychologically uninteresting' and have 'no conflicts'. What they are thinking of is the smooth faces of the Chinese who, even in the most difficult times, manage to avoid being consumed by problems and fretted by cares. There is certainly some truth in this assertion, although the converse might equally well be maintained; namely, that it is in this very ability to preserve a healthy vitality and spiritual balance, that the psychological interest of the Chinese lies.

It has always been the East Asian ideal to strike a balance between, or to overcome one's conflicts, thereby achieving a reposeful and harmonious maturity; it is therefore not surprising that something of this is to be discerned in their faces. And yet it would be quite wrong to say that they are not subject to any kind of conflict. Conflicts between individual psychic functions are, it is true, largely unknown to the East Asian; he seldom identifies himself with an individual function or allows himself to be carried away by it. To that extent there is no dichotomy. But, to my mind, there is a very real conflict in him between mask and reality. Perhaps, to employ a paradox, this could be called a 'total' cleavage, since it is less concerned with the individual functions than with the whole man. In this respect the whole man, with all his functions and personal characteristics, is proved incapable of approaching the ideal of personality.

When some sort of psychic disturbance affects an East Asian, one has always the feeling that it goes very deep and affects him to the very core. He is prone to depressions, but not to schizophrenia. Because of his 'total' character his reactions take place always in the totality of the mind: joy and sorrow are felt by the whole psyche. When he is miserable or in trouble he gets little help from his intellect, for he has no faith in intellect alone; and he can just as little fall back on his feelings (or any sort of belief), because he has equally little faith in feeling alone. Should the centrum—the source of all psychic functions—become affected, a sickly and incurable impression of utter hopelessness results. There is no sight more affecting and depressing than East Asians when melancholy and downcast; there is no approaching or helping them. With their black hair and dark eyes, they go about like real and living symbols of pessimism and negation. It is as though the spring in a watch were broken, as though the man were in a decline. Such depressions usually pass after weeks, months or years, but in bad cases, where they take on a morbid character, may end in suicide or in madness.

The present-day state of affairs in China and Japan has meant that these conditions are of relatively frequent occurrence there. Such Chinese of the younger generation as had studied abroad, for example, were often among those affected. As long as they remained at their foreign universities they seemed lively, highly intelligent, active and filled with a decidedly positive enthusiasm for national affairs. Shortly after their return to China the same young people would emerge as listless, weary pessimists, rarely speaking any longer of reforms and of the future, and at best only able to summon up enough of their former vitality to fulfil their family obligations. The tremendous problems facing modern China were too great to be tackled by the less strong personalities. Many a young character was oppressed and crushed by the times to such an extent that he became a pathological case. In Japan, however, these manifestations are even more frequent: our observations show that there is here a marked incidence of schizophrenia also.

The Japanese—contrary to the Chinese—strike many foreigners as 'slightly mad'. We consider the peculiarity of the Japanese character less responsible (otherwise the same would have to be true of the Chinese too!) than the high degree of psychic conflict to which the island race has been subjected during the last few decades. East Asians undergo psychical changes, too, and the Japanese have perhaps changed more quickly than the Chinese. Japan was modernized by 'command from above'; modernization was imposed as a patriotic duty and the Japanese embarked in consequence on a period of almost convulsive spiritual over-exertion which often bordered on the pathological. In China, where both central authority and guiding idea were lacking, the process took a more natural and fortuitous course. Foreign influences entered wherever they found an open door, and were welcomed in cases where the advantages they offered were readily apparent. The Chinese changed very slowly and in a way that suited their personal convenience. To some extent—much against their will, it is true—they had to submit to external pressure, but nothing happened methodically or coherently. They were not exhorted to set up factories, to build textile machinery and warships, and to study science and technology. Nobody saw to it that railways, municipal transport and power supply undertakings were financed with Chinese capital. Nobody compelled Chinese children to attend school, nor were secondary scholars and students spurred on to learn and to study until they verged on a nervous breakdown. But the Japanese, sighing wearily beneath their burden, did all these things. Furthermore, the Chinese Communists will no doubt from now on try to whip up the people in a similar manner to even greater efforts.

When Japanese are assailed by melancholy, it is every bit as bad as with the Chinese. Everything seems as black as black can be and, if they speak at all, they tell you that the Japanese are a useless people, that the imperial idea is ridiculous nonsense, that modern Western civilization will collapse from within, and that it would be much the best thing if the whole world were to come to an end. Many of them drive themselves on through life for years in this frame of mind, constantly meditating on, and proclaiming disaster. Others, again, are subject to acute fits of depression and at such times appear completely broken. Occasionally they merely lay themselves down silently for days and weeks on end, without the doctor's being able to discover the slightest sign of fever or any symptom of physical disease. Sometimes these attacks are wholly overcome, at other times they recur periodically at ever-shortening intervals. For a psychiatrist, Japan would probably be richer in 'finds' than would China—but he would have to reconcile himself to learning his business all over again. He would be unwise to believe that the accumulated case histories and theories contained in our psychological books would get him anywhere.

The inner restlessness of the Japanese grew considerably from the time of the Manchurian Incident onwards. Ruth Benedict, who gives detailed consideration to the phenomena of Japanese

depression and Japanese boredom in a book previously referred
to, says in connection with the mood of this period, 'The typical
Japanese swing of mood is from intense dedication to intense
boredom, and the psychic shipwreck which many intellectuals
suffered was in the traditional Japanese manner.' Depression
and the feeling of being drained of all content—in other words,
boredom—can be very closely related psychologically, particularly in contrast to the intense dedication of which Ruth
Benedict speaks. She attributes these gloomy states chiefly to
Japanese vulnerability; in which she is right in so far as this
vulnerability is patently complementary to the inordinate
ambitiousness of the Japanese. This argument would, however,
apply also to other peoples and individuals, and still not explain
the specifically Japanese-East Asian nature of such conditions.
I believe that one can only fully appreciate the depth and
so to speak the horror of these conditions of depression, if at
the same time one takes into account the 'total' character of the
East Asian.

During the period of the Manchurian Incident and the China
War one had the constant feeling that the nation was not yet
inwardly mature or prepared enough for its far-reaching plans
and ambitions. The China conflict drove Japanese youth, where
it was intellectually awake—even in the army—to positive
despair. Melancholy, blackest pessimism, nervous breakdowns
and suicides were common. The conflict appeared to have
neither aim nor end. Had it in fact any purpose at all? What
good could they do the Chinese? The whole thing made no
sense. The object was allegedly 'to restore order in China'. But
in accordance with what principle? Every Japanese knew that
China, unlike, say, Manchuria, could not be regarded as
colonial territory, and nobody counted on military, or any
other sort of domination there as a permanency. Was there
anything Japan had to offer to China? Punctuality on the
railways, surfaced roads and factories? But that, after all, the
Western countries could also do. The Japanese imperial idea
was inapplicable to China, and had already proved a knotty

problem in the case of Manchukuo. Modern Japan had become great by virtue of its Shintoist creed, and the latter was not for export. That did not get one any further.

Pearl Harbour came as a release after these years of mounting discontent and groping. Their Chinese cousins were forgotten and receded into the background. The conflict with the white race as a battle-cry appealed instinctively to every Japanese; it was something that he could immediately understand. His resentments found an outlet. These feelings and sensations were so powerful that rational considerations were temporarily discarded.

*

In spite of their 'mad fits' and pathological states, one never gets the impression that the East Asians are psychically unsound, feeble, tired or senile. Nor are they fatalistic, as many maintain; they combine—as is usually the case—both the fatalistic and the non-fatalistic. The East Asians are complex, but not depraved or degenerate. In general they are psychically —and physically—strong and sound.

In point of fact, the remarkable thing is the way in which these ancient peoples have managed to keep themselves so fresh and youthful. We spoke elsewhere of the humanity of the East Asian, of his capacity for joy and sorrow. There is clearly a connection between those two traits. Even fits of depression and other sorts of weakness are not indications of inner vacuity, dullness or indifference. They are rather expressions of a deep and noble capacity for suffering which is the prerequisite of all true and genuine regeneration. These people have made up for their lack of material advancement by husbanding their spiritual resources, and so preserved their strength down the ages.

One thing at all events is certain—that the East Asians have preserved their firm belief in themselves and in their future. Chinese Communism, regarded objectively and unpolitically, must be treated as an attempt to find a new pattern in China, following the decades of chaos. Whether this experiment will, like the efforts of the preceding Kuomintang government, also prove abortive and a flash in the pan, time alone will show. In any event, China seems determined not to sink to the level of a weak and third-rate power. Nor is Japan by any means 'finished'; she will certainly live again to play her part. Military imperialism reveals only one side of this versatile and talented people.

NOTES

[1] Li Chi, *The Book of Manners.*
[2] C. G. Jung, *Die Beziehungen zwischen dem Ich und dem Unbewussten.*
[3] Hermann Hesse, *Das Glasperlenspiel.*
[4] Jacob Burckhardt, *Weltgeschichtliche Betrachtungen.*
[5] Junyu Kitayama, *West-östliche Begegnung.*
[6] C. G. Jung, *Das Unbewusste im normalen und kranken Seelenleben.*
[7] Kitaro Nishida on 'Goethe' (Quarterly of the *Goethegesellschaft*).
[8] Cf. E. H. v. Tscharner, *China in der deutschen Dichtung.*
[9] Op. cit.
[10] Goethe, *Maximem und Reflexionen.*
[11] Daisetz Suzuki, *Zen und die Kultur Japans.*
[12] Hermann Bohner, 'Shotoku Taishi' (Mitteilungen der Deutschen Gesellschaft für Natur- und Völkerkunde Ostasiens).
[13] Op. cit.
[14] *Seami, Der Neun Stufen Folge,* transl. and introduced by H. Bohner (Mitteilungen der Deutschen Gesellschaft für Natur- und Völkerkunde Ostasiens).
[15] Lafcadio Hearn, *Kyushu.*
[16] *Analects,* Book *XVII,* 20.
[17] Cf. G. B. Sansom, *Japan: A Short Cultural History.*
[18] Alfred Weber, *Abschied von der bisherigen Geschichte.*

Chapter 7

ANTIPATHY TOWARDS TECHNOLOGY

FOREIGNERS domiciled in East Asia like as much as anything to discuss their experiences of the Chinese and the Japanese regarding technical matters; and the East Asians' failure to grasp these subjects never fails to arouse the foreigner's incredulity or irony. What fantastic stories were spread during the second World War by the Japanese press and propaganda! Tales of successful attacks on enemy tanks with Samurai swords were by no means the wildest. There was a delightful story describing how a Japanese pilot brought down a hostile aircraft by bombarding it with round rice-cakes. This amazing episode was reported in all seriousness by the entire Japanese press. There was a great deal of similar propaganda about the bamboo spears which everyone was supposed to hold in readiness against the possibility of an American landing.

In Japan shortly before the war it happened that the engines of a steamship were wrongly installed, with the result that the vessel was able to steam backwards only. The fate which met a machine-tool ordered some years ago from a foreign country also serves as an illustration. The foreign engineer drew attention to the fact that a certain lever had to remain in the regulation position, since otherwise the machine would come to pieces. On the following day the Japanese returned and declared pleasantly that the engineer was indeed right; they had experimented by putting the lever in the wrong position and the machine had indeed broken down!

The story is told of a similar incident in China a few years ago, which might have had far more serious consequences. The Chinese mechanics at an airfield belonging to one of the big civil airlines had been negligent in the examination and maintenance of the aircraft. The superintendent of the airfield—a foreigner—thereupon warned them that unless they were more conscientious an aircraft might crash. A fortnight later the mechanics accused him pretty bluntly of being a liar. In what way? Well—had he not told them a fortnight ago that the aircraft would crash unless they were regularly serviced? Since then they had not overhauled a single machine—but in spite of this not one had crashed!

*

The fact that such occurrences are more frequent in China than in Japan does not mean the Japanese have more inborn technical aptitude than the Chinese, but only that they are more conscientious. The Japanese has learnt to do his duty—whether he understands it or not. The Japanese railway employee, for example, can be relied on carefully to test the brakes of every single railway train if it is part of his duties to do so. It is in defence matters that the technical care and thoroughness of the Japanese is seen to best advantage, because every piece of equipment with which the soldier or sailor is concerned—aircraft, guns, vehicles and even rifles—is the property of the Emperor. For this reason every object in the military sphere is handled with love and reverence. The Chinese —at least until quite recently—were without a similar sense of national duty and responsibility, and as a result various East Asian weaknesses and deficiencies appeared in them more patently than in the Japanese.

To drive with a Chinese or Japanese chauffeur is sheer torture, since they have no sort of feeling for the engine. On no account, for example, when going uphill, will they change into a lower gear until the car has come almost to a standstill. As soon as they have got up some sort of speed again they at once change back into third or top gear, so that the vehicle is once more slowed down to the point of stopping and the gears have to be changed all over again. By way of amusement I once counted while a Japanese driver changed gear in this way no less than 120 times on a short stretch of mountain road.

The East Asians will tell you in all seriousness that this uses up less petrol. But that is not the only reason—they merely want, like children, to see whether after all it is not possible to make it in third. That it is theoretically impossible never even occurs to them.

In China—except in Shanghai—the life of a strongly-built American truck can be reckoned at eight months at the outside. Everything belonging to the truck is either lost or neglected. If the ignition key gets mislaid somebody simply knocks the mechanism to pieces and holds the two wires together (if he can!) for the rest of the journey. Accidents are always happening on the muddy, slippery mountain roads, but it never occurs to anyone to take a rope or a shovel along as a precaution. When military vehicles carrying officers get bogged down, the latter never on any account get out to direct operations. That is beneath their dignity, and, what is more, there is not one among them who is himself able to drive a car.

A Japanese or Chinese, furthermore, never drives his own car. In the first place, driving is the job of the chauffeur (and no one may deprive him of his livelihood!), and secondly, he gets not the slightest pleasure from driving. Motor racing seems quite as stupid to East Asians as horse racing, and has consequently never been introduced. Horse racing on the other hand is enormously popular—but only because of the totalizator, for all East Asians are born gamblers. This passion for gambling is from the psychological viewpoint of course an adjunct to their leaning towards oracles and fortune-tellers.

This East Asian attitude towards technical matters, which strikes us as so peculiar, can be seen or detected everywhere and in every little thing. Every now and then one discovers in some factory or other, machines which are supported by pieces of wood or held together with string. On looking more closely into the matter, one finds as a rule that an appropriate procedure for adjusting the machine in question has already been laid down but has evidently not been understood by the operator. But no matter—the chief thing is that it works. The East

Asians are not concerned about how long it will continue to work properly in this improvisatory fashion. After all, many defective machines are just not repaired at all; in such cases there is always manpower to fall back on. Instead of pressing a button, one can equally well detail a particular worker to go every five minutes to a lever fifty or a hundred yards away, and so set a particular machine in motion.

During the war years, when there were no foreign engineers and advisers, a marked decline in technical efficiency was noticeable in Japan.

*

When the East Asians, during the last few decades, began to take over our technical achievements, they proceeded on the false assumption that it was a matter of acquiring something once and for all time. It did not occur to them that there were such things as technical progress and development. For example, they believed railways, which were introduced into their countries at the end of last century, to be something fixed, absolute and immutable.

When they began to realize that what they had taken over was not final and unchanging, and that every few years there would be something new to copy, they were possessed by a great yearning to bring to an end what they held to be a pointless and disquieting game on the part of the white races; but at the same time they shut their eyes to this realization and just refused to believe that the stream of new inventions would go on endlessly—that there would forever be new aircraft, new guns, new artificial fabrics, new machines and so forth.

Then gradually it dawned on them that the importance lay not so much in the things which the white race happened to produce, but in the ideas that lay behind them. The events of the last few years must have brought the Chinese and Japanese a good deal closer to such a realization.

The Japanese think of their defeat less in political and military, than in scientific and technical terms. Whereas bad

policies and lack of military success can be ascribed to an un-
lucky constellation, a failure of the people's capabilities cannot.
This latter cut them to the quick. It was the squadrons of giant
American bombers, the hoards of American ships of every
description, the countless motor vehicles, the giant bulldozers
capable of clearing the rubble of burnt-out cities in next to
no time—it was all this that broke the heart of the Japanese.
It was the realization that it was not they who had invented all
this; it was their awe of the mysterious white race.

It had been their belief that they too had progressed 'thus
far'. They had been convinced that they had fully adapted all
important inventions to their own needs. Now they had to
recognize the extent of their error. They began to see that they
had conceived the reckoning with the West in terms too frivolous
and superficial. They saw that, although they had bought and
copied many things from the white races, they had not had
the slightest inkling of the true nature of those things! Since the
collapse I have not met a single Japanese schoolboy who did not
say that he wanted to study science or some technical subject.

It is this perception of their own inadequacy in the trial of
strength between the nations that goes to the very fundamentals
of the Japanese people's attitude to things. That free and
democratic America should have vanquished imperial and
authoritarian Japan was felt to be a question of quite secondary
importance.

In recent years this realization has been brought home to an
ever-increasing degree to the Chinese also. In the first place
they were confronted with the shameful fact that the Japanese,
whom they regarded as their actual inferiors, were victoriously
advancing on all sides, and for no other reason than that they
had achieved a higher degree of 'Westernization' than the
Chinese. At the beginning of the war Chiang Kai-shek even
went so far as to say that the Chinese should in this respect
follow the example of the Japanese. Many Chinese, despite their
ancient vanity and conceited pride in their own culture, betrayed envy and admiration when they referred to the Japanese.

Then there was the further fact that it was principally those Chinese divisions that had been trained and equipped by foreigners, which fought with most distinction against the Japanese; at the beginning of the war it was still the troops that had been trained under German supervision, and later— to a far greater extent—it was the American-trained divisions, notably those raised and equipped in India without any Chinese participation.[1]

The Chinese probably realized much sooner than the Japanese what issues were ultimately involved in the tug-of-war between East and West; perhaps that is why they so often seemed at a loss and oppressed by the size of the problem. Only the Chinese Communists appear to be unabashed. They are attempting with a cruel determination to carry through a modernization, an adaptation to twentieth-century require- ments, which in their opinion cannot be achieved by more moderate means.

Our earlier expositions, and in particular our description of the nature of East Asian thought, will have made it clear in principle why the development of the Western type of science and technology was an impossibility in East Asia, and why these peoples have difficulty even now in understanding the nature and significance of our achievements in this field. The remainder of this chapter will be devoted to the special question as to whether there has at any time been evidence of tendencies in East Asia towards a development which might have run parallel to that of the West.

*

At one time there were, in fact, in China clear symptoms hinting at such notions. Their only exponents were Mo Ti (also called Mo Tse), philosopher and founder of a religion, and his school. Up to now we have said nothing about this movement because it exercised no lasting influence on Chinese thought. Mo Ti (who lived towards the end of the fifth century B.C. and was therefore a little later than Confucius) and his disciples played an important rôle for over 200 years—but almost all trace of their work was lost during subsequent generations. The Chinese began, almost contemporaneously with the Greeks, to develop a system of logic and dialectics, but in China it was never carried beyond the earliest stages; Mo Ti's system was attacked and was ultimately lost in oblivion. Mo Ti is the only great Chinese philosopher of whom, until well into the twentieth century, no biography had been written. There is no mention of his name in any chronicle, or in any of the innumerable and voluminous Chinese histories. Attacked and discredited as he was by other Chinese philosophers, foremost among them the Confucians, he was known to the Chinese people 'right up to the present era only as an abominable heretic'.[2] Not until our present century was he rescued from oblivion and subjected to a detailed evaluation by Hu Shih[3] and others, who pointed out with every justification that in the changed world conditions of today China should by no means look only to foreign countries but might also link up with her own traditions.

By comparison with the doctrines and philosophies of life which have prevailed in China for centuries, Mo Ti with his intellectual affinities with the West strikes us as distinctly un-Chinese.[4] When the Christian missionaries came to China, the educated Chinese found 'nothing new' in Christianity. They pointed to the Mohist school and explained that the same ideas had emerged in China 2,000 years ago, only to be refuted there and then.

Mo Ti was at once religious and intellectual. He believed in a God having both personal consciousness and will, to whom man should do service and submit himself. He also believed in a 'world beyond' which is real and distinct from 'the world around us'. The basis of his teaching was universal love for mankind regardless of family or other ties. He was more individualist than collectivist. In the words of Richard Wilhelm,[5] he regarded 'mankind not as an organism split up by a natural process into an infinite series of relationship gradations whose units are the family and the clan—as Confucianism conceived things—but as an association of mere individuals, all owing one another the same universal love'. In this, Mo Ti set himself up against many things that were sacred to the Chinese; in particular, he laid no stress on the family as the centre of things. He also antagonized people by his opposition to the usual death rites and the wearisome funeral observances which he regarded as pointless, expensive and a waste of time. He was, moreover, strongly ascetic in his outlook and attacked luxury in all its forms: for him this included the fine arts, music and literature. He was probably the first who theoretically justified his anti-militarism and pacifism; the arguments he used in this connection read like a modern treatise.[6] Mo Ti founded a religious organization, which was developed by his successors into an austere discipline, the like of which China had never before seen, and has not witnessed since. At the head of this organization stood a 'pope', to whom all were sworn in obedience. The first head of this Church, its first 'pope', was Mo Ti himself, and he had a number of successors.

Mo Ti, who was far from being a mystic, tried to prove and to justify his theories rationally. Not only is he the first founder of a theistic Church in China, he is also her first logician. What is more, he was interested to a marked degree in technical matters and their practical application; many practical suggestions in this field are thought to go back to him.

*

There is, therefore, a great deal to be learnt from what Chinese philosophers have had to say about Mo Ti. Naturally, all of them have rejected his thesis in the most decided fashion. The greatest of them have nevertheless acknowledged the integrity of his aims, and are not blind to the greatness of his personality. Let me quote certain passages from Hu Shih's paper on the Chinese logicians. Mencius, that celebrated figure who declared that Mo Ti's teachings would lead mankind 'to live like wild animals', admits elsewhere that 'Mo Ti loved all men, and would gladly wear out his whole being from head to heel for the benefit of mankind'. Chuang Tse, an equally celebrated figure, wrote:

> The life of the Mohists is toilsome and their death ritual is too simple. Their way is too primitive. It makes men sad and sorrowful. It is difficult to practise . . . It is against human nature and men cannot stand it. Though Moh Tze himself could bear it, how about the world? . . . But Moh Tze was certainly a glory to the world! What he could not attain he would never cease to seek, even though he be in privation and destitution. Ah, what a genius he was!

Thus Mencius, the Confucian, thought that the rejection of the family system and the morals that held society together would lead to a situation where men would of necessity live like beasts—exactly the same argument that is still adduced against individualism in East Asia today. What comes out above all in Chuang Tse's assessment is the wise prudence of the Chinese, according to which is it not man's place to strive, like Faust, for the unattainable. The aim of human society should be an attainable, a 'practicable' harmony. In characterizing the Mohists as 'primitive', Chuang Tse is thinking of the way they make too little allowance for human character, of how they have too little experience of life and knowledge of men and affairs.

The disciples of Mo Ti continued the attempt to supply an intellectual and logical basis for his religious doctrine, whilst his later successors, the so-called neo-Mohists, turned aside from the religious aspect of the doctrine and preoccupied themselves more and more with studies of a purely dialectical and logical nature, which degenerated into sterile sophistry. Nevertheless, they also pursued scientific studies and carried out experiments. According to Hu Shih, those works of the Mohist school which have been handed down contain theories of logic, grammar, mathematics and optics, as well as of psychology, ethics, politics and economy. Amongst other things, their writings contain references to various experiments in mathematics and optics, for example with concave and convex mirrors. According to Hu Shih these treatises are, with the exception of a few minor works of geometry and medicine, the sole surviving evidence of the scientific achievements of ancient China. (To prevent misunderstanding, let me explain that the term 'scientific' is used here in its Western not in its 'universistic' Chinese sense). The neo-Mohists were also familiar with the principle of causality, as well as the 'theory of opposites'; in other words categories which underlie much of Western thought.

The Confucian Sun Kuang, who exercised a greater influence on those times than Mencius, called the logical theories of the neo-Mohists 'perverted', and above all, 'heretical'. This is reminiscent of what we said above about Chinese tolerance and intolerance (cf. p. 122 et seq.). The Confucians repudiated not only religious doctrines but also (and much more readily) intellectual theories as soon as they came into conflict with their own 'universistic' conceptions. Sun Kuang stigmatizes in particular those paradoxes which were advanced by the neo-Mohist dialecticians, much as they were by the Greeks. He maintains that every wise ruler should perceive the meaninglessness of such sophistries. National unity could only be maintained through the Tao and not through useless argumentation. He even demands the punishment of those who do not adhere to the established 'universistic' outlook, and continues:

> Therefore a wise ruler establishes authority over them (the people), guides them by truths, reminds them from time to time by ordinances, makes truths clear to them by expository treatises, and forbids their deviation by penalties. By these means the people can be converted to truth as readily as if by aid of the gods. What use is there for arguments and debates? (As quoted by Hu Shih).

It is in Sun Kuang that the anti-Mohistic views of the Confucians find truly classic expression. Hu Shih, moreover, holds him primarily responsible for the decline of Mohism, for Sun Kuang quite deliberately intended that man should be the sole concern of philosophy, thereby banning nature and science from the realm of all serious studies. In the eyes of Confucius, in whose day no Mohist movement existed, there could be no question but that man stood at the centre of the universe: it was, so to speak, an unpolemical fact. For this reason Sun Kuang, who was out to defend Confucianism against the Mohists, formulates his ideas with considerably greater definition. For example:

> You vainly seek the cause of things: Why not simply appropriate and enjoy what they produce? Therefore I say: to neglect man and speculate about nature is to misunderstand the facts of the universe. (As quoted by Hu Shih.)

He maintains therefore that it is wrong to seek 'the cause of things', and elsewhere he says that it is vain to speculate 'why something is as it is'. 'These', he continues, 'are things the knowledge of which does not benefit men and ignorance concerning which does not harm men . . . they belong to the speculations of unruly persons of a degenerate age'. On Sun Kuang's assumption, then, all Western science and philosophy would derive from the 'speculations of unruly persons of a degenerate age'. We find here the introverted viewpoint of the Chinese at its clearest: he who neglects man and speculates about nature will misunderstand the facts of the universe.

Mo Ti's pacifism and anti-militarism was also sharply attacked, although he did not specifically deny that defensive wars were justified. These theories, and also those of universal love for mankind, were held to be too much in conflict with the military necessities of the age. Hu Shih quotes amongst others a contemporary of Mo Ti who expresses this attitude: 'If the principle of disarmament triumphs, then our strategic passes will be defenceless. And if the doctrine of universal love triumphs, then none of our soldiers will be willing to fight.' The Chinese were, generally speaking, of a peaceable disposition, but as a consequence of their practical and realistic mentality and their slight regard for 'theories', it is only on rare occasions that they have acknowledged the principle of pacifism.

*

It was inevitable that the opposition of the majority of Chinese thinkers should cause Mohism to founder. The Mohists were different from the normal run of Chinese. Their sombre heroism and earnestness were in themselves qualities which cannot exactly be regarded as typically Chinese. In its external manifestations Mohism perished as a result of Huang Ti's persecution of intellectuals and of the great book-burnings of 213 B.C., which have already been mentioned (cf. p. 123). Confucianism, too, was attacked by the government in precisely the same way, but the remarkable thing was that soon afterwards it shone forth again in all the glory it was to retain over the next 2,000 years, while Mohism never recovered but fell into complete oblivion.

Of the decline of Mohism, Richard Wilhelm[7] writes the following:

It is important to consider the reasons why the essentially theistic belief in universal love failed to take root in the East, while in the West it provided the basis for religious life for centuries. There are various reasons. The activistic conceptions of Mo Ti suited the demands, so to speak, of a 'younger' spiritual stage. The Chinese were too experienced to harbour the naïve conviction that it was possible to improve the world by means of universal love for all mankind. This has emerged no less clearly in the history of Christendom than in the fate that befell Mohism in China. But Christianity retained its authority at least in externals, while Mohism perished. The reason for this may lie in the fact that Christianity did not have to compete with a philosophy of life such as Confucianism, with its ideals of maturity, revealed clarity and humility. What is probably ultimately responsible is the fact that in the West the tendency was, by its own preference, towards the development of the individual—of the human soul in its anthropocentric aspect—whilst the development of the East was for a very long time inseparably bound up with the family basis of society.

From these observations of Wilhelm we might get the impression that it was first and foremost the religious teachings of the Mohists that antagonized the Chinese. I believe, however, that neither the religious doctrine, nor on the other hand even the intellectual approach of the Mohists can be held exclusively responsible. It was their basic psychological disposition which was in opposition to the 'total' psyche of the Chinese. The cleavage between emotion and reason in the Mohist teaching was similar to that in Western culture. This coincidence can scarcely be fortuitous, since the division into separate spheres of emotion and reason is on occasion undoubtedly a sign that a certain phase of psychic differentiation has been reached. It is the more remarkable that the Chinese should have rejected the consequences of this differentiation already 2,000 years ago.

The temporary appearance of the Mohists on the Chinese scene furnishes fresh evidence that civilized peoples are endowed in a like manner with all the psychic potentialities, but these have been variously developed. Today the Chinese are once again beginning to study the Mohists, a side of their culture that has hitherto been neglected and suppressed, just as we are evincing renewed interest in the Western mystics.

That the Chinese and Japanese have developed no science or technology cannot be ascribed in any way to an 'incapacity' on their part; it is due essentially to their *Weltanschauung* and to psychic restraints. The difficulties that confront the East Asians in these fields are attributable rather to the unbalanced training they have had for hundreds, nay thousands of years, than to any constitutional incapacity or lack of intelligence.

Many basic elements of this ancient training are still prevalent in the East Asian school system. The retention of a large number of their traditions, while restricting the introduction of Western ideas and methods, was the only possible course open to the East Asians, if they did not wish to jettison their indigenous culture entirely, and so become a mere imitation of the Western world. The problem of the script in use, which we have already discussed (cf. p. 58 et seq.), is a case in point. It is most difficult to learn to think logically when at the same time one has to learn 2,000 written characters by heart. The question now is whether the Chinese Communists will do away with the old pictorial script. When they tried to do so many years ago, they met with no success. As is well known, East Asian children who go to school in America or in Europe develop along quite different lines from their compatriots at home, but it is equally true that Western children who go to Chinese or Japanese schools acquire an East Asian mentality. The latter does not happen often, however, (because foreigners in the larger East Asian cities mostly maintain their own schools for their children) and we propose therefore to give an instance.

A foreign merchant living in a Japanese provincial town was forced to send his two children, until the age of twelve, to a Japanese primary school. They were thereafter placed under a European tutor, who had the greatest difficulty in teaching the children mental arithmetic, grammar and history according to our own methods. They were incapable of adding twelve and five together in their heads, yet with the help of the abacus (or counting table) they could do the most complex calculations in next to no time. (Where figures of several digits were concerned, their abacus enabled them to be even quicker than the teacher who wrote his figures out in the usual way on a piece of paper). Grammar was a quite hopeless case, for the children were unable to grasp the logic of sentence construction. In history lessons, indeed, they remembered everything, even the most unimportant details, but the sequence of the dates quite defeated them. They did not in the least care whether Napoleon lived before or after William the Conqueror; in other words the idea of historical development was something quite strange to them. These fair-haired children had become typical little Japanese in mental outlook.

*

Further proof that it is less incapacity than disinclination that has determined the attitude of the East Asians, can be found in the numerous inventions made by the Chinese but seldom put by them to practical use. We need only think of the mariner's compass, gunpowder, vaccination and the taxi-meter! The compass, although invented 2,000 years ago, was not used in navigation but rather in connection with 'universistic' practices. Hu Shih[8] thus describes his feelings on contemplating this invention:

> When I look at the mariner's compass and think of the marvellous discoveries which the Europeans have made herewith, I cannot but feel a sense of shame to recall the supersititious uses which I myself have seen made of this great invention of ancient Chinese genius.

The fact that the Chinese made no use of gunpowder for warlike purposes has, contrary to the somewhat superficial interpretation placed upon it, nothing to do with their alleged pacifism. It was rather that the thought of using gunpowder for practical purposes just never occurred to them. If it had in fact been their peaceable disposition that set them against the military use of gunpowder, they would have been able to put it to other uses, for example in road and canal building. But this they did not do, until the Westerners made their appearance.

Vaccination against smallpox was discovered as long ago as the Tang period (618–907), yet this preventative measure is scarcely ever employed.[9] The taxi-meter, which was discovered at the same time, remained only a sort of toy. It is quite possible that the Chinese have been familiar with the principle of the steam engine for centuries.

In physics and chemistry, in biology and medicine the Chinese knew many isolated facts of significance, but these were never co-ordinated into a scientific system; rather were they incorporated into the framework of the 'universistic' system. On this Wittfogel[10] says:

> Such fragments of knowledge were practically all acquired as the result of empirical collection and observation, or were by-products of alchemistic experiments. Only elementary progress was made towards formulating the results, or even the problems, in terms of ideas.

From all we have said about the cosmic view of things, it is understandable that the Chinese were bound to make very considerable strides in the field of astronomy. Thus we learn that it was a Chinese who first discovered sun-spots. It was not, however, until 400 years after Hipparchus that the precession of the equinoxes became known.[11]

Their achievements in the field of mathematics were also noteworthy and we can trace their origin back partly to Mohist beginnings and partly to foreign influence. Thus, the Chinese knew the theorem of Pythagoras, and determined the value π. They also applied themselves to solving complicated equations prior to any other peoples. According to Wittfogel,[12] the Sung Period (960–1276) saw the development of a method of finding roots and of solving all manner of equations, such as was not discovered in Europe until 1819 by the Englishman Horner.

If we except the experiments of the Mohists, the Chinese knew next to nothing about the principles of mechanics. In a strictly empirical way they nevertheless put mechanical forces to various uses. They were familiar with the action of the lever and the windlass without knowing—or asking about—the cause of this action. Similarly they made use, from a very early period, of the wheel, the cylinder, the screw and the cog-wheel, as also later on of the capstan, the block-and-tackle and the rock-drill.[13]

Next to the numerous artificial dykes and canals, one of the most impressive instances of ancient Chinese mechanical achievements is provided by the installations at the salt mines in Szechwan province, which are still in operation today. Here one can see—and marvel at—the way elementary rules of mechanics have been applied in practice, with no more than bamboo, wood and hemp ropes, to build up a highly-organized mining system. Naturally, none of it is worked by machines, but by oxen, water- or man-power.

On the other hand the Chinese reached the heights of achievement in the utilization and adaptation to artistic ends of nature's raw materials. They produced silk, paper, porcelain and lacquer. It was in the sphere of handicrafts that the preference of the Chinese—and of East Asians generally—for the concrete and readily understandable, and their rejection of the abstract and theoretical, found its most beautiful expression. Silk, paper, porcelain and lacquer are close to nature; they are not materials giving the impression that nature has been coerced or even transformed, but rather directed into given channels.

The East Asians have no love for our fine, smooth, shiny white paper—it seems strange and abstract to them because one cannot tell how it is prepared or of what substances it is made. Our types of paper give the East Asian no 'sense of material'. He prefers a coarser paper in which the fibres of the original wood-pulp can still clearly be recognized. He likes pottery when it is not wholly glazed, but when a small portion underneath is left free so that one can imagine how the glaze was poured over the clay mould. Silk also is close to nature in the eyes of the East Asian: in earlier times he never wove the very fine threads that find favour in the West. Once again, this was not because he was unable to, but because he did not wish to. With silk, exactly as with paper, one must be able to see of what, and how it has been prepared.

All East Asians used to dislike manufactured, chemically-treated or artificial materials. Some rich Japanese will even today spend a small fortune on a bamboo or wooden fence, such is their aversion for cheap cement walls or iron railings.

*

The East Asian way of making inventions and engaging in 'scientific' pursuits resembles in many respects that of the alchemists. The Western alchemists had certain theories but no general corpus of knowledge in our sense, nor did they do any systematic scientific work. Every alchemist worked on his own account, and each probably had to tackle his problems afresh from much the same starting point. The East Asian philosophers approached things in a similar way, but this is not inconsistent with the fact that Chinese thinkers took the doctrines of the old philosophers, for example Lao Tse or Confucius, as their starting point, for each of them proceeded from the basic problems and questions posed by the older masters.

In reading old—or even new—East Asian books one often has the feeling that they were, so to say, written down by the 'first man'. Everything seems much closer to the beginning of things; nothing is referred back to, except that a poem or the words of some philosopher of ancient times are now and again quoted. No explanation is given as to the grounds for the author's statements. Scientific and historical topics are discussed as though no one else had ever written about them before. Even those East Asian scholars and research workers who have received a thorough scientific grounding now and again relapse into this method of approach when they are left to themselves and no longer subjected to the critical scrutiny of Western scholarship.

Also germane to this issue is the 'concept of work' already discussed on p. 197. The European scientist looks upon himself more as a small brick in the vast structure of learning, in which he occupies a clearly defined place. Personal considerations are of purely secondary importance. The East Asian as a member of an *organic* community still has difficulty in conceiving himself as part of a rational and theoretically determined whole.

The East Asian's instinctive aversion to works of a compendious and systematic nature derives from his 'humanistic' attitude. His consistent adherence to a spontaneous and human approach to things does not call for the systematic compilation of a clear and coherent body of learning or, in other words, for the evolution of science. And without science there can be no modern technology. One cannot at one and the same time serve both man and the objective principle.

*

Most sinologists tend to be horrified by the vast accumulation of written material, mostly concerned with history and literature, that the Chinese have accumulated down the ages. They consider it quite pointless and unnecessary, and speak of a misdirected expenditure of effort and of spurious Chinese learning.[14] They forget that we, too, carry an enormous weight of ballast around with us, and that our libraries also are filled to overflowing—and to the East Asian this ballast seems for the most part quite as ridiculous as do the mountains of 'universistic' wisdom to many of us. It is at any rate far from certain which side could to advantage jettison more of its accumulation of written matter.

Let us briefly consider this vast literature whose content is so expressive of the Chinese mentality. In the first place there are the endless commentaries not only upon the classical, but also on the later Taoist and Buddhist philosophers and writings. Of these Hackmann[15] has the following to say:

> From the habits of mind of the commentators the closely-related work of the compilers developed, and there is no other nation on earth that has produced such monumental achievements in this field as has China. The knowledge and wisdom of past centuries, texts and commentaries arranged according to both subject matter and field, were collected into anthologies (some of them comprising thousands of volumes and representing in themselves alone an extensive library) and presented to the public. Encyclopedias with a vengeance! But how very different from everything produced under the same name in the West since the eighteenth century! The Chinese encyclopedias represent, as it were, the detailed findings of academic erudition set forth in a huge mass of verbiage, which tends to stifle all learning unless a certain amount of order and supervision is introduced.

What are the contents of these thousands of volumes? They are meticulously detailed descriptions, mostly of a historical or geographical nature. Everything is conscientiously taken into account—topographical details and natural occurrences, famous men and women, strange beasts, obsequies and abortions, river courses and bridge-building, harvests and crop failures, administration, temples, town walls, house building: in short, everything that is liable to happen in town or country. Cultural matters also are dealt with in detail—painting, calligraphy, poetry, numismatics, ceramics and so forth.

Not one of these accounts is anything more than a compilation of a succession of facts. A logical or causal relationship is never perceived, nor is anything ordered according to logic. This 'science' is a consequence of associative and analogical methods of thought. There is, however, one point which Hackmann fails to make: the East Asians are by nature much better fitted than we to survey such masses of material. They are more able to take a general view of the whole situation, and have better heads for detail (cf. p. 267 et seq.). We, on the other hand, have difficulty in reviewing and memorizing large agglomerations of detail not systematically arranged in accordance with our own methods. Most of us fail to grasp the 'universistic' principle of order and are therefore too prone to speak of meaningless and unco-ordinated masses of material.

*

One frequently gets the impression that the East Asians deliberately improvise on occasions when it would be our practice to take careful thought for the future and, in making our preparations, to allow for all possible eventualities. This can be discerned in every detail of daily life, in the way houses, bridges and roads are built, in industry, in legislation—in fact everywhere. This propensity towards dealing with things *ad hoc* —which must multiply the difficulties in the way of technical and scientific work—derives, of course, in large measure from the East Asian consciousness of the transitory nature of things. But not only from that: to it must be added their deep-rooted aversion to the idea of causal relationship. They make a regular habit of applying the human attribute of spontaneity to other spheres where it is out of place. They fight shy of issues that are quite clear and straightforward, and even accuse you of having 'the typical outlook of a Western materialist' when you try to bring home to them the necessary logical consequences of some measure or occurrence. What we consider already to be 'facts' are not so to the East Asian until they have specifically taken effect. Pearl Buck, the American authoress who is celebrated for her books on China, once wrote: 'The Chinese do not like to face facts', a remark which we must understand in the light of what we have said above; that is, that the realistic Chinese will fully acknowledge facts that have already taken place, but not the consequences and circumstances to which they must necessarily give rise. What Sansom[16] says of the Japanese can be ascribed to precisely the same cause: 'They seem to have preferred to work on empiric lines, promulgating laws to meet occasions as they arose, but not anticipating them'.

Cut off as we were in Japan during the second World War, we had opportunity enough to study the illogical and contradictory ways of the East Asians. In their efforts to control their war economy they frequently issued regulations which were wholly contradictory, or took measures without the least regard for their inevitable consequences. When, for example, rationing of rice and rice-wine was introduced, it was clear from the outset that it would cause great hardship to the tens of thousands of owners and employees of small shops where these products were sold, and which would have to close down while rationing lasted. But nothing was done about it until this hardship actually began to make itself felt: belated efforts were then made to absorb the people thus deprived of their livelihood elsewhere into the productive machinery. This should have been settled beforehand, for the war industries had long—and well before the shops closed down—been searching urgently for labour.

It sometimes happened, both in China and Japan, that the government would introduce measures of this kind, and would then sit back and calmly await the outcome. Should the result not be satisfactory, then further improvisatory steps were taken. It is really astonishing how far one can get by such methods, for things often fall quite naturally into place without the logical and expected consequences. It is just in political and economic affairs that events do not proceed according to cut-and-dried principles of cause and effect, as is the case, say, in technology; in this field, illogical behaviour at times gets one just as far as does logic.

The same reason, namely sceptical antipathy towards causal connections, also lies behind the long-standing East Asian hesitation to interfere with the processes of nature. Why did the Chinese not make greater use of vaccination—their own invention—against smallpox? In the last resort—from fear lest the natural course of events, and therewith the rules of the cosmos, might be disturbed by arbitrary intervention of this sort on the part of man. There was the suspicion that the evil might reappear somewhere else if it were 'artificially' suppressed. According to the doctrine of 'change', everything unpleasant was to be explained by causes lying deep in cosmic and human events. The laws of 'change' were not to be approached through rationalism, however; they could only be fathomed and influenced through the 'universistic' attitude of mind. Here we have again, therefore, a fundamentally unscientific approach!

*

Right up to most recent times nearly all East Asians have preferred to study the arts rather than the sciences. Even in Western universities they came in search of those subjects in which they were traditionally interested: ethics, philosophy, art and literature. To occupy oneself with other things was regarded by the youthful élite as something completely beneath them. They came in search of a Western Confucius, Western social theory and Western poetry. All other matters, in their opinion, were not proper subjects for a university. It was only out of a patriotic sense of duty that the Japanese succeeded in largely overcoming this attitude; to these, admittedly, no Western standards can be applied. In Japan, too, the greater number of students consisted of long-haired and pasty youths whose pallor betrayed the incipient artist or philosopher. It was for these reasons that, in time, a chronic shortage of physicists, chemists and engineers made itself felt. (Japan was nevertheless the only Asian country that at least did not have to suffer from a hopeless shortage of doctors.) In the second World War, when Japan was to a greater or less extent thrown back on her own resources, the maldistribution—from the national point of view—of the student population was brought into full relief, for neither the Navy nor the Army were in a position to meet their requirements in scientifically and technically-trained personnel. From radio-operator to aeronautical engineer, from motor mechanic to rocket expert—these were everywhere in short supply. Thus it was, for example, that modern war material, which the Japanese had been able to get to the Philippines in plenty of time, could not be used operationally because of the lack of technically-trained supporting troops.

For this reason the Japanese Government, in the middle of the war, decided on a drastic measure: they simply stopped the study of the arts for the duration of the war. In this way they compelled students either to change faculties and go over to the sciences, or to interrupt their studies and volunteer for the forces. Among the Japanese suicide pilots were many of these former pale and literary youths.

The youth of Japan—and of East Asia in general—does not go in for technical hobbies. Interest in such things is not yet sufficiently awake (cf. also p. 205 et seq.). Technicians do not therefore start off with a natural interest acquired at home, or with the benefit of experience acquired while pursuing their youthful hobbies. Nothing is learnt light-heartedly, but only through a 'sense of duty' and often in desperation. In the last decade the Japanese Government has done everything possible to awaken an interest in technical matters among the people and especially among the youth of the country. In consequence, at the beginning of the war a hobby period (for girls too!) was introduced at primary schools to teach the principles of gliding. Thereupon every single Japanese child felt it his duty to make a toy aeroplane out of bamboo and paper stuck together, and soon in the whole of Japan no schoolchild was to be seen without such an object in his hand.

In China, where there is no tradition of 'service to the Emperor', the state of affairs in this respect is far from encouraging. It is all but impossible to describe how complete is the dearth in China of experts and technicians of all categories. The few who have studied in foreign or their own native universities, are so dispersed throughout the vast country that they seem scarcely to exist at all. All the Japanese failings in this respect reveal themselves here, too, but to an even higher degree. It is significant that Chinese Communism—as, for example, is evident from the statements of Chinese generals concerning the Korean war—gives special attention to the matter of scientific and technical reserves of manpower.

Chinese students used to have an even greater aversion to the sciences; they had a greater fear of letting themselves down, or of losing 'face', in the event of their having to boil their chemical fluids themselves or having to carry their own land-surveying instruments about the country. (Sometimes they actually employed special servants and porters for such purposes!) Chinese engineers were for the most part too 'genteel' to do anything else but sit at a desk and prepare plans. They regarded their practical execution as 'tinkering' and beneath them. It would not have occurred to a Chinese oil-boring specialist in charge of a boring site to visit the scene of operations if something should go wrong. There were certainly exceptions, but they could be counted on the fingers of one hand.

The Chinese National Government, it is true, did not remain absolutely inactive in face of this situation. In the years before the Sino-Japanese War attempts were made to develop the scientific faculties of the universities by means of improved financial grants, and active propaganda was started to get people to enter them. Furthermore, preference was given to those taking scientific subjects when selections were made for the allocation to students of state or other (mostly American) awards for studying abroad. Now, in all probability, the Communist régime will send students of science and technology by the hundred to Moscow.

Not once during my many years' stay in East Asia did I come across a single instance of the literary glorification of technical progress or a single enthusiastic description of a technical achievement. In this connection one heard only references to practical value, national duty and necessity. I can only recall a hymn in praise of flying from the pen of the great Indian poet, Rabindranath Tagore, but in East Asia I encountered nothing of this kind.

A gradual change in this attitude is certainly taking place, as has been mentioned before; hence the great impression made on the Japanese by the American landing in the autumn of 1945. Even during the war this amazement was manifested, when the B29's—those great silver birds—appeared over the island kingdom glistening either in the sun or in the light of the searchlights. At first all danger was forgotten and the sight of these giant bombers was declared ecstatically to be 'beautiful in the extreme'. Not all East Asians today agree with the Chinese peasant who, on seeing an aircraft for the first time in his life and being asked for his impressions, coolly replied 'Why should it not fly, when it is built to do so?'

*

What of the future, where development of science and technology in East Asia is concerned? Many genuine qualities of the East Asians which were formerly suppressed, and still are to some extent, would certainly make great achievements possible, were they to be directed into proper and legitimate channels.

The East Asians are today undergoing a psychic change. Were the Occidental on his part also to undergo a psychic change—and tendencies in this direction are appearing amongst us,—will the unceasing development of technology come to some sort of a halt? Will a period then begin which will see the consolidation of all that has hitherto been achieved in the technical field? Will development of mind and soul be allowed precedence over applied labour? Will humanity strive to accustom itself to the new stage of civilization and technology to which we have attained by enormous strides, instead of continuing its headlong and unheeding progress into the unknown?

These are questions which one was always asking oneself in East Asia. One could imagine an ideal and desirable solution in a synthesis of Eastern introversion and Western extraversion —a 'critical-total' world culture; an encompassing outlook which nevertheless acknowledged in each sphere of life certain dominant rules; a 'universism' which acknowledged the fact that different laws applied at different levels; a science that was aware of the limitations of its methods.

*

Once spiritual needs are experienced, however, man will spontaneously turn his attention more and more to inner things, and this alone would indirectly bring about a gradual reduction of the rate of technical progress. In other words, nothing can grow and prosper when humanity has lost interest in it. Technology has no 'life of its own', it is no independent self-subsistent system of causality, but is essentially the work of man and is dependent on human volition and human striving. Technology cannot be developed *ad infinitum* if man is psychically unable to endure it.

Let us now enquire whether, over and above the psychological ones already advanced, there are not other grounds for thinking that the period of restless technical progress might gradually come to a stop.

We ourselves are still far from being accustomed to the things we have created and are still creating: nylon tooth-brushes, plastics, air conditioning, dried milk, and automatic devices of every description have still an element of strangeness for us.

We are neither able nor willing to retrace our steps: we merely wish to be clear about our situation and our aims.

The organic 'assimilation' of technology is the problem of our time, and this task can only be performed by men who are psychically sound. The man who represents to an advanced degree the 'split' type, and has no deep spiritual roots, feels that technology is something 'daemonic'; he overlooks the fact that technology can itself have nothing daemonic about it. What he is really referring to is the daemonic element within himself.

Let us examine these questions quite dispassionately, and turn first to science.

Modern physics has reached a transitional stage. A progressive differentiation of things explicable by logic may well be arrived at in many branches of physics, but that would only mean shifting a few boundaries and would make no difference in principle to the fact that atomic physics is advancing into regions where problems can no longer be solved by reference to purely scientific aids and means. Indeed, atomic physics, as already indicated, can prove mathematically and by logical methods that our questing *must* lead back to such beginnings, since otherwise all physical laws hitherto discovered cease to be valid.[17] In all works of reference consulted on this point I found the opinion expressed that no revision of the modern physical conception of the world is to be expected in the foreseeable future.[18]

If, then, physics has already progressed so far, will not the urge to carry out further research gradually slacken off? Will not many young people whose desire for knowledge hitherto led them to study physics, now, as a matter of course, choose philosophy as their 'main subject' and physics only as a 'subsidiary one'?

These considerations do not, of course, affect the possibility of further progress in the sphere of practical and technical application of physical knowledge. But in spite of this a drying-up of potentialities in the field of pure research would also mean that the endless possibilities for practical innovation would slacken, since all notable innovations have their origin in the results of theoretical and pure research. It was not the will to construct atom bombs or atomic power units that led to the discovery of the inner structure of the atom, to modern quantum and wave mechanics, but the scientists' impersonal and disinterested urge for truth and knowledge, unrelated to any thought of practical utility, coupled with the white man's natural instinct to experiment.

A quite different picture emerges in regard to psychology and biology. Of biology, Bavink[19] says that it is 'actually still at the same stage as was physics at the time of Galileo'. It is, of course, no coincidence that these two youngest of the sciences should be at the beginning of their careers, for the scientific approach hitherto employed was to a certain extent inappropriate for these subjects. In the interpretation of, and research into organic life, the logico-causal attitude of mind can be of only limited help. Unless we broaden the conception of 'science' that we have entertained up to now, we may not apply the term 'science' to psychology and biology.[20] Many scholars are nowadays afraid to acknowledge this fact. To act in an 'unscientific' manner is still accounted reprehensible, people having apparently forgotten that it is worse still to be untruthful. If methods of enquiry that are widely identified today with scientific research fail to produce results, in many spheres, why should the fact not be frankly acknowledged?

Psychology and biology which concentrate on the natural and organic, on man and life, reveal — properly regarded — a conservative tendency rather than a progressive one. The emergence particularly of psychology is proof of the increasing propensity towards introspection.

This must not be taken to mean that in our view all innovation should cease forthwith. Nobody would wish this, for we live in an age of transition and are yet far removed from the attainment of a state of what Ernst Jünger[21] called 'Chinese constancy'. It is first and foremost the United States that is faced with an immense historical task—that of leading our Western culture to its consummation and thereby opening up a new epoch of quiet and stability. It does not necessarily denote a deeper insight into historical and predetermined necessity if we Europeans smile at, or reject the Americans' faith in progress, just because we are more aware of the limitations of progress. For the time being, we shall be unable to dispense with this 'faith in progress'. Should we not actually rejoice that there are still people who are less sensible of the bitter conflicts of our time than we Europeans, and are, therefore, able to carry on with their work untroubled and with confidence?

*

Our present-day striving after a new equilibrium does not necessarily entail the sacrifice of the intellectual function. It only means that it must be subordinated to the total psyche. We are neither able, nor do we wish to go back to a stage of spiritual undifferentiation. Differentiation, into which we emerge from the undifferentiated state, must be organically endurable if the germ, the spark of life is not to be extinguished. Today we have reached the highest pitch of differentiation, a stage that brings hidden dangers with it, and we must direct our attention towards establishing the extent to which the living entity, the organism, is able to endure this state of affairs. Our age has seen remarkable achievements in the intellectual sphere, certain of which—for example those of Albert Einstein—may well not have their equal in the whole history of the world. That there should be an organic reaction to this is not only natural but also desirable. Whether we possess the vital forces and powers of regeneration whereby we can attain once more to a state of equilibrium, remains to be seen.

It is in this respect that we can expect to derive both benefit and guidance from the age-old views and experiences of the East Asians. Our problem is more difficult than theirs ever was, in that we are more differentiated than they: but on the

17

other hand, the fact that we have their example to draw on makes our task that much easier.

The East Asians for their part are faced by the reciprocal problem of the necessity for a higher degree of differentiation. Theirs is a difficult task, because the sole object of their study for thousands of years has been the idea of totality. True, they have our example before them and this makes for a certain alleviation of the difficulty. From this example they will be able to study the limits and dangers of differentiation and so will be able to turn our experiences to their own advantage. A productive interchange of this sort should enable humanity ultimately to rise to new heights.

The East Asians will the more readily find a point of contact with the modern world if they are able to discern some ultimate purpose, some conceivable outcome to all our endeavours. So far they have recoiled from the unco-ordinated urgency of the Occidental, from his blind and headlong progress. What is the point of all this, they asked. What has humanity to gain from it? Why should we, too, have to lose our souls? They were in full agreement with Goethe's remark[22] that 'unrestricted activity, whatever its nature, can end only in bankruptcy'.

The East Asian's understanding of our efforts and the path we have trodden hitherto will doubtless be facilitated by the fact that the most modern developments of science have brought scientific thought closer to the Oriental's way of thinking. Should we—and not they themselves—be able to demonstrate the correctness of many of their views on things, they would then presumably alter their opinions of the pointlessness of our scientific endeavours.

It is sometimes claimed that the younger generation in the West is able to comprehend the new cosmic picture presented by modern physics more rapidly than the older generation, since the latter is still too much under the spell of the logical approach. The East Asians, by reason of their traditional methods of thinking, would accordingly seem better placed today than ever before. And it is a fact that in the last twenty years Japanese and Chinese scientists have made important discoveries and formulated new laws in the sphere of atomic physics.[23]

The East Asians will perhaps even prove themselves capable of gradually overtaking us in technology and the sciences. It is true that we have always been more differentiated than they, but we must remember that it was not until the eighteenth and nineteenth centuries—particularly the latter, of course—that we made our greatest advances. Goethe and Napoleon still travelled at much the same speed as Julius Caesar, and all three of them in their turn no faster than did the Chinese before they adopted our modern methods of transportation. Until right into the nineteenth century the food supply of Peking or Tokyo was effected in essentially the same way as it was in London or Paris. The supply problem in the case of Tokyo, which was called 'Yedo' in those days, may well have given rise to even great complications, for in the eighteenth century Tokyo was the largest city in the world. The economy of China and Japan was not in past centuries autarchic in the primitive sense, as is generally supposed: both, on the contrary, had trading relations with as many other countries as were in those days accessible to them. It was not until the nineteenth century that the marked discrepancy in levels of 'civilization' and technology became evident.

It is my belief that the encouragement of mutual understanding between West and East, in which each provides a stimulus for the other, constitutes one of the most productive forms of intellectual activity that can be conceived at the present time. All concerned cannot but gain therefrom, and at the same time secure the means of raising themselves to a higher plane. And the attractive thing about this prospect is that this higher plane will be the same, or very much the same, for all peoples.

NOTES

[1] Concerning the great work carried out in this direction, particularly by General Stillwell, cf. Theodore H. White and Annalee Jacoby, *Thunder out of China*. The official German military mission was recalled by Hitler in 1938; Chiang Kai-shek yielded reluctantly to this request, and in the end no doubt for political reasons. At the head of this mission was General v. Falkenhausen, later Commander-in-Chief of the occupying forces in Belgium.

[2] Richard Wilhelm, *Geschichte der chinesischen Kultur*.

[3] Hu Shih, *The Development of the Logical Method in Ancient China*.

[4] Marcel Granet, in his *La Pensée chinoise*, to which frequent reference has been made, warns us not to look at Mo Ti one-sidedly through Western spectacles. He holds, for example, that one of Mo Ti's basic conceptions, 'Kien ngai', cannot be rendered as 'universal love' (amour universel), and he doubts, too, whether the Mohists really knew of the principle of causality and the 'law of transformation'. We have here kept mainly to the statements of Hu Shih and Richard Wilhelm. It may be that these two writers stress somewhat uncritically the likeness between Mo Ti and the Western mind, though their interpretation seems to us to be in essence correct, as is evidenced already by the reaction of Chinese thinkers coeval with Mo Ti.

[5] Richard Wilhelm, *Chinesische Philosophie*.

[6] Quotations taken from Hu Shih, op. cit.

[7] *Geschichte der chinesischen Kultur*.

[8] Op. cit.

[9] According to K. A. Wittfogel, *Wirtschaft und Gesellschaft Chinas*.

[10] Ibid.

[11] Ibid.

[12] Ibid.

[13] Ibid.

[14] Cf. de Groot, *Universismus*, and H. Hackmann, *Der Zusammenhang zwischen Schrift und Kultur in China*.

[15] Op. cit.

[16] G. B. Sansom, *Japan: A Short Cultural History*.

[17] Cf. C. F. v. Weizsäcker, *Zum Weltbild der Physik*.

[18] Cf. the works of Bavink, Jeans, Weizsäcker, etc., already drawn upon.

[19] As quoted by K. v. Neergaard, *Die Aufgabe des 20 Jahrhunderts*.

[20] Cf. K. v. Neergaard, op. cit.

[21] Ernst Jünger, *Der Arbeiter*.

[22] Goethe, *Maximen und Reflexionen*.

[23] The Japanese atom-physicist, Yukawa, predicted the existence of mesons already in 1935, and the Chinese Lin is the brilliant discoverer of the basic laws of turbulence—to name only the best-known. Whereas the Germans possessed only one cyclotron before the second World War, there were two of these machines for splitting the atom in Japan. One of the few technical journals dealing with pure physics is published in Tokyo.

Chapter 8

COMPLEMENTARY STRENGTHS AND WEAKNESSES

I<small>N</small> East Asia the highest forms of knowledge and wisdom co-exist with religious practices that are primitive in the extreme and border on superstition; enlightened disciples of Buddhism or Taoism live peaceably side by side with nature-worshippers and conjurers of demons. Illumination and mystic experience; the pragmatic wisdom of Confucius; ancestor- and emperor-worship; worship of gods, holy men and Bodhisattvas; animism; magic; fear of the ghosts of the dead and of men able to turn themselves into animals—all exist here side by side. Nor do the inferior spirits and demons hang back among the shadows; their existence is officially sanctioned; they have their shrines and attendants and are treated with every respect.

The ancient Indian conception (the Upanishads) assigns the highest place to those men who strive after the Absolute, the second place to those who worship a personal God, and the third to those worshipping some form of reincarnation (for example Rama, Krishna or Buddha); next come those who worship ancestors, gods or wise men; and the fifth and lowest place is assigned to those who venerate spirits and demons.

All these categories are present in India, whilst in East Asia the second is wholly lacking. There the incidence of the first and fourth is most pronounced, although the third also shows itself, above all in East Asian Buddhism, and the fifth, in popular superstition.

The absence of the conception of a personal deity alone, this most significant intermediate stage, allows one to conclude, with certain reservations, that the East Asians, as compared with other peoples, are comparatively lacking in religious apti-tude. We can, in this connection, ignore both the temporary phenomenon of Mohism and the question of the form in which monotheism originally existed in ancient China, for neither played a decisive part in the development of the East Asian outlook.

*

These facts must be considered in relation to the markedly differing levels of spiritual development obtaining in the East Asian world, and its propensity towards the esoteric. Many feel able to adhere to a religion which stresses the emotional aspect, but only few strive after perception of the ultimate truths, for to do so presupposes knowledge and spiritual culture. It is for this reason that culture has in East Asia—as opposed to the West—always been valued as something ethically positive and good in itself.

In East Asia a higher and a lower level of consciousness have always co-existed. In principle we can no more refer to a 'progressive growth of consciousness' in this connection than we can to a 'development' in East Asian history. The higher consciousness existed in East Asia at the dawn of history, and the lower is still there today exactly as it has always been. To believe that mankind as a whole could ever aspire to a higher level of consciousness has always been counted as a Utopian dream by East Asian thinkers. For reasons of spiritual hygiene, therefore, they welcomed the existence of lower and more primitive forms of religion, which provide scope for projections from the unconscious. C. G. Jung's[1] remark about the Indians: 'The philosophy of the Upanishads implies a psychology that long ago acknowledged the relativity of the gods', applies equally to East Asian philosophy. The relativity of the gods was recognized at a very early stage, but no attempt was ever made to expound this to the many who possessed neither the intellectual prerequisites nor the necessary degree of maturity.

Oriental realism, then, which renounces the impossible, stands in direct contrast to Christian idealism. It is also behind the conception that regards all striving for the unattainable as something dangerous and even immoral. Only harm is done when the uninitiated experience too much, or when they only half-understand—or completely misunderstand—what they experience. This attitude of all esoteric sects and behind all cabbalistic instruction is so deeply ingrained in East Asian consciousness that we can discern it not only in religion but also, as we saw earlier (cf. p. 181), in the arts and crafts. The Occident itself once inclined towards this outlook, especially under the influence of the Catholic Church, but has lately retreated further and further from it—and today it is doubtful, to say the least, whether this retreat has been wholly to our advantage.

For East Asia the following statement is in general true: the higher type of man perceives, and the masses worship. Perception is identical with redemption and is not only a way by which the latter can be attained. Expressed differently—loving is indeed a prerequisite of perceiving, for perception without love is impossible; but as a goal perception takes precedence over love. This has its counterpart in the Indian conception which assigns the highest place to those striving after cognition, while the monotheistic religions are awarded second place before all others. The big difference, however, lies in the fact that the Indians, with their much greater capacity for religion, have frequently struck off along the second path, while the East Asians have less often been aroused to similar depths of feeling in matters of faith. There is a psychological connection between this and the fact that the Indians, in contradistinction to the East Asians, have developed their own system of logic, even though the latter may to us appear in many respects unsatisfactory.

Meditation and prayer—these two words sum up the fundamental distinction between the religious life of the Far East and that of the West. As we have already seen (cf. p. 135), it is only in certain Buddhist sects which worship Amida Buddha and stress the idea of redemption that prayer has made its appearance.

*

The extraordinary significance of mysticism for the few is something which we may take for granted. But what value has it for the many? Let us try to present the reverse side of the East Asian attitude—so to speak, its complementary draw-backs—in order to reveal its limitations and weaknesses. In such an attempt we are, it is true, faced with almost insuperable difficulties, for where could we find a comparative 'Ideal Culture' against which to measure that of East Asia? We can indeed point out that in the West we neither pay priests to exorcize demons nor are given to phallic worship, but can we maintain that we have therefore attained a higher degree of human maturity than the East Asians? We identify ourselves with our feelings, ideas and prejudices in a way that is, when all is said and done, absolutely primitive, and quite fail to perceive how utterly they have us in thrall. Our psychologists say that these unconscious identifications can be more dangerous psychically than is the worship of gods and spirits, because these latter beings at least provide some sort of outlet for those who cannot attain a high degree of self-knowledge and, therefore, of self-mastery.

We can see, then, how difficult and also perhaps how pointless it is to try to pass judgment on issues concerning values. In his commentary on *The Secret of the Golden Flower*[2] C. G. Jung says:

> We would like to climb the heights of a philosophical religion, but are, in fact, incapable of it. We can at best grow up to it. The Amfortas wound and the Faustian conflict in the Germanic man are not yet healed; his unconscious is still loaded with contents which must first be made conscious before he can be free of them.

This assertion is certainly correct; but on the other hand, we must bear in mind that even in East Asia it was only given to an élite to 'climb the heights of a philosophical religion', and that this élite—it must once again be stressed—was, at all times quite conscious of its special position and therefore remained esoteric and without any urge to reform the world.

The pious illusion that human progress and the reform of

mankind are realizable ideals has been the prime force behind our tremendous accomplishments in the field of civilization. Christianity's first achievement amongst Western peoples was to uproot them from the more primitive forms of religion and concentrate their rich and vital emotional potential upon the worship of God. In this way all the other gods, spirits, demons and magic powers, which until then had peopled nature and the world, gradually vanished. As belief in them became weaker, nature and the world became, as it were, 'de-spiritualized' by Christianity; all that remained were material things—things 'of this world'—whilst everything mysterious was assigned to God in the 'world beyond'. For this reason the convert to Christianity did not find it so difficult to obey the Biblical command: 'Let the earth be thy servant'. The development of science and technology only became possible because not only the élite but also the greater part of Western humanity had lost its fear of spirits or mysterious natural forces. In Europe the 'little man' did not fall into a panic because somewhere or other a railway tunnel was being built; whereas in China even nowadays the little—or even the bigger—man fears that the whole district will be visited by disaster when such 'geomantic' upheavals are instituted.

It must be admitted, though, that herein we made a mistake. We presumed that in reality neither spirits nor magic existed in nature because, in accordance with Christian doctrines, we failed to find evidence of their actual presence. As our beliefs weakened, however, the supernatural again took a hand, only this time not in nature but in ourselves. We are beginning to recognize the 'relative' existence of the gods, a knowledge which the Indians and East Asians have long possessed.

It was during the period when our faith was strong that the foundations of our modern civilization were laid. In the Christian religion all men are equal before God, and everyone has his own peculiar and personal relationship to Him. This conception, which Protestantism specially emphasized, became one of the fundamentals of later individualistic, liberal and democratic theories. The Occident has, then, laid constant stress on individualism and equality, although in gradually changing forms; in other words, it formerly believed in the possibility of redemption, and then came to believe more and more in the capacity of every individual for self-development.

If we regard this civilization—and in particular its special characteristics, science and technology—as something positive, it immediately becomes clear where lie the advantages in our manner of approach, as opposed to that of the East Asians. Even the price that has had to be paid for them, namely our present psychic and spiritual difficulties, is one that we willingly accept. We realize today that our basic conceptions were partially wrong, but that we nevertheless accomplished great things on the strength of these illusions of ours. The strength of our unseeing faith was to some extent crowned with success.

The East Asians became resigned earlier, and attained earlier to wisdom. Their point of view was justified, in so far as general human progress and improvement of mankind in the true sense of the word are impossibilities. For, technical progress signifies not an improvement but merely a change in our means of living. Each epoch in a civilization brings its own problems and difficulties in its train; and the technical era has been no exception.

*

When the East Asians rejected the theory of progress, they did so with extreme thoroughness. But in Western eyes this theory is integrally bound up with the purpose of life and the essence of human and universal history. To be sure—and to this extent the East Asian attitude is justified—we do not conceive of the theory of progress in strict relation to man, but in relation to the transformation and modification of the world in which we live. In other words, there are spheres and provinces in which the theory of progress has application, and others where it has not. Whilst we applied the theory of progress indiscriminately and fairly uncritically to all and sundry, the East Asians, organic thinkers as they were, equally uncritically rejected it in every detail.

To us the East Asian approach betrays its weakness in an exaggerated degree of realism and resignation. Misled by the assumption that with all peoples and at all times, the way to perfection is the same and is always equally hard, the East Asians have taken it for granted that everything else, too, remains basically unchanged, and subject only to similar periodic alterations and transformations. They failed to note that this assumption is at variance with the facts of history, for it is not only our own planet and the entire cosmos that are being subjected to a unique and historic process of evolution; national character also changes and evolves, even if not in the sense of an advance towards human perfection. The East Asians themselves, it is true, thanks to their individual outlook, number among those peoples who hitherto have changed and evolved the least. But the universe is characterized not only by eternal change but also by eternal evolution.

Westerners in East Asia repeatedly experience feelings of revulsion whenever this all-round lack of development is encountered. It is true that we place a high value on oriental wisdom and mysticism and also realize that they can provide us with the most valuable stimuli; nevertheless we are at the same time convinced that these excessively narrow and one-sided oriental conceptions must be widened, just as we ourselves are ready to revise our own conception of things.

I doubt whether anyone who has not lived in China can form a correct picture of the dread of spirits in which the Chinese perpetually walk, and of the extent of their superstitions. With the exception of certain very recent examples, all Chinese books and novels are plentifully furnished with incidents involving the supernatural; and this indeed is the case with Japanese literature also. Yet most Western readers skip too rapidly over these sections or dismiss them as the poetic fancy of the narrator. Constant reports of suchlike occurrences even appear in Chinese and Japanese newspapers. In China these stories most often concern the dark deeds of the Kwei, the wicked demons with which the police were sometimes called upon to deal! In Japan the favourite story is that of the fox which can change itself into a beautiful woman. Every year or so someone claims to have seen quite plainly how in the end the lady revealed herself as a fox—an occurrence which is then described in the press in the greatest possible detail.

But in East Asia today a change can be detected in the traditional attitude of tolerance and indulgence in such matters. Not only the ruling classes, but millions more besides, have come into contact with Western civilization and are now therefore at a loss to know what attitude to adopt towards their entire tradition. Like the masses in Europe, the masses of East Asia too are seeking something new to cling to. In China one sign of this was the big increase in the numbers of the Communist party, long before that party came into power. It may be observed, incidentally, that the Communists have actually succeeded in shaking to a considerable degree the faith of their supporters in ancestor-worship and the family system. One thing only has eluded them, and that is how to get rid of spirits, for these are said to be still just as active in the Chinese Red Army as they were in that of Chiang Kai-shek.

*

Let us now turn our attention to certain significant traits in the East Asian character. Let us cast our minds back to the war years and think of the widespread devastation in China and Japan. The East Asians reacted to this quite differently from us. To such an extent are they permeated by the organic conception of growth and decay, and therefore of the transience of all earthly things, that despite their positive attitude to life, they are less affected by material loss. When, during the war, foreigners in Japan grieved at the thought of the destruction in Europe, they found the Japanese somewhat lacking in sympathy. The latter certainly showed a certain measure of commiseration and regret, but at the same time expressed their inability fully to understand the much talked-of 'destruction of European culture', for, after all, destruction in wartime was confined only to material things.

Not long after the event the *Neue Zürcher Zeitung* published a gripping article by Benno Reifenberg on the destruction of Frankfurt and the ruins of Goethe's birthplace. In East Asia such an article would be out of the question. There Goethe's house would have been immediately rebuilt and the new house would breathe for everybody the same spirit as the old. The old building would have been to them merely a symbol that could easily have been replaced by an equivalent symbol without any wailing or gnashing of teeth.

Naturally we explained to the Japanese that the Western peoples' attachment to these things was not due to their material attributes but to associated historical or personal traditions. But on this point there is a fundamental difference. In our case the memories are literally vested in the things themselves. Not so with the East Asians: in their case spirit and tradition live on independently of material things—or behind them, if one prefers to put it that way. Material objects are merely replaceable symbols.

The East Asians, those worshippers of antiquity and pre-servers of tradition, retain in their possession fewer material mementos from former times than do the European peoples. They regard all material things as having only a provisional and temporary value. Most travellers are not clear on this point when they arrive in East Asia and expect to be confronted with antiquities in the European sense. I have, for example, myself seen how foreign tourists gazed in astonished awe at the 'ancient' half-ruined buildings and other remains of the old imperial residence in Jehol, not far from Peking, in Western Manchuria; whereas any historical account of the subject would have told them that these antiquities were not built until the seventeenth (indeed most of them not until the eighteenth) century, only to be allowed to fall into decay again in the century following. The famous Forbidden City of Peking dates partly from the fifteenth century, but most of its buildings are of more recent construction. Peking, however, is quite an exception: in most other Chinese cities—for example in Nanking—there are scarcely any traces of the former splendour. In China one will search in vain for old private dwellings and public buildings, or even for really old temples and monasteries, for most of such places have been several times burnt down and rebuilt. In point of fact, it is only the massive old town walls and the canals that are really old. There is no point in looking for ruins as old as those of Greece or Rome. The few exceptions only serve to prove the rule.

This failure of buildings to survive is due to the fact that in China wood was used for building in days gone by—as it still is in Japan. Furthermore, it is only seldom that anything is repaired or restored in East Asia; to do so is regarded as pointless, since all earthly things are subject to decay—much rather build something completely new, in full consciousness that this too will one day pass away and in its turn be replaced by something new. The Chinese have little understanding for the great concern felt by foreigners over the gradual dilapidation of the beautiful imperial city of Peking (cf. p. 140; note 2). It might even be a source of pleasure to them when a tree grows through the roof of one of their old temples, for it reminds them of their melancholy philosophy of the transience of earthly things. A Chinese once said to me in Peking: 'We do not understand your museum-like concern for old things; we Chinese have confidence that coming generations will in their turn build something new'.

There is, nevertheless, a special reason why monastic buildings in a tolerably good state of repair are often allowed to fall into decay, while new ones are built alongside them: the faithful reckon it more deserving to donate money for the foundation of a new temple than to subscribe to the repair of an old one.

A typical example of the East Asian attitude is afforded by

the great shrines of Ise, these most holy of holy places in a Japan abundantly rich in sacred things. These shrines, dedicated to the Sun Goddess, are pulled down every twenty years and then rebuilt with new timber from the sacred forests. This is said to have been going on for over 2,000 years, and is certainly an extremely ancient practice. That human beings every other decade deliberately carry out this work of destruction seems proof enough that it is the *genius loci* that matters rather than the buildings themselves. Feeling in Japan ran high when a chance American bomb fell on a relatively unimportant building which happened to belong to the shrines of Ise. This reaction was naturally not on account of the destruction in itself but because of the affront to the Sun Goddess. (General Tojo, the Prime Minister, humbly apologized in a public speech for the negligence of the Army, which had been incapable of preventing the incident.)

Ninety per cent of Tokyo, a city of eight or nine million inhabitants, was burnt down during the war, and probably therefore constitutes the biggest single scene of destruction associated with it. But, for the Japanese, the city has lost none of its essential spirit. Tokyo remains Tokyo even though it takes over an hour to go by train from one end of the burnt-out area to the other. In their imagination the Japanese already see the houses which their children and their children's children will build on the old site.

It is astonishing how much damage, destruction and decay the East Asians, and in particular the Chinese, will put up with. Sometimes one has the impression that they are inwardly so tranquil and so locked up in themselves that they are not easily put out by external shortcomings; whereas most Westerners are ceaselessly engaged in tidying up the outside of things, almost as though, by so doing, they hoped to create the inner tranquillity which they feel to be lacking. The East Asian is not unduly put out if a window-shutter refuses to close or if the front door bell does not work. It is quite common for a whole family to clamber awkwardly around a broken floorboard just inside the door for weeks on end, or for a householder to replace a broken lock by a piece of string for an equally long period, before it occurs to anyone to repair the damage.

*

The East Asians' tolerance in human affairs is also due to the 'total' nature of their character. They are tolerant because they view man, his actions and his reactions, from all sides and therefore pay more heed to the general facts of the case than to the position of the individual. This tolerant understanding is enhanced by the East Asians' great and characteristic gift of humility, which is probably one of their finest virtues and has its origin in their conception of the relative insignificance of the individual, and in their awe and dread of the mysterious forces of the universe. East Asian humility and modesty is therefore akin to piety: it is strange, but even the sober, realistic and sensible Chinese is more pious in his manner than are most Western people. And it is precisely this lack of humility in the Western world that strikes the East Asian as our most distasteful attribute.

'Self-importance' is unknown in East Asia; it is only assumed —as for example, when a minister attends a public function or a scholar opens a learned congress. On such occasions an official air of importance, dignity and unapproachableness is worn for the occasion, but only so that the dignity of office may be suitably expressed. In China and Japan even the most celebrated personality considers himself of less consequence than does the average European, filled as the latter most often is with a sense of his own importance.

Chiang Kai-shek is more modest in his manner than any subaltern or lesser official. One has only to recall the diary that he published after his imprisonment in Sian-fu in 1936. The tone of humility and self-accusation which is its key-note made a psychologically inexplicable and strange impression on most foreigners. A similar spirit informs the notes written by the

Japanese statesman, Prince Konoye, before his suicide in November, 1945.

Yet we must not overlook the fact that this East Asian humility has also its drawbacks, since it can be accompanied by a lack of frankness. It is considered immodest and ill-bred to think it worthwhile expressing one's own insignificant opinion. This training in reserve can be carried to such lengths that (especially in Japan) one friend does not dare tell another what he really thinks. This gives rise to that atmosphere of uncertainty and mistrust that we have already mentioned. Such universal modesty or humility verges on insincerity.

The East Asian gift of patience is, psychologically, easy to explain: it has the same roots as the quality of biding one's time, that gift of letting things ride, which is typical of the 'total' attitude. Many people do not hesitate to characterize this patience as a virtue, but we should consider whether it does not occasion many an unfortunate or embarrassing situation. Bertrand Russell, who calls the Chinese 'the most patient of all nations', does indeed voice the opinion[3] that 'the evils produced in China by indolence seem to me far less disastrous from the point of view of mankind at large, than those produced throughout the world by the domineering cocksureness of Europe and America'. On the other hand, the Chinese writer, Lin Yutang, in his book *My Country and my People* considers his fellow-countrymen's excessive tolerance of chaotic conditions and their aversion to reaching clear-cut decisions as a serious shortcoming. Lin Yutang seems to see the situation in a truer light. For have not circumstances in China during recent years been more horrible than those caused in Europe by the second World War? Even in peace-time millions used to die of hunger in China as the result of floods and bad harvests.

After every natural disaster one sees on the roads thousands suffering from frightful skin diseases due to starvation, and children covered from top to toe with boils and ulcers: the same is the case after any big military operation. In China, indeed, there are people who have sunk so far in their misery and distress that they seem half animal; they go about in rags, almost naked, even the women. They crawl about on the ground like dogs, begging. There is nothing like it in all Europe. China can be so terrible that the majority of authors and journalists—I make no exception—are well-nigh incapable of reporting conditions there 'realistically'.

In Japan, too, we discovered during the war that a number of embarrassing situations could be attributed to excessive forbearance on the part of the people. When a nation is too patient the Government can do much as it pleases and many a reform that it would be quite able to effect remains untackled. In Nazi Germany there was open 'grousing', but in wartime Japan there was only a faint undertone of complaint. The Nazi Government did at least have to manage the country's administration and economy efficiently in order to maintain itself in power and prosecute the war, but the Japanese Government could get away with the most incredible blunders, incompetence and corruption without the nation losing patience. The Japanese put up with being bombed and burned in their sleep because the sirens failed to sound in time, and they starved because the Government was incapable of getting supplies of soya beans and other foodstuffs from Manchuria. One of the first expressions that a foreigner picks up in Japan is *Shigata ga nai* ('Nothing can be done about it').

*

The best way of obtaining an insight into East Asian matters is to take up some form of East Asian occupation. Practical experience is of paramount importance here, since it is scarcely possible to comprehend the 'total' approach to things by purely intellectual means. It makes a great deal of difference whether I 'understand' something about Chinese pictures, or whether I have had lessons in painting from a Chinese master. I think that the person who has spent many hours struggling, albeit without success, to transfer a bamboo shoot satisfactorily on to paper with black ink, has assimilated and understood more about East Asia than the collector and admirer of priceless pictures. A very good key to the understanding of East Asia is undoubtedly the mastery of its handwriting and calligraphy— at all events more can be learnt from this than from the study of the language alone. But, when all is said and done, it is im-material in what way one goes to work, for in all fields the basic experiences are the same; and the first thing that our East Asian instructors teach us in every case is invariably the same: do not only think, do not only reflect, but imitate, repeat, practise! One must not set about feeling one's way into a subject too energetically or too consciously; sympathy and understanding must come gradually and without coercion.

In Tokyo I attended a Japanese school whose principal function was to assist Japanese returned from overseas to brush up their native language. It was a great strain on one's patience, for everything had to be ceaselessly repeated after the teachers, and the same texts read over time and time again. The teachers, with the exception of the headmaster who had studied in America, actually took offence when I asked questions. It was as though I had made a *faux pas*. When finally I ventured to suggest that there might be no point in repeating aloud, several times over, a sentence which was meaningless to me, the answer was that the meaning of the sentence would ultimately be revealed to me of itself. It would have been quite hopeless to attempt to point out that the Western mind works differently; that we understand things more quickly and retain them better when we have also an intellectual grasp of them.

Experience of the East Asian confirms the general conclusion that a lower level of intellectual development is accompanied by a corresponding stronger development of the faculty of memory; one might almost say that the East Asian culture is to a considerable degree built up on the basis of memory and the kind of values associated with the latter. Two aspects must be differentiated at this point: the natural development of memory in the East Asian, and the intensive cultivation of this faculty as a result of the characteristic demands of East Asian culture.

It is the latter's conservative, retrospective element that demands this. Imitation of one's ancestors and contemplation of antiquity is only possible with the help of memory; there is no wish to conceive of the past in purely intellectual terms, still less to carry on logically from where the intellectual achievements of former times left off.

*

Thus it happens that memory largely takes the place of intellect in East Asian education and culture. Intellect can only comprehend intellect; but where traditions have not an intellectual basis one must find other means of feeling one's way into the spirit of the ancients. No purpose can be served by the rational analysis of poems and pictures; one must read them or look at them, as the case may be, over and over again until the sense is revealed 'of itself'. Similarly, in reading Lao Tse or the *Book of Changes*, one finds that progress beyond a certain point is impossible by means of reason alone; one must read them time and time again until their message is revealed. Their meaning becomes apparent only to him who is mature enough; it will not avail the 'immature' person to try to take them by intellectual assault.

The East Asian learns by identifying himself as closely as possible with the object or the ideal, not only by means of his feelings and his understanding, but with his whole psyche. Expressed in concrete terms: imitation and learning by heart are the fundamentals of East Asian education. In recent decades we in Europe have partly abandoned these principles, which used to play a large part in infant education and at schools, on the assumption that it is more important to teach children to think for themselves at an early stage. Yet, so far as I can see, a certain reaction to this dangerous over-valuation of the part to be played by thinking has already set in.

Learning important texts by heart has the advantage that opinions and sayings of the wise men of antiquity are always ready at hand. In this way every experience, every act of judgment or perception can at once be related to some classical precedent. What has been learnt by heart thus becomes constantly richer in content as life progresses. A thought or an experience that makes no appearance in the classics does not 'count'; one might say that it has no existence.

Imitation, viewed psychologically, rests on the same principle as learning by heart, namely on memory; it is a question of retaining what has been learned by heart, or imitated by visual observation—as for example in the case of fencing, painting or handicrafts—so that it is always present in one's mind. This is all very well where intellectual comprehension is not called for; but when preconceived notions are brought to bear on a subject to which they are unsuited, the result can often be grotesque and humorous in the extreme. When, for example, in 1853 Commodore Perry and his fleet appeared off the coast of Japan, the Japanese immediately sent off a number of boats containing draughtsmen whose task was to make drawings of the 'black vessels' of the American fleet. They literally believed that they themselves would be able to build steamships with the help of such drawings. It took some time before they discovered that it was first and foremost a question of understanding the principle of the steam engine, and that everything else would follow logically therefrom. Until most recent times the principal activity of Japanese spies in both the military and industrial spheres was to obtain photographs and drawings: they were unable to make much use of theoretical explanations or treatises.

Nevertheless, the East Asians have the liveliest gift for recalling past moods, sensations and feelings. They 'know' exactly how they felt on any given occasion, whether it was a social gathering, a moonlight evening on the terrace, or waiting for someone at a railway station.

Or let us take the case, for example, of memory for music, which is specially strongly developed in the Japanese. It is impossible to ascribe this solely to their aptitude for music; their considerable powers of memory must also be held generally responsible. The indigenous musical tradition of the Japanese rests almost exclusively on an ear for music and powers of retention. Performers on the *koto*, perhaps the most beautiful of Japanese instruments and the most difficult to play, are almost without exception blind men.

The observations made by foreign music teachers in Japan of their pupils' behaviour in this respect are highly characteristic. It often happens that in keeping with East Asian tradition a pupil will imitate exactly, not only the teacher's manner of execution, but also the movements of his hands and his head. At the same point in the music he will bend forward over the keyboard or boldly toss back his head, precisely as the teacher did when playing the piece over to him. The difficult thing is to teach the Japanese, when playing, to form their own conception of the music and to give expression to their own feelings. The younger pupils even regard this as showing a lack of respect and as unmannerly presumptuousness. Naturally the best pupils gradually grow out of this traditional attitude, but their playing as such is further impaired by a characteristically East Asian quality, and one which we have already discussed: namely, that necessity for self-mastery which is hammered into them from early youth. A conductor will not make a very sound job of conducting an orchestra if his sole concern is constantly to keep a rein on his own feelings and to try at all costs to prevent himself from making an undignified or comic gesture. Practically every foreign conductor in Japan has a difficult time of it in so far as it takes the Japanese some time to get used to the lively play of his features.

Our own music, especially since the sixteenth century, is essentially individualistic. Were the East Asians to take over our music and to develop it independently of, and uninfluenced by us, their self-restraint would certainly in time make something pretty tame out of it.

*

There is a further small peculiarity of the East Asian which most foreigners find difficult to understand; it is linked up with the question of imitation. It is well known that when the Chinese and Japanese succeed in manufacturing in their own country what was originally a foreign product, they like to make use of the trade marks of the appropriate foreign firms and of such qualifications as 'Made in England', 'Made in Germany', and so on—indeed they often slavishly copy manufacturers' labels in their entirety, with the original place names, details of diplomas won at exhibitions, etc. The reason for this lies not only in a deliberate and conscious wish to mislead the consumer, but in the belief that name and product are inseparable, and that a product is no longer the same thing when it is called by another name.

To amplify a little. Terminological exactitude has long been a problem in Chinese philosophy, and one to which Confucius paid a great deal of attention. Terminology plays a large part in assigning things, and also men, to their proper place in the universe and in human society. When conflicts of opinion and misunderstandings arise in regard to the names of things, it follows that the entire—'universistic'—system will be flung into disorder, with consequent disturbance to the harmony of human relationships and of the universe. This philosophical conception has gradually come to apply to all departments of life in East Asia; a tendency developed to label everything and, consistent with East Asian conservatism, to stick to a name once it had been given. But at bottom it is not only the notion of assigning things to their proper place that gives this question of nomenclature its great importance, but rather the notion that the image and the symbol existed *before* the thing itself. To grasp this relationship, we should perhaps remember how Pao Hsi contemplated the images in the sky and then created the tools of man (cf. p. 48). The name is therefore the immediate designation of the primordial image or symbol from which the thing is descended. As 'idea', therefore, it is of greater significance than the thing itself. But the idea is creative and casts a magic radiance upon the thing without which the latter could not exist.

Correct labelling, then, has always been an important matter in East Asia. In Japan a gift is no gift unless there is attached to it the customary 'musubi' (a thing like an envelope made of red and white paper and various lucky charms). Every Japanese wears the family coat-of-arms on his black, ceremonial kimono, and the jacket of every apprentice and shop assistant carries, in giant letters, the name of his firm on its back. Throughout East Asia all firms choose their house signs and label their goods with care and artistry. The sea of written signs and pictorial trade marks in the narrow Chinese and Japanese streets is familiar to everyone who knows East Asia.

Why the East Asians imitate trade marks is therefore understandable. It is the old and, if you will, naïve idea of the small manufacturer that name and product are inseparable. His exact imitation can even be regarded as testimony of his great respect for his foreign prototypes—for have not the foreigners been producing such goods for centuries (so it seems to him at least on the strength of conditions in East Asia), and did they not, in their thorough and efficient way, give a great deal of careful thought to the correct and appropriate markings for the goods?

Let me, in this connection, refer to *400 Million Customers*, a book by the American writer Carl Crow who, in discussing conditions in China, gives countless examples illustrating this peculiarity of the East Asian attitude. In China it was a matter of great difficulty to import new goods with new markings. We have only to recall the affair of the old, rusty and worn-out horse-shoes which the Chinese used to import from Hamburg. When, for some reason, supplies from Hamburg ceased, the Chinese refused to buy old horse-shoes in other countries, because none of them bore the familiar markings. As far as I remember, firms in those countries then resorted to the simple expedient of adopting very similar markings.

Although the small Chinese and Japanese manufacturer still thinks in these terms, the big internationally renowned Japanese firms have long ago adjusted themselves to our methods. The Japanese did not conquer the world markets by means of

foreign trade marks and false references to the country of manu-
facture, but under the sign of the 'Three Wells' of the House of
Mitsui, and that of the 'Three Diamonds' of the House of
Mitsubishi, which used to carry the designation 'Made in
Japan' throughout the world.

*

The East Asians have the gift of summing up complex situations fairly quickly and of retaining the details in their heads.
In their mind's eye they see a sort of variegated mosaic-like
image within the framework of which the relationships of the
various individual parts are then examined. Two national
games in China and Japan—chess and the 'Go' game—offer
good examples of this.

It is generally assumed that the East Asian form of chess
(there is no great difference between the Chinese and Japanese
versions), like the European, comes from India, although there
is no certain proof of this. At all events the East Asian version,
even if it has derived from the same source, has developed
quite differently from ours and in a way that is strikingly
characteristic. In the first place the board is bigger; it consists
of eighty-one, i.e. nine times nine squares and not eight times
eight as with us. (In Japan until the twelfth century it consisted of as many as 144 squares, and in times more remote it
was even bigger.) This already goes to show that the East
Asians have comparatively little difficulty in surveying a complex situation of some magnitude. But what makes East Asian
chess especially difficult, is the rule that all pieces captured by
a player may be put back into play on his own side whenever
he pleases. This gives rise to more varied problems than in
European chess, in which the number of pieces in play
diminishes as the game proceeds. The East Asian game mostly
ends with a tremendous battle, in which each player brings
his entire forces, his own pieces and those he has captured,
to bear. In East Asian chess it is not strict logic that counts,
but a more comprehensive system of thinking in combinations.

It is characteristic that no single figure has the same un-restricted possibilities as has the Queen with us; it is more a question of co-operation between all the pieces on one side, so that even here we discern a manifestation of the collectivist outlook.

The 'Go' game, which is more popular and widespread than chess, possesses East Asian characteristics to an even more striking degree. It is, furthermore, of pure East Asian origin and is believed to have been known at the very earliest periods of Chinese history. It first came to Japan in the eighth century, and has become even more of a national game there than in China.

The 'Go' board consists of eighteen times eighteen, i.e. of 324 squares. It is played with small stone counters, of which, traditionally, there should be 181 black and 180 white, though in practice the full number is seldom used. The object of the game is to fill with one's counters as big an area, or as many small areas, consisting of adjoining squares, as possible. One's opponent, using similar tactics, tries to prevent one from doing this. At the same time one tries to encircle one's opponent, for counters thus encircled count as 'dead' and are out of the game. The winner is he who at the end has the most 'live' counters on the board. This is the basic principle behind what are, in themselves, highly complicated rules of play.[4] The 'Go' game is concerned even less with logical thinking than is East Asian chess; it is rather a question of summing up the whole large mosaic on the board, and taking advantage of every opportunity that arises.

'Go' has been played for some years both in the United States ('The American Go Association') and in Germany ('*Der Go-Bund*'). It appears that after Pearl Harbour more attention was paid to this game by the Americans than ever before, per-haps on the assumption that it might help towards an under-standing of what seemed at first the bewildering mentality of the Japanese. It is patent that both games, 'Go' and the East Asian form of chess, have a certain interest, from a military point of view also, as keys to the understanding of East Asian reactions; for the strategy of a 'Go' player is different from that of a Western chess player.

It was not primarily due to strategic, but rather to technical reasons that the Japanese lost the second World War. Their strategy would have proved correct had not the Americans in a short space of time been able to effect so astounding and unprecedented a degree of technical progress. Hence the latter's ability to sweep with iron hand across the Japanese 'Go' board and to fling down the complicated positions built up at such great pains. In the end many of the strongest Japanese positions (we need only think of Rabaul!) lost all their value because they were by-passed and cut off by the rapid American advance. The Americans won the Pacific war with only few, albeit logically correct, chess-board moves, of which the Philippines landing was the grandest in concept. But, as has already been pointed out, this was only made possible by the Americans' material superiority, for they could not have afforded to undertake these bold thrusts had the Japanese been their equals in the matter of equipment.

The Japanese defeat of 1945 is in fact only the exception that proves the rule, for the Japanese have never before lost a war. Their military and strategic talent will remain latent within them. It is pointless to forget or to ignore this circumstance simply because, at a recent stage of world history, the Japanese were not up to the technical requirements of the day.

The East Asian mentality, as revealed in the two games mentioned above, is also active in the world of commerce and in other spheres. And there is no doubt whatever that it has its advantages—we need only think of the enormous economic achievements of the Japanese which had already outpaced those of most European nations, of the organization of their big concerns, and of all they built up within a few years in Manchuria in the way of industry and mechanical transport. The port of Dairen, whose installations were among the world's most modern, was already on the point of outstripping Shanghai. The 'Asia Express', which ran between Mukden and Dairen, had few equals in speed, comfort and punctuality. We must not be misled by the fact that the Chinese have up to the present time achieved so little in this field; that has less to do with a lack of ability than with a world situation that was unusual in every respect. The Chinese achieved great things wherever they were able to link up with their own traditions, as for example in banking; many foreigners have long preferred to do business with the Chinese banks because they are as reliable as the foreign ones, and at the same time prompter and more accommodating. What the Chinese have achieved in the sphere of commerce, despite their political disintegration, is well known, as is also the position of economic power they enjoy throughout South Asia and Indonesia.

One of the big Japanese concerns (these have now been partially broken up by order of the Americans), or one of the big Chinese banks, is naturally organized differently and functions differently from its Western counterpart, but is clearly no less efficient. If Western concerns are structurally complex, those of Japan are even more so. It is often difficult to comprehend how it is possible to supervise these highly ramified organizations effectively. Diagrammatic representations are of little help towards understanding the internal organization of a Japanese concern, because of its fluctuating, animated, mosaic-like character. But there is very little the Japanese do not know about getting results from these illogically assembled and illogically functioning machines.

Every foreign business man will admit that the East Asian is his equal as a competitor, and often a very dangerous and astute one at that. He mostly possesses astonishing all-round vision and is ultra-quick in his reactions, whether, say, in judging the state of the market or concluding a given deal. The foreigner, newly arrived in Shanghai, used to have from the outset in the ricksha-boys a good opportunity of studying this business acumen—these ragged fellows could sum up in an instant the current exchange rates, the war situation and the price of rice, and adjusted their fares accordingly.

*

Before we conclude this brief survey of certain East Asian characteristics, we must glance at a particularly disagreeable and repulsive chapter, namely that concerned with East Asian cruelty. Many foreigners unacquainted with the East Asians believe, with the experiences of the last war in mind, that the Japanese are as cruel as the Chinese, or more so. This is a mistake, however, for the two races differ considerably in regard to this very point.

Although the Japanese are capable of extreme brutality and barbarism, they have little of the refined and perverse cruelty of the Chinese. One gets the impression that in China it is largely a matter of subtle methods of tormenting evolved in the course of a very long civilization, whereas in Japan it is more the heedless barbarities of a younger race. The Chinese subject their prisoners of war and other adversaries to a lingering death, and enjoy the spectacle of their dying agonies; the Japanese on the other hand, will just as soon run wild with their bayonets and indulge in panic-striken orgies of killing. The enjoyment of the agonies of the dying is not, for the most part, their object.

Many foreigners who are genuinely fond of the Chinese on account of their many amiable qualities—their humour and commonsense, their intelligence and thoroughness—find it impossible to reconcile themselves to this murky side of their character. This, to us incomprehensible, trait vitiates the sympathetic approach of the well-disposed foreigner. Many times one imagines one has attained a fair measure of understanding of the Chinese, only once more to be reminded of the cruelties that interpose an unbridgeable gap between ourselves and this anciently civilized people.

That the Chinese have devised the worst forms of torture known to history in any country of the world is a fact that is familiar to most foreigners. Many will even have read Chinese novels and stories in which scenes of horror occur. But most readers are inclined to transpose such incidents into the past, failing to realize that they still occur today, exactly as they did one or two thousand years ago.

Latterly one has not had to rely on second-hand accounts of such stories, for the methods used by the Communists in putting to death captured Government troops, and vice versa, have been openly described in certain Shanghai newspapers. Prisoners were tied to trees and gradually killed by knife-thrusts or by having pieces of flesh cut from them. We can perhaps spare the details of other methods employed. When Japanese soldiers refused to allow themselves to be taken prisoner by the Chinese, it was by no means solely due to their heroism; they knew what was in store for them.

Hardly any of the Japanese prisoners of war that the Chinese did succeed in taking used to arrive at their place of destination: they were tortured and killed on the way. Chiang Kai-shek did everything possible, not least from reasons of prestige, to stamp out these abuses. Trustworthy military policemen were dispatched to the scene of the more important battles, large monetary rewards were offered for the production of a living Japanese—but all in vain. According to the statement of a foreign bureau that dealt with such matters, there were in the summer of 1945 in all China—after five years of war—only three living Japanese prisoners of war to be registered.

At the beginning of the war cases occurred of the Japanese using living Chinese prisoners as targets for their bayonet drill. The purpose of this despicable practice was not, however, to enjoy the sufferings of the victim, but to teach their soldiers how, if possible, to kill the enemy with one thrust of the bayonet. It was a crude and barbaric method of inducing battle-hardness, for the normal young Japanese feels just as badly about having to kill somebody as the average European. A big difference between the Japanese and the Chinese is that the former have great difficulty in overcoming this initial reaction, and that for the most part it is only in a kind of frenzy that they are capable of such brutalities.

During the entire Sino-Japanese War the Japanese had to endure successful Chinese propaganda against Japanese cruelty and brutality. According to our ideas this propaganda was, of course, entirely justifiable, for one need only think of the excesses committed by the victorious Japanese army in Nanking in 1937, which did on this occasion in fact recall the customary Chinese practices! Many of us foreigners did not understand how it was that the Japanese, who had every justification, failed to reply with the appropriate counter-propaganda. Right at the beginning of the war, for example, at Tungchow near Peking two hundred Japanese, including many women and children, were shot and beheaded without any apparent reason, after they had been fastened to one another by wires drawn through the nose. I was in Peking at the time and have had this story confirmed by a Chinese and a Japanese eye-witness (a few Japanese were saved by faithful Chinese friends and servants). There were frequent similar occurrences, but they invariably involved small and isolated groups of Japanese soldiers or civilians and an undisputed preponderance of Chinese.

The Japanese gave no publicity either to the Tungchow incident, or to any other. I have often discussed with Japanese people the reasons for this reserve, but failed to elicit the true cause. For the most part they became embarrassed when this subject was broached. Did they think that these incidents would be regarded by the world as proof of the anti-Japanese attitude of the Chinese? Did they, who were the self-styled champions of Asia and brothers of the Chinese, feel, 'in the name of all Asian peoples' as it were, the ignominy of such occurrences? Or was it some deficiency in the Japanese propaganda, their inability to understand the psychological reactions of the West?

The answer most probably lay in this final consideration. The Chinese were much more adroit in this respect, probably alone for the reason that a much greater number of them— drawn furthermore from the ruling classes—had either been brought up or had studied abroad. It was, indeed, striking how Chinese propaganda, destined for internal consumption, differed from that destined for abroad. Thus atrocity stories were principally intended for foreign consumption, for they could not be expected to make much impression on the Chinese people, accustomed as the latter were to the greater excesses of their own troops. The inhabitants of large areas of China have on occasion been a good deal more afraid of their own soldiers than of the Japanese.[5]

Acts of cruelty in China do not only result from wars and civil strife, they have also figured at all times in the administration of justice. In modern China they were banned, at least officially, from the legal sphere, but even in this connection improbable things could still happen in the more remote districts.[6] A Chinese prison is an institution from which not many emerge alive, and in which human beings are sometimes reduced to the level of animals.

The Chinese not only frequently left their wounded to die because it was impracticable to render them any assistance, they also on occasions killed them off. Once in Shansi Province a temple containing severely wounded men was soaked in petrol and set on fire. The Governor ordered machine-gun fire to be opened on sick and wounded soldiers who were asking for food.[7]

As the war proceeded, conditions in the army became a good deal worse. Training establishments for Chinese recruits finally resembled the worst of concentration camps. This is how Theodore H. White and Annalee Jacoby described them in their book *Thunder out of China*, which appeared in 1946:

> Conditions in combat units were horrible, but by comparison to conditions in induction centers they were idyllic. Recruits ate even less than the starving soldiers; sometimes they got no water. Many of them were stripped naked and left to sleep on bare floors. They were whipped. Dead bodies were allowed to lie for days. In some areas *less than 20 per cent lived to reach the front*. The week that the stories of Belsen and Buchenwald broke in

Europe coincided with the height of the conscription drive in China; the doctors who dealt with the recruit camps about Chengtu refused to be excited about German horrors, for descriptions of the Nazi camps, they said, read almost exactly like the recruit centers in which they were working. Near Chengtu one camp had received some 40,000 men for induction. Many had already died on the way; only 8,000 were still alive at the camp at the end of the drive. One batch of 1,000 inductees was reported to have lost 800 recruits through the negligence of its officers.

To treat prospective young defenders of the fatherland in such a manner is surely something we cannot understand. The chief reasons for the mass deaths of Chinese recruits were indifference to human suffering and the covetousness of the officers who pocketed the funds with which food was to be bought for the troops.

At the beginning of the war conditions were still—to some extent at least—different. Steps were being taken, as a result of the exertions of foreigners or out of purely humanitarian considerations, to help soldiers who were sick and wounded. I myself saw how simple peasants in the fields put their work on one side to hurry to the assistance of a wretched group of sick and wounded soldiers who happened to pass by. Yet I also witnessed how, at a railway station, the passengers carelessly jumped over a number of severely wounded who were lying there—some of them already dead—knocking them with their luggage as they did so.

*

The East Asians' ability patiently to endure very great physical pain may go some way towards explaining the cruelty of the Chinese and their indifference to the sufferings of their fellowmen. Chinese and Japanese can be operated on without anaesthetics in cases where it would be quite out of the question with us. They can go on marching for days on end, despite severe wounds and sickness, on the scantiest nourishment. To exercise a certain control over their bodies is something that

19

comes naturally to them; it is part of their strict training in self-discipline. I was once able to observe how Chinese wounded, who had arrived in Hangkow after a three or four days' journey in goods-wagons without even straw to lie on, refused to accept the offer of food or water. Some of them explained that they were so pleased and grateful that such care had been taken of them, up to then, that they did not like to eat and drink in case some unpleasantness should ensue. They could hardly expect anyone else to clear the 'unpleasantness' out of the railway-truck for them!

But we must, while considering this matter, also bear in mind the fact that the East Asian has no great fear of death. So long as there are relatives to arrange the funeral and other male descendants in the family, the death penalty holds no great terror for him. The prospect of death only terrifies him when it is to be preceded by torture.

The Chinese possess the same lack of compassion for all living creatures. One can find them watching patiently and intently while some horse, who has been shot and whose entrails are hanging out, struggles hard to take a few paces; or standing in the street and staring with just as much interest at some old man who is dying. In Kunming I once met some students who had cut their ponies' mouths open with knives because, not knowing how to ride, they had let their mounts bolt. They assured me that the ponies were now 'quite tame' and safe to ride! In Peking I had to witness how an elderly man at the point of death, whose mouth was already flecked with foam, lay on the ground in violent convulsions, while the Chinese standing around shook with laughter at his every movement.

One has only to question one of the fairly numerous foreigners who were witnesses of the 'exodus of the beggars' from Nanking which took place, as far as I remember, in 1934 or 1935, for confirmation of this callous attitude. All who saw this declared that the sight of it would remain with them till the end of their days. The beggars were driven from Nanking by order of the Government, since the new capital was to have a 'modern and progressive' appearance. Nobody knows what was the ultimate fate of this endlessly long and dismal procession of shrivelled, ulcerous and wretched figures.

China is both a fascinating country and a terrifying one. Many Chinese maintain that Westerners are degenerate because they can endure so little pain, dirt and misery. There may be some truth in this, but it is difficult to form a judgment because the problem of Chinese cruelty has never been psychologically investigated.

Lin Yutang, who describes his Chinese fellow-countrymen in terms as pertinent as they are amusing, for understandable reasons prefers to ignore this darker side of the Chinese character. Nevertheless he has not failed to make certain short, and quite incidental, excuses for Chinese cruelty. After he has explained[8] that it is not 'dirt but the fear of dirt' that is a sign of decadence, he continues: 'Nor is cruelty, natural in all children and savages, a sign of degeneracy; it is rather fear of pain and suffering that is a sign of it. The dog which remembers only to bark and not to bite, and is led through the streets as a lady's pet, is only a degenerate wolf.' According to this, cruelty is the expression of healthy and unimpaired vitality. But it is precisely to the Chinese that this does not apply, because their cruelty has at the same time too much that is shrewd, ingenious and even hyper-sophisticated about it.

All peoples racially akin to the Chinese possess the same in-human tendency, just as they are all equally superstitious. The past and present performances in this field of the inhabitants of Indo-China, Siam and other territories, in no way fall short of those of the Chinese.

*

However, we must draw a distinction between these people and the Japanese, who have only a slight racial affinity with the Chinese. Certain severe forms of torture were not introduced into Japan until the sixteenth and seventeenth centuries (cf. p. 174). Taken all in all, Japanese traditions in respect of cruelty do not differ much from those of the West. In all wars of the modern era the Japanese have conducted themselves well, and have observed the rules—except in the conflict with China and in the second World War! In many instances there was some measure of excuse for the bad treatment of prisoners-of-war and civilian internees, the chief of which was the acute food shortage. A soldier or prison warder who is hungry is seldom disposed to treat his prisoner better than himself. Ruth Benedict[9] affirms that, as a result of the inadequate and primitive conditions that prevailed on the Japanese side, the Japanese soldiers were at times treated no better than the prisoners-of-war. She writes:

> According to our standards the Japanese were guilty of atrocities to their own men as well as to their prisoners. The former chief medical officer of the Philippines, Colonel Harold W. Glattly, said after his three years' internment as a prisoner of war on Formosa that the American prisoners got better medical treatment than the Japanese soldiers. Allied medical officers in the prison camps were able to take care of their men while the Japanese didn't have any doctors.

Apart from this, however, Japanese officers deliberately mishandled and humiliated their white prisoners. 'Political reasons' were to some extent responsible for this, inasmuch as the other 'coloured' races were to be shown what liberties could be taken with white men. Over and above such deliberate political factors there was, of course, also the long suppressed resentment against the whites, which erupted suddenly among the Japanese. Certain Japanese N.C.O's. in particular behaved as though all their lives they had had no fonder wish than one day to be able to thrash a white man and see him writhing in agony on the ground.

Among the worst episodes of the Pacific war must be accounted the 'death march' on Bataan; the construction of the road and railway in the Siam-Burmese frontier area by British prisoners-of-war, thousands of whom lost their lives; and the massacre of the Japanese in Manila and other parts of the Philippines.

Behind all these events lay different motives. It was principally the East Asian characteristic of indifference towards the sufferings of others that was responsible for the march of prisoners-of-war across the Bataan peninsula which caused the death of equal numbers of both American and Philippine soldiers. The Japanese themselves were battle-weary and tired and did not trouble themselves about the state of the prisoners. Cold-bloodedly they allowed them to starve and die of thirst. Political and practical considerations lay behind the forced labour operations in Siam and Burma, intensified of course by the same lack of humanity. He who is himself able to suffer and endure a great deal—and the Japanese had to undergo unheard-of privations in all their campaigns—and is himself indifferent to death, takes it for granted that others, too, react in the same way.

Whereas there had previously been one or two isolated instances of slaughter, the massacre on the Philippines took on the semblance of a veritable running amok. The panic-stricken Japanese, who had lost every vestige of reason, murdered not only Philippinos, foreigners and prisoners-of-war, but also their own fellow-countrymen. As the Japanese troops withdrew into the mountains they brutally and indiscriminately bayonetted and murdered Japanese civilians—men, women and children alike; in short, everyone who was unable to look after himself and presented only a useless encumbrance. Some Japanese women were even called upon by crazy, grinning soldiers to witness the bayonetting of their children. To obtain some measure of psychological understanding of the Philippine massacre one must remember these aspects, too, and think not merely of the Japanese officers who, in the streets of Manila, ran their swords through every Chinese within reach. Some of these officers are said to have shouted: 'If we are to be defeated, then everyone else shall perish too.'

It has already been pointed out that the East Asian is dangerous and unpredictable once he effectively loses his long pre-served composure; the events in the Philippines and to a certain extent those in Nanking also, can be ascribed in my view to a form of mass-psychosis. In China we are faced with a similar phenomenon in the notorious outbreaks of mob violence, in which quite innocent people fall victim to popular fury. Every foreigner is assailed by an uneasy feeling when confronted with an excited crowd of Chinese, even on occasions when its anger is not directed against the foreigners. In Japan itself such outbreaks of mob violence are very rare on account of the higher degree of order prevailing; but the war years showed what the Japanese, too, are capable of doing. With the Japanese on such occasions, in contrast to the Chinese, the element of self-destruction comes more conspicuously to the fore. Also connected therewith is their tendency to joint suicide (as for example in the case of unhappy lovers), and even to mass self-destruction. Japanese soldiers, in face of superior (real or imaginary) American forces, killed themselves in dozens without even trying to make a fight of it. Hence the not unjustifiable assertion of many Americans that the Japanese are cowards at heart.

*

Perhaps the lack of sympathy and indifference towards one's fellow-men in East Asia can be ascribed in some degree to religious factors. Presumably they have something to do with the absence of the Christian concept of loving one's neighbours, which is so deeply rooted in us Western people that we feel it to be something entirely natural, indeed, a norm. This is painfully evident in East Asia, for all Westerners, even though they have no aptitude for religion or are indeed avowed atheists, react alike in this matter. We feel, for example, that it is natural to save a drowning child; the East Asian, however, thinks it unnatural to risk his life if he is not related to the child, which in any case might turn out to be 'only a girl'. The East Asians are never so lacking in sympathy towards members of their family as they are towards strangers. Should a Chinese be condemned to death by torture, then the members of his family will exert themselves to bribe the officials to arrange a quicker death for him. In the case of 'death by knifing', for example, this could be achieved through someone aiming at the heart from the outset.

The fact that the Japanese with their sentimentally and emotionally charged religiosity are less cruel than the utterly unsentimental Chinese, may also argue in favour of a religious explanation. East Asian Buddhism, with its strong accent on faith and universal love, has always been more of a living force in Japan than in China. The religious argument, at all events, cuts both ways, for only too often in history has it been the religious fanatics who have perpetrated the worst cruelties!

NOTES

[1] C. G. Jung, *Psychologie und Religion*.
[2] Richard Wilhelm and C. G. Jung, *Das Geheimnis der Goldenen Blüte*.
[3] Bertrand Russell, *The Problem of China*.
[4] The May 1942 issue of the English-language Japanese periodical 'Contemporary Japan' (Tokyo), contains a paper on the 'Go' game, accompanied by diagrams.
[5] Cf. Theodore H. White and Annalee Jacoby, *Thunder out of China*, in this connection.
[6] Cf. Ralph Townsend, *Ways that are Dark*, in this connection.
[7] These events, which I witnessed during the summer of 1938 in Hankow, were confirmed by an American journalist, who had covered the areas in question.
[8] Lin Yutang, *My Country and my People*.
[9] Ruth Benedict, *The Chrysanthemum and the Sword: patterns of Japanese culture*.

Chapter 9

EVOLUTION VERSUS CYCLIC CHANGE

AN unknown object must first be described before an explanation can be given of how it came to be made. In this book, therefore, we have reversed the normal procedure and have placed the historical aspects, not at the beginning but at the end of our discussion. This seemed the more justified, since to have discussed historical factors first might easily, in view of the undue emphasis they would thus inevitably receive, have created a misleading impression of East Asian affairs. An historical approach is necessary for an understanding of the West, but this is not necessarily so with regard to East Asia.

At what point did the West and the Far East begin to develop along such widely different lines? How far back do the roots extend? To the very beginnings of things? These are questions we cannot answer with any degree of certainty; all we can say is that distinct tendencies towards divergent developments were present even in earliest historical times.

True, it could be argued that this is the very crux of the matter; for would the differing courses taken by West and East need any further explanation if, for example, it could be proved that both have different racial origins? Indeed, this opinion predominates today, namely that the human race is descended, not from a single racial group, but from several; but this cannot be fully substantiated. One anthropological theory has it that the East Asian is descended from the chimpanzee and the Occidental from the gorilla! This hypothesis would deny us common ancestors even at the ape stage, and would presuppose quite different 'missing links'. And, indeed, the skull of Sinanthropus Pekinensis, whose bones were found near Peking, has a different shape from that of the, admittedly later, Neanderthal man. But be that as it may, it is sufficient for our purposes, i.e. for the description and explanation of the contrast between West and East, if we confine ourselves to historical times.

*

In the course of the history of our Western culture everything has altered over and over again, from earliest times down to the present—our outward circumstances, knowledge, philosophy, religion and finally man himself—for our culture has been carried on by a succession of different peoples and races. One thing only has remained unaltered, and that is the principle governing the course of this development: the principle of evolution. Apparent already in ancient times, and emerging ever more distinctly as the Middle Ages receded, it presented itself with increasing clarity to the mind of man until it finally produced its finest flowering in the dynamic faith in progress of the nineteenth and twentieth centuries. Once we had detected this underlying evolutionary trend—this principle of perpetual change, of irreversible progression—we made it the guiding principle of our lives. It was this that became the dominant note of our culture, not the concept of eternal flux and eternal recurrence which became the governing impulse in East Asian culture.

In early Greek times the Western world still had points of resemblance and contact with the Chinese, though strong tendencies towards differing lines of development emerged shortly afterwards. Heraclitus[1] still reminds us of Chinese thinkers, whilst in Aristotle and Confucius we already seem to see two diametrically opposed worlds. Strictly speaking, it would be more accurate at this point to contrast Aristotle (and his predecessors and successors) with Mo Ti and his school, the first and last of Chinese logicians. But how can we explain the fact that Aristotle had so fundamental and overwhelming a significance for our culture, whilst the Mohists, his Chinese counterparts, vanished without fame or influence? As we have already seen, it is not the chance facts of history that must be held responsible for this, but more fundamental causes inherent in the structure of the psyche (cf. p. 232 ff.).

For us Aristotle, the logician, far more than Plato, turned out to be of decisive significance; for the East Asians it was Confucius, the philosopher of 'totality'. Nor must it be forgotten that the concept of the individual was evolved as far back as in Greek times, with the help of analytical thinking, then being developed; whilst in China, with its synthetic way of thinking, it is only in Mo Ti that we find any hint of such a concept. The seeds of a divergent development were therefore already present before the rise of Christianity and the dawn of Western science and technology.

*

We shall now consider one or two salient features of our Western development, as far as they are relevant to our theme.

Let us first of all recall how strongly the classical era influenced the subsequent development of Christianity. If I may be allowed this entirely subjective observation—I believe that no one can discern and comprehend this influence as immediately and strongly as the person who has spent a long time in East Asia. It is not so much the Christian revelation or the nature of the creed that seems so utterly foreign to the East Asian observer, as the forms assumed by Christian thought and feeling, not to mention its framework of dogma. It is the rational element in Christianity, which has its roots in the classical world, that seems so typically Western when viewed from a distance. As compared with this, all other aspects of Christianity—its diverse traditions and contrasting interpretations—fade into insignificance. As long as it retains this preponderantly rational character, it is never likely to achieve the dominating position of a world religion.

Closely connected with the concept of the individual, which reaches back to Greek philosophy, is the idea of a personal God, such as came to be manifested in Christianity (cf. also

p. 144 ff.). Other elements of Greek and, above all, Hellenistic philosophy, such as mysticism, pantheism and the concept of the divine as something absolute and impersonal, exercised only a transient, at all events never a dominant influence on Christianity. In this late classical wisdom, which in a certain sense represents the highest point reached in the development of ancient thought, and was supplanted by Christianity, we find, significantly enough, ideas akin to those of the Chinese.

By the standards of late classical times, the victory of Christianity denoted something like spiritual and metaphysical impoverishment. The Christian religion found its support less among the educated classes than among the broad masses, and the average intellectual level of many of its spiritual leaders was not so high as that of the philosophers of the Alexandrine school. In the words of Jacob Burckhardt:[2]

> In the fourth century the Church overcame the Arian heresy, and from the time of Theodosius onwards Empire and Orthodoxy became one and the same thing. And from then on not only was the Church, as an entity, superior to the Empire, but succeeded in displacing almost every other form of literature; we lose touch almost completely with what is being thought outside the Church; life in its entirety takes on an ascetic hue; there is a general rush for the monasteries; the cultured world of old, sorely tried by the civil power also, seems content to pass away without issue. Church and barbarians are the only spokesmen, and prelates the mightiest personalities; the main pursuits, even of the masses, are the cult and the clash of dogma.

In the attempt to defend Christianity against attack and to establish it spiritually if not materially, increased efforts were made to provide the creed with a philosophic backing. This did not involve so much a search for metaphysical perception as the intellectual underpinning of a truth already attained and—entirely without the aid of philosophy!—accepted from the start. Faith, as a purely emotional factor, was so uncommonly active and powerful that man was thrown once and for all out of any sort of 'total' equilibrium. But once faith is 'split off' from totality, it can no longer feel at one with reasoning, with the result that the latter is virtually forced to follow a separate, rational path.

Christian thinkers, above all the later 'barbarians', therefore quite naturally linked up with the Greek rationalists. Though it was primarily rational thought of a more emotional type, yet the intellectual approach was in both cases determined by one and the same method, namely by logic.

Perhaps every nation, as part of its development, necessarily passes through a rationalist phase, the duration of which varies in accordance with its nature. All the historically unique achievements of the Western world took place within this phase. This may well, of course, have been due to some unique set of circumstances, but does not affect the thesis that rationalism represents a transient and surmountable phenomenon.

The ages at which individual human beings are at the peak of their achievement likewise vary: one man may be at his best at eighteen, another at thirty and yet another at sixty years of age. It is a striking fact that nations always 'favour' youth during their rationalistic, and age during their 'total' periods.

We believe, then, that the rational tendency in Christianity was strengthened by the conversion of the youthful, Northern European races, and by the latter's increasing influence in the spiritual and religious spheres; though, of course, this youthfulness could not in itself constitute a determining factor in the subsequent development of the nations concerned.

*

When the Germanic races succeeded to the heritage of the classical world, Christianity already possessed a 'split' character, in that it was at once emotionally charged and underpinned by rational props. Up till then the Germanic peoples had been quite primitive, and no doubt possibilities of spiritual development in various directions lay open to them. The fact that they came to acquire culture in just this dualistic form has been, as we all know, of enormous and unique historical importance. Within the framework of a vital Christian culture, which was at first primarily emotional, these dual aspects, known already to Greek rationalism, grew to problems of immense proportions; time and again these problems have convulsed the history of European thought, though they have remained practically unknown to the 'totally' orientated East Asians.

Much has been written, with an eye to the interpretation of contemporary happenings, on the manner and method of the Germanic peoples' accession to the culture of Christianity and classical antiquity. The chief question to be investigated in this connection is why Western culture, which until the close of the Middle Ages still retained some of the static qualities of classical times, thereafter gradually acquired an ever more dynamic character. To sum up: 'split' as they were into emotion tinged by religion and rationally conditioned thought, the Germanic peoples advanced in both directions without realizing that a yet more pronounced divergence of feeling and intellect would inevitably follow. Let us hear what Alfred Weber[3] has to say about the way in which these races adopted the Christian ethic:

This ethic, with its rejection of earthly things, demanded from those in whom vigorous life pulsed, the deflection of the most vital instincts. When, at the moment of first spiritual awakening the essential earnestness of this act of deflection became apparent to these fresh, vital and vigorous forces, it was seen to be the only possible course. Thus it became the basis of European dynamism, the effective key to that which gives the latter its individual character. From the time of the fantastic explosion of the Crusades and the austere new monasticism, i.e. from about A.D. 1000 onwards, we can as little understand Europe's continual intellectual eruptions and its proneness to incessant revolutions (both materially and ideally motivated) as we can the succession of technical achievements made possible by its science, and finally, its capitalist incursion upon the world, unless we start from this same deflection of the most vital forces, unless we are prepared to recognize all about us, the eruption of surplus energies accompanying this deflection—energies which other nations allow to run a quiet and natural course, but are here consciously seized on and directed into definite channels. Everything here is tensed, concentrated and heavily charged—seeking a way either of remoulding thoroughly what is within, or of venting itself explosively on the outside world.

As Oscar A. H. Schmitz[4] once expressed it: 'The way from Plato and the stoa to Christ was not difficult: that from Wotan and Thor could not be other than violent'. It was principally in the sphere of German culture that these tensions reached, at times, the limits of endurance; a circumstance that, not altogether without justification, has been ascribed to the fact that large parts of Germany, as opposed to countries further west (especially England), were converted to Christianity, not by peaceful means but by sword and fire. These arguments can, of course, only be put forward with some reserve, and within the framework of a universal historical survey. In Scandinavia, for example, which was likewise converted by force, things have in general developed more peacefully than in Germany. But as we are concerned only with the contrast with the East Asian world, we can pass over these nuances within the various European nations. The tensions extended throughout the whole Western world, and had everywhere, in the last analysis, the same causes.

*

What made it possible for Western man, with his cleavages and conflicts, to become the creator of our modern culture and civilization? To what extent, indeed, is it possible to give an explanation of these processes? In discussing this question we will confine ourselves to the origins of science and technology, since these phenomena have no counterpart anywhere else in the world, and give the West its striking and special character.

Only since the end of the nineteenth century onwards have we grown increasingly sceptical and critical. Deprived to a great extent of our earlier blind faith, we have begun to cast around us for some meaning to our history. And today we are discovering, with some degree of astonishment, that the long journey we have made—which some might call only a detour—seems to be leading us to a new 'totality'. In the course of this journey—or detour—we did, however, bring science and technology into being. As Hermann Keyserling[5] once put it, we were 'the hands of God—but hands are blind'.

Science is rooted in our philosophy, or, to put it more generally, in the straightforward logical methods of thought that have prevailed in the West. It is, perhaps, unnecessary to give an account of the various phases in the development of Western thought—of scholasticism, of the swing towards empiricism since the twelfth and thirteenth centuries, of the growing influence of Greek thought, and so forth. This can be found in any history of philosophy. The decisive factor in our development was that, thanks to our Western way of thinking, the effort to reconcile reason and belief could lead only to an ever-increasing degree of autonomy on the part of the intellect, and to a steady widening of the gap between the latter and belief. The gradual rise of reason to a state of pre-eminence did not therefore come about through a weakening of faith but, on the contrary, by virtue of the very strength of faith. People believed that, if God existed, he too must be a reasonable being, and that it should also therefore be possible to investigate and to prove his existence and the Creation by using rational methods. These efforts had as their result not the 'discovery' of God or the Divine, but rather, as men turned from the abstractions of a sterile scholasticism to investigation of experienced facts, the discovery of science. At first nothing was altered in principle, for philosophy and science continued to assist in the investigation of God and his works. It was not until later that this work, begun in the name of God, proved a direct source of uncertainty about religious dogmas and the very existence of God.

As belief in God declined, many remained convinced that science was the proper means for investigating the 'unknowable', although this opinion has always been strongly opposed. Both parties to this conflict of opinion are, in my view, in a certain sense right. The scientists, because science is today on the point of leading us back to the 'unknowable'; and the faithful, because science confronted now with the prospect of the 'unknowable', is for the first time clearly proving that it is not itself able to fathom it. In the words of Goethe[6]: 'Man must persist in the belief that the incomprehensible can be grasped; otherwise he would cease to explore.' We have retained this belief long enough to accomplish great things. In the *Wanderjahre*, furthermore, Goethe expressed the opinion that the age of technology must be furthered to the utmost, so that it may all the more rapidly pass away. He recognized, then, more than a century ago what many of us are now for the first time beginning slowly to realize: namely, that we can only overcome our disequilibrium and our problems by working and fighting on to the very end. Nothing can come of taking up an anti-scientific and anti-technical—in other words a reactionary—attitude; we must, rather, strive to ensure that science and technology reach a stage of maturity, harmony and complete naturalness. It seems to me that things are developing in exactly the direction indicated by Goethe.

*

From time to time we hear it said that the natural sciences could have originated only after man had lost his fear and awe of nature, and that this changed attitude towards nature emerged during the transitionary phase between the Middle Ages and the modern era. This conception gives rise to the impression that medieval people saw in nature something inspirited, divine or at least magical, and that the subsequent advance of reason led to the 'despiritualization' of nature. We, however, believe, on the contrary, that from the very beginning Christianity prepared the ground for the birth of science by assigning the idea of God to the world beyond, and by conceiving of nature, in dualistic fashion, as its counterpart.

The stronger the faith of medieval man, the less was his fear and awe of nature. In fact, in nature that which was still felt to be mysterious really derived from pagan traditions, i.e. from classical influences still surviving in Christianity itself and in the Germanic heritage.

The Japanese writer Kitayama[7] describes the Western attitude towards nature in the following words, which at the same time point to counter-currents reminiscent of East Asian ideas:

> In the Christian world God created man in his own image. As his servant was the world given to man. The world and man therefore stand in opposition to one another; man and nature. God is imprisoned by man in churches. This is the God served by man, and man must be served by nature: a seemingly unshakable hierarchy. Now and again, however, it was burst asunder, as for example by Meister Eckhart and Saint Francis, when the world and God were seen in fact to be a unity, rather than the work of man. In this way, by the mystics and later by the Romantics, bridges were built between East and West.

Such a commandment as 'Let the earth be thy servant' exists in no East Asian religion. Buddhism did not simply disavow nature and the divine powers vested in it. East Asian Buddhism, in particular, was strongly influenced by the mystical, 'universistic' ideas prevalent in East Asia. It beheld in nature manifestations of the Buddha.

If those who lived in the Middle Ages had had as intimate a relationship with nature as the East Asians, it would indeed have seemed as inexplicable and as inconceivable as any miracle, had they more or less 'suddenly' and without any special reason begun to 'despiritualize' nature and to inaugurate the natural sciences. In reality, however, they had long been out of touch with nature. The saints and wise men of Western countries withdrew first of all into the barren and desolate wilderness, and later behind the stone walls of their monasteries, to wrestle with their God; those of China lived in the green solitudes of their pleasant hills and forests in small makeshift cabins, sunk in mystic contemplation of nature. Chinese culture, according to Kitayama,[8] can be understood by someone without 'a natural disposition to the mystic contemplation of nature', as little as can the culture of the Japanese.

If anyone wishes to have this contrast presented to him in a tangible form, let him compare a Gothic cathedral with a Japanese shrine! In the case of the cathedral the building materials are used only as a means to an end—to the end of erecting the house of God. Stone is piled on stone, the most bold and daring forms are evolved—all is done with genius but without consideration for anything but the ultimate object. How different is the fashioning of a Japanese shrine where every material—mostly wood—is handled lovingly and in a manner suited to its individual characteristics; where to recognize the grain of a wood and to know what tree it comes from is part of the holiness of the shrine; where one sometimes scarcely knows whether it is the wooden pillars of the temple or the native trees of the forest that are before one. The shrine or temple, furthermore, is always open to the elements even in the ice-cold northeastern part of the country, and unlike our own churches has no place from which nature is entirely excluded. Cathedrals are situated mostly in towns, whereas shrines are nearly always away from habitations and are often indeed situated in the middle of parks.

East Asians are for the most part full of admiration for our cathedrals but they experience at the same time feelings of alarm and terror. They are stirred by the spectacle, but it leaves them unsatisfied. In the words of the Chinese, Chang Hsin-hai[9]:

> The Gothic cathedrals are beautiful and noble in their own way, but the symbolism of aspiration somehow leaves the soul unsatisfied. Look on the other hand at the palaces in Peiping! Look especially at the Temple of Heaven; what a different impression you receive! What harmony, what tranquillity, what peace!

To one who has recently come from East Asia it is instantly clear that the experience of nature cannot have exerted any very strong influence on the builders of our churches. Rather were they concerned with God, the personal God of the world beyond, not God in nature, not God in all things, animate or inanimate.

It was not because the analysis of nature came close to profanation that the Christian Church later turned against the natural sciences—how many early works of science originated in monasteries and monks' cells!—but because in due course it became apprehensive lest the Christian dogma and its concept of the world might, as a result of the steady advance in scientific knowledge, be shaken to its very foundations.

The natural sciences owe their origin to the Christian attitude towards nature, and to the circumstance that the tendencies toward psychic cleavage present in Christianity were intensified by the European peoples. The first scientists were devout Christians and did not for this reason have the feeling that they were desecrating anything by their activities.

*

These tendencies were enormously strengthened by the rise of Protestantism. The Catholic Church, with its universal outlook, its superior sense of realism and knowledge of the world, was replaced by idealistic Protestantism, which taught that every Christian being could alone and unaided find his way to God. Protestantism further intensified the tendencies toward cleavage, and thereby helped to accelerate the development of Western man; in that he rejected the cults and practical religious usages of the old Church, the individual now felt himself able, with only a modicum of guidance from the Church, to enter into a relationship with God in which he stood more or less alone. Luther could certainly not have been aware of the consequences of his defection, of the process of progressive 'atomization'—as we might call it today—which he had set in train; yet their advent was inevitable as soon as man, now on his own, was more and more compelled to seek God along every path open to him, in particular along the path of science and reason.

The intellectual origin of technology, with its roots in rational thought, can be deduced from the historical facts. Before the birth of modern technology at the beginning of the nineteenth century we can distinguish, strictly speaking, two points of origin: the philosophical and the scientific. These two in their turn, however, are derived from a common source, namely the rationalism of earlier centuries. Basically they represent only a further subdivision of this same way of thinking.

Already in the eighteenth century and in some instances much earlier—one has only to recall Leonardo da Vinci—principles were established, inventions made and working models constructed, which at first found only sporadic practical application. It was not until the second half of the eighteenth century, after rationalist 'enlightenment' had gained the upper hand and ushered in the era of narrow causal thinking and faith in progress, that the 'leap into technology' inevitably followed. Among rationalist thinkers, it was principally Adam Smith who gave a direct intellectual stimulus to the development of technology. In demonstrating the advantages of a market system of economy and of free trade as opposed to a mercantile economy with its fixed trade links, he lent a decisive impetus to the modification of economic theory. And in England, as it seems to us in retrospect, machines harnessed to the task of economic production were put into operation on a large scale from one day to the next. Until there was a world market and free competition, there was no occasion for the employment of machines, for the producer would have been unable to dispose of the increased production achieved with their aid.

The question as to what extent purely material factors had a bearing on this process does not materially affect our argument. Here, of course, just as in any other sphere of human activity there has been an interplay of material and spiritual factors. For, without the simultaneous conquest of the world the new economic theories would not have been able to carry the day successfully. But let us not forget that in the last analysis this world conquest, too, was nothing more or less than a consequence of our dynamic character; like thought, science and technology, it can trace its origins, psychologically regarded, to the powerful differentiations of Western man. The Western mind is like a concentration of rays each representing capabilities, talents, enterprises, dreams and desires; all these have at every stage of our history mutually influenced one another. Without cleavage there could have been no science—and no world conquest.

There is, true enough, little that is wonderful about the dry and prosaic evolution of technology. If, nevertheless, we exist today in a state of constant bewilderment at jet aircraft and atom bombs, and fail absolutely to understand how it can all have happened, the answer lies in the last resort in the rapid tempo of technical development, and not in the nature of technology itself. Between a simple and a complex machine there is only a difference of degree. What has confused us is that we have so rapidly attained this high degree of complexity. Fundamentally regarded, there is nothing puzzling about it: we are concerned here with nothing more than manifestations of the colossal energy expenditure on the part of 'split' man seeking to express his personality in the several 'spheres of cleavage', be it technology, in political endeavour, in one of the branches of science, in art or in anything else.

*

At the heart of East Asian culture lies the struggle to achieve human perfection. This struggle is everywhere and at all times of equal severity: it remains unaffected by the material circumstances of life or by contemporary events, both of which are purely external considerations. It is this basic attitude that is responsible for the fact that the East Asians have at all times exhibited so little interest in any modification or improvement of their everyday living conditions. Thus, it constitutes also the deepest root of East Asian conservatism.

The unfolding of East Asian culture is the outcome of a quest to live up to those ideals which have come to be recognized once and for all as valid. The Chinese never entertained the idea of throwing off their 'universistic', monarchical constitution, but devoted much thought to improving it; it never occurred to them to abandon their ancient form of handwriting, but they strove to surpass their forefathers in calligraphic excellence; they did not try to produce new (e.g. artificial) fabrics, but sought to spin their silk even finer; they were not at pains to devise an original literary style, their endeavours were rather directed towards imitating the classical writers. They did not attempt to find more lovely precious stones than jasper, but attached importance to chiselling the latter ever more finely; their philosophers did not wrestle with new ideas, but with the correct way of expounding the old.

When, during their efforts to perfect what already existed, they happened to come across something completely new, such as the compass or gunpowder, they failed to understand how to turn these things to account. The 'development' of East Asian culture consists in the elaboration of that which already exists.

But whence come these standards, these ideals? We have already mentioned the fact (cf. p. 47) that, in the Chinese view, culture unfolds as a consequence of the realization of images perceived intuitively by their sages. Thus the Chinese are from the outset unable to conceive that things might be discovered, fashioned—in short, 'developed'—by experience or reflection: the 'idea' has, in their view, been present from the start and all that was called for was its realization and improvement. Just as it was through intuition that man was raised from the primitive to a higher level, so his subsequent development resulted from intuition also, and not from any consequential manner of thinking and acting.

*

That some of the largest flood-control and irrigation schemes originated over 2,000 years ago is a significant fact of Chinese history, though admittedly the construction of the famous Imperial Canal was not begun until the first centuries of the Christian era, and the greater part of it not completed until the seventh century. The construction of dykes and irrigation works was a matter of life and death to the Chinese in ancient as well as modern times, for without them agriculture and intensive settlement were impossible. These water systems, some of which were conceived and executed on a vast scale, and which served both as a protection against floods and for irrigating the fields (above all, the paddy fields), are thus extremely old; they remained basically unchanged in later times, having been at most improved here and there.

A good example of this is furnished by the irrigation works in Szechwan Province, which were built during the Chin Period (third century B.C.) and are among the largest and the most important in the world. The focal area of the province, the Ming Plain through which flows the Ming River, has since become the most fertile part of China, whereas before the Chin Period it was for the most part a desert area. The whole province has about sixty million inhabitants, of which probably more than half live in the Ming Plain, which is about the size of Bavaria, and a little smaller than Indiana. This represents an unusually dense scale of settlement for a purely agricultural region. In the Ming Plain the farm-houses, which are mostly quite large, stand so close to one another that one cannot at first properly see how the peasants are able to support themselves on the little land there is left between. There is a rice harvest, however, three if not four times a year, and purely vegetable crops are gathered four or five times annually.

He who still believes that the Chinese are a 'primitive' people because they have no science and technology in our sense, should one day visit the irrigation and land reclamation schemes in Szechwan which for over twenty centuries have enabled millions of human beings to maintain themselves!

The principle underlying these works, which still survive in their entirety, is briefly this: the Ming River was diverted every autumn from its own natural course to a new channel dug specially for it, and then in springtime re-diverted to its original course. In the winter the inhabitants of the adjoining districts remove the silt deposited by the river from the original river bed, and in the summer from the new channel, with the result that the water—in contrast, for example, to that of the Yellow River—has never been known to rise sufficiently high to cause really serious flooding. Both arms of the river are connected with the paddy fields by a complex system of small canals.

The work of diverting and dredging the river is, nowadays as in former times, all done by hand. The diversion is effected by alternately closing and opening an artificial dam consisting of enormous bamboo baskets filled with stones. The extent to which the Chinese have used bamboo in all their technical contrivances is quite astonishing. There is, for example, still in existence at Kwanhsien, north-west of Chengtu, the capital of Szechwan Province, an ancient suspension bridge across the Ming River which can carry all but the largest motor lorries: it is made entirely of bamboo.

The many floods from which China has suffered in these last few decades cannot be wholly ascribed to unavoidable natural calamities, for they are to some extent due to neglect of the dykes, weirs and other installations. As political authority declined, the work of maintaining and improving these installations ceased to be carried out with the same punctiliousness and care as formerly. These tasks require a communal effort, in some cases on a very large scale, and can only be performed with the help of a certain amount of state planning and direction.

The above examples should suffice. These age-old systems of water control and conservation appear to us to be grandly conceived projects of a unique and intuitive character, rather than the product of a prior 'technical' development, although even China had, of course, achieved a certain degree of technical progress. Nor did they serve as the starting-point for subsequent progress. The Chinese have never presented the world with any novel or revolutionary ideas on the subject of canal and bridge building or related matters, although they themselves have been preoccupied for centuries with irrigation schemes and methods of river control. They went on steadily building in accordance with their original, 'once-for-all-time' conception, just as their entire culture has its origin in those 'fixed celestial images' which were seen by the sages.

*

Perhaps we can come most near to understanding this static attitude of the East Asians, together with the 'unhistorical' (as it seems to Western eyes) nature of their history, if we consider their ideas of time and space. As we have already pointed out (cf. p. 88), in East Asia these two conceptions are not separated in a dualistic way, and we do better to speak of a 'space-time-union'. According to East Asian ideas this concrete 'space-time' flows on in a series of constantly repeated transformations; its passage is not 'once for all' and non-recurring. This concept of the passage of time can be explained graphically as a cycle, or better, as a system of superimposed cycles.

But the 'space-time-union' and likewise the idea of concrete time is only, in the end, an illusion produced by our imagination. In reality there is neither space nor time—a view shared by both Buddhism and East Asian philosophy. Time, according to the expression used by the Japanese philosopher Nishida[10] is 'eternal rotation in the eternal present'; we are therefore required to imagine all temporal events as compressed into a single moment in time. We have similar conceptions in Christianity, which has it that a thousand years are but as a day in the sight of God. Bavink[11] gives this expression a modern twist when he says that 'God's works on earth cannot be thought of in terms of time as understood by man'.

This conviction of the illusory nature of time has entered more deeply into East Asian consciousness and is more widespread than is the case with us. It is almost as though every East

Asian were aware, or at least suspected, that space and time are only functions designed to keep life going, and thus nothing more than a sort of cosmic device (or, for that matter, man's conception of the cosmos).

Concrete time, as we experience it, is so to speak only 'outward' time, whilst 'inward' time—the 'eternal rotation in the eternal present'—is something that can scarcely be grasped rationally, and can only be apprehended through direct vision, through one's own experience.

It is impossible to appreciate East Asian culture fully unless one tries to get a reasonably clear idea of those two concepts, —inward and outward time. External time is not regarded, as it is in the West, as progressing in a straight line, but as cyclic. This is one of the two root causes of the anti-progressive spirit of the East Asians.

The other is bound up with the idea of inward time. Someone who is to a high degree aware of the illusory nature of time and space can no longer give his whole and undivided attention to the temporal sequence of events; he will tend to regard this sequence as being of only secondary importance. He will direct his gaze only upon the climaxes, i.e. the moments when man attains to the Absolute; but even so he will remain indifferent as to *when* this happened, for the time-scale of events will appear only as an illusion. Yesterday, today and tomorrow become indistinguishable to someone who sees past, present and future as one. In this way the East Asian's consciousness of inward time fortified his indifference towards historical development.

One might say, then, that the East Asian 'space-time-union' is a cyclic phenomenon that ultimately resolves itself in nothingness.

Despite this final resolution in nothingness the idea of outward time remains an extremely vital one. The East Asians have no feeling for our modern conception of time in abstract and mechanical terms. Time, which for them is something alive, will not allow itself to be forcibly fitted into a cut-and-dried conceptual mould. An hour is not in their eyes necessarily always an hour; a lot depends upon what happens during that period. The Japanese have had to accustom themselves to a considerable degree to our mechanical time system—and so also to our equally mechanical working routine—but there is in them still a great deal of resistance to it. The result of this, in practical terms, is what the Westerner throughout East Asia characterizes as 'unpunctuality'.

It is impossible for the East Asian to do 'three hours' work' or to go for 'an hour's stroll'; instead, he works for as long as the job demands, or strolls for as long as it pleases him to. If he is made to regulate his activities or his pleasures by the clock, he is robbed of all his enjoyment of them; he feels injured and impeded. He neither forgets that three minutes are often worth more than a whole hour; nor, on the other hand, that things exist which can only mature or become effective over long periods of time.

Chinese and Japanese are very loth to arrive punctually at their place of work, and do not take their meals with the same punctual regularity as we. They eat when the meal has been prepared and when it pleases them to eat. They do not stop working when the bell goes, but carry on until some reasonable stopping point is reached. Although they would very much like to, many Chinese cannot get themselves to go to the cinema because they are unable to accustom themselves to exact programme timing. All East Asians prefer those cinemas that repeat the same programme continuously every two hours from two p.m. until midnight, because it does not then matter much at what time one arrives. Theatrical performances last several hours in China and Japan—formerly they even went on for days on end, but nobody ever remained for the whole performance. They were made so long and so varied, only so as to ensure that everybody derived pleasure from some part of them. Before the war the modern Japanese theatres started at four or five p.m., but the greater part of the audience did not arrive until about six, and many not until eight. People were always coming and going. East Asians, particularly the rural inhabitants, do not like to consult the time-table before travelling by train, but go to the station as soon as they have completed their preparations for the journey and await the next train to their destination.

Even in present-day Japan many peasants still tell the time by the old form of 'double hour' which was originally brought over from China, and varies in length from winter to summer. The time from sunrise to sunset was divided into six 'double hours', so that in summer the latter can be twice as long as in winter. This organic method of telling the time—similar to that prevailing in Europe centuries ago—is so appropriate to the farmers' daily routine that, despite the modern Japanese craze for watches, it has not quite died out even yet.

*

Now we must examine how the East Asian's 'space-time' concept affects his historical ideas, which at first sight strike us as so strange a mixture of exalted historical sense and a complete lack of it.

The East Asians do not regard history as a continuous process, but as a panorama. They therefore lack any sense of how far dates and events are removed from them. They remember the most astonishing details from the pictures in this panorama, and sometimes know the dates within the various dynasties or periods of government; but they cannot accurately say whether the relevant emperor or dynasty was at the helm centuries or thousands of years ago.

Unlike us, they have never thought in terms of a chain of connected dates, but often used very short periods as the basis of their chronology. These periods may be determined by the length of an emperor's reign or by other special events, mostly of an auspicious nature. The current year, 1952, is the twenty-seventh year of Showa in the Japanese chronology, for 'Showa' will be the posthumous name of the present emperor (who ascended the throne in 1925). The Chinese, by contrast, are at present in the forty-first year of the Republic, the last emperor having been overthrown in 1911. It is possible, moreover, that the Communists have already—I have not been able to ascertain this—introduced yet another new system of reckoning dates. In that case the time of writing this would no doubt be called Year 2 'of the Chinese People's Republic'.

Some years ago the Japanese Government attempted to introduce a system of chronology on the Western model, whose reference point was the year 666 B.C., reputedly that in which the first emperor, Jimmu, ascended the throne. According to this system the present date in Japan would have been the year 2618. It did not, however, succeed in establishing itself.

The East Asians have, therefore, no fixed point in their chronology such as we have in the year of Christ's birth; chronologically they remain somehow suspended in mid-air—exactly as in their attitude to life they conceive neither of a beginning nor an end, but only of eternal flux.

While the average educated East Asian has difficulty in visualizing as a continuous sequence the past of more than half a century ago, many things remain alive irrespective of their remoteness in time, and can be resuscitated, if circumstances so require, without regard to their age. Thus the origin of the 'new' Japanese constitution of 1889 can be partly traced to the old imperial constitution of 645; the Pao-China system, reintroduced in severer form by Chiang Kai-shek to combat the Communists, dated from the eleventh century, but existed far earlier in much the same form.

This characteristically East Asian historical sense explains why things can succeed one another chronologically in East Asia, while continuing to be co-existent. Sometimes, in the course of time, things change a little, the new will now and again find its way in from outside; but in spite of this, ancient forms continue to exist exactly as they have always done. Even after the giant American bombers had begun their work of destruction in Tokyo, the old rattle of the night-watchman, which must date back more than 3,000 years (it is already mentioned in the 'I Ching'), could still be heard in the modern centre of the Japanese capital. Customs are still observed in China and Japan which can be traced with certainty to the Stone Age.

When the East Asian surveys his history, he does not actually look backwards; it is the eternal present that he contemplates. We therefore do wrong when we say, for example, that an East Asian 'looks back' towards his 'ancient sages', for this is a term derived from Western concepts of time and historical development. He just regards them as if they were still living.

East Asians have a well-developed sense of history, inasmuch as the past remains alive and is ever-present to them. Thanks to their great powers of memory their historical knowledge is extremely rich. They have, however, little sense of chronological sequence in history and of the causal relationships between successive happenings; in this sense they are 'history-less'.

*

The Chinese had very early reached the highest levels of conscious, 'total' thought. This cyclic thought does not permit of further spontaneous development. Expressed graphically, it resembles a closed circular system which, as it revolves about its axis, repels by centrifugal force all attempts to break in.

Only a very powerful blow from outside could have made any serious impression on this way of thinking; but before the encounter with the West, China received no such blow. If we ask ourselves why none came, then we can only broadly indicate the geographical factors. In Europe we see races mingle with one another and follow successively upon one another within the confines of a relatively small and sectioned area, whilst the irruptions of foreign peoples into the broad areas of China have produced the effect of ripples on a pond; the waters in the depths remained unstirred. In former times there was only one recognized centre of East Asian culture; this was China with its fertile valleys and plains. But in the West, where geography imposed no such restricted choice, the centres of culture kept alternating.

Chinese culture had its origin in the most fertile and climatically the most favourable regions in East Asia, where, furthermore, the fertility could be exploited by such technical means as were then available. We need not go deeply into the question as to how far this culture can be regarded as autochthonous, and to what extent it might be necessary to seek its origins in the impacts and minglings of different races. Nevertheless it is a fact that at a very early period an indigenous culture developed in North China, which has continued, by and large, to exercise a decisive influence.

This culture bore, from the very outset, a collectivist stamp, and depended not least on the necessity for considerable communal efforts in the matter of flood control and irrigation. Such conditions paved the way for a 'universistic' *Weltanschauung*.

Chinese culture has developed far more autochthonously than has that of the West, which throughout 2,000 years has constantly had to wrestle with foreign cultural influences. China, it is true, had to contend as frequently as we with external foes, and in her case too it fructified her spiritual life; but it did not 'throw her into a ferment'. Viewed historically also, China's spiritual development was effected through introversion, and not through extraversion. China's reaction to conquest by foreign barbarians and domination by their rulers was to deliberate calmly; she 'meditated' and permitted no foreign culture to influence her decisively. National catastrophes have thus constantly served to strengthen China's individual characteristics, and have failed to shake or to weaken her.

The Chinese system was something new—indeed, something of a revelation—to China's foreign invaders, who were mostly nomadic tribes. Even if, as nomads, they were hostile to agriculture, they had to admit that to live off the land without damming back the waters and controlling flood violence was scarcely possible. They could not therefore but acknowledge the way in which the Chinese took this work in hand and organized it. From this it was no great step to accepting also Chinese conceptions of communal living. It was not only because the intruders were dazzled and impressed by the refined and lofty character of Chinese culture that they succumbed quickly to Chinese influence, but above all because they were gripped by the spirit of the river plains, by the spirit of Chinese communal culture. China has always been able to furnish spontaneous and convincing proofs that her attitude among all others, was the right one, and not therefore subject to change or outside influences.

In recent years China has for the first time failed to bear this out, in that a dogma deriving from outside, from the West and from Moscow, has established itself there. The rationalist school which, in the form of Mohism, succumbed over 2,000 years ago, has been revived in the shape of Marxism. In contrast to the relatively young Russian people, one of the oldest peoples of the world, the Chinese, are to be conditioned in the rationalist-marxist school. So the Communist 'challenge'—to revert to Toynbee's phrase—here encounters an entirely different state of affairs from that prevailing in Russia, and therefore the 'response', too, will be correspondingly different; in other words, Chinese Communism will certainly assume a different aspect from the Russian version.

Many friends of China—among which I count myself—when arriving at this conclusion, are bound to indulge in a certain measure of 'wishful thinking': we tend to hope that Chinese Communism will assume a more bearable, a more human and reasonable form than the Russian variety. But let us not harbour any illusions. What is already now happening in China is to our idea terrible enough, but in all probability it will become far more terrible. Mass executions are taking place, and thousands of persons whose baser instincts are being whipped up by propaganda, are screaming, 'Kill them! Batter them to death!' Hundreds of thousands—perhaps millions—

must still die, before the Communist State conforms to the requirements of its bosses.

If the peasants do not adapt themselves to collectivization, they will purposely be left to starve, just as in the Soviet Union, until they give in. If an inundation occurs somewhere, no help will be forthcoming should the Communist authorities consider it more politic at the time to issue the available provisions to the army. Indeed, one or two famines and cataclysms may even be welcomed, for they will enable discharged Communist soldiers to be settled on land thus made available. No, one must have no illusions. There are traditions, furthermore, in China when it comes to huge communal undertakings such as irrigation and building schemes. In carrying out their plans the authorities in Peking will no more be put out by the deaths of thousands than were their predecessors two thousand years earlier, when the Great Wall was being built.

*

Japan, who not only developed her own primal and indigenous characteristics, but took over a foreign culture (namely that of the Chinese), was at no time subjected to penetrating stresses or upheavals of a fundamental nature, her assumption of Chinese culture having been a voluntary and gradual process. At no time did a foreign invader foist a strange culture upon the Japanese; but the Yamato, with their gradually awakening interest in cultural life, brought over from China what in their view Japan needed. Unmenaced by any enemy until well into the twelfth century, they were able to devote as much time as they pleased to the appropriation and assimilation of Chinese culture. They were able, moreover, to repulse the attacks of the Chinese and the Mongols, which started towards the end of the twelfth century, with fair speed and success. Japan's assumption of Chinese culture—and also of Buddhism—was on the whole an organic and healthy process; nothing was adopted in an uncritical fashion.

21

The spiritual development of Japan also was introverted to the extent that it was conditioned entirely by her own spiritual needs. The Japanese have never had either a general or a particular interest in China. There are many important Chinese artistic and philosophical movements of which not a trace is to be found in Japan. Other Chinese traditions, however, which long ago died out in China itself, continue to flourish in Japan. Understandably enough it was the China of the Tang period, during which Japan borrowed more than at any other time, that has had the most lasting influence on the island kingdom. The Japanese have preserved or developed many influences from Tang times, whereas they were inclined to be more critical towards later Chinese creations and achievements.

Japan was therefore not unacquainted with conflicts of one sort and another, but she has always resolved them harmoniously and has always found the way back to her mystic and 'total' primal character.

Today also, as a result of powerful American influence, the island kingdom finds itself in a state of flux and tension. But once again everything is being resolved by way of reforms and a process of adaptation. Japan, which in recent decades had already modernized herself to a far greater degree than China, is spared bitter revolution.

*

A peculiar feature of East Asian history is the concept of national 'isolation', which the West with its world-wide contacts has never known. In the last few centuries both China and Japan have been at pains to seal themselves off hermetically from the rest of the world—an attempt which, admittedly, only fully succeeded in the case of the latter.

China began to shut herself off in the sixteenth century, firstly as a measure of protection against the Portuguese. She was later forced nevertheless to make repeated concessions, for, in addition to the Portuguese, both the Dutch and the English insisted, often by force or the threat of force, on opening up various ports and harbours. In the nineteenth century, as the Manchu dynasty grew progressively weaker, she was compelled to permit access to numerous ports (including those on the larger rivers, such as Hangkow and Chungking), to admit further foreign nations and to grant the latter certain special areas for settlement.

Japan was entirely cut off from 1603 until 1856, except for a tiny area on the island of Deshima near Nagasaki where the Dutch had a trading concession. Even so, the Dutch lived there behind a barbed-wire enclosure, as it were, for none of them were allowed to leave their little settlement. In 1618, moreover, the Japanese were forbidden on pain of death to leave their islands.

The reason for these measures was in every case the same: fear of the West and its disturbing influence, against which they wished to protect themselves. It was suspicion of the motives of the Westerners, and the fear that they intended the conquest of all Asia. They followed, with rising anxiety, the course of the white nations as they established themselves in India, on the Malayan peninsula, in the Indonesian archipelago, and in the Philippines. But in addition to this they became aware betimes of another thing: the threat to their culture and to their very existence from these foreigners who, despite their strength and power, were nevertheless regarded by the East Asians as ignorant, uncivilized and barbarous.

Their first reaction to what they sensed to be this dangerous onset of Western man was essentially that of the introvert—not active defence, not counter-blow and counter-attack but withdrawal to, and concentration within their own positions, behind which they sought to isolate themselves.

In doing this they ultimately lapsed into the great illusion of all introverts, namely, that it is possible to live apart from the world and independent of it. Introspective and unprepared to adjust themselves to circumstances, they did not see that the world, represented at this period by the Occident, was equally unprepared to pay much regard to their self-centredness and smug exclusiveness.

It was the last attempt on the part of the East Asians to preserve their traditional way of life; they assumed that theirs was the only true and definitive culture, failing to realize that other paths were open to mankind.

All that the East Asians were fundamentally capable of visualizing was their own, or 'total' type, just as our own was all that we ourselves could comprehend. Bertrand Russell[12] is of the opinion that 'our industrial and commercial civilization has been both the effect and cause of certain more or less unconscious beliefs as to what is worth while; in China one becomes conscious of these beliefs through the spectacle of a society which challenges them by being built, just as unconsciously, upon a different standard of values'.

There seems no other explanation, from the psychological point of view, but that the Westerner—the extravert—represents the aggressive and challenging factor, and the East Asian —the introvert—the defensive and resisting one. It is therefore rather superficial to condemn outright the world-wide expansion of the white man with such catch-phrases as 'imperialism', 'oppression of the coloured races' and the like, as is often done by certain narrow and tendentious 'intellectuals'. The Westerner and his way of life have also served a useful purpose in history.

It is appropriate at this point to compare the East Asian concept of isolationism with the Russian 'Iron Curtain' policy. Pretty much the same attitude is, at the heart of it, responsible for both developments, except that the East Asians sealed off their countries to preserve their traditional culture and social organization, while the Russians' object is through isolation to attain a higher pitch of maturity. The Russian attitude is thus ultimately based on the desire for self-examination and self-development. The Russians have always had, as the history of their thought and religion shows, a strong leaning towards introspection and mysticism.

Russia is today striving, with unprecedented energy, to adapt herself to the modern technological era, an aim which in the days of the czars was pursued more or less superficially.

This might well explain the fanatical rationalism of the Russians, which in its present form is certainly only a passing phenomenon. The Russians will never develop a 'split', dualistic and dynamic culture as the West has done. Their aim is to attain to a higher degree of civilization and to remain there when they have reached it. They reject the Faustian urge as decisively as do the East Asians.

Their introverted method of pursuing this aim surely belongs to the Asian traits of the Russians. Developments so far show that, like the East Asians before them, they have become the victims of an illusion; for the Russians have not succeeded in peacefully building up a new social order and culture behind their iron curtain. Ever since the foundation of the Soviet State there have been constant passages of arms, both diplomatic and military, between them and the rest of the world. They have not foreseen that the world at large would automatically become just as mistrustful of a great power that withdrew from its midst, as they themselves were of other nations. The Russians were compelled more and more to devote their attention, their energies and their resources to the outer world, instead of to the task of internal reconstruction. But there is nothing that the introvert dislikes more than to be diverted from his preoccupation with himself; this sets up an unendurable tension within him that most often manifests itself in feelings of hatred towards his neighbours. Russia, still in the early stages of her development, has not yet attained to a state of equilibrium with her surroundings. She does not understand that an introvert is only pardoned when he is not dangerous, just as the extravert only meets with approval when he lives and works for others, instead of only for himself. We are under no obligation to any nation that withdraws into isolation and, at the same time, adopts a threatening attitude towards us; just as we receive no thanks for having given the world a new civilization, because in doing so we never lost sight of our own advantage.

Now China, too, has once again isolated herself—this time not in order to preserve her ancient culture, but for much the same reasons as the Soviet Union. And the world can no more forgive the Chinese their self-absorbed 'lone-wolf' attitude, than the Russians. Their reactions are the same as those of Soviet Russia: hate towards the outside world and defence by aggression (Korea!).

In this chapter we have attempted to explain why Western culture 'developed', whilst that of East Asia remained for centuries essentially the same. Today the East Asian world has got to come to terms with a number of problems that are new to it. These are: in the philosophical sphere, the concept of 'development'; in that of psychology, the necessity for a more extensive differentiation (and particularly for the cultivation of a rational mode of thinking); in the religious sphere, the undermining of the hitherto generally accepted religious forms and beliefs, and the growing perplexity of the masses; in the social sphere, individualism. They are therefore the very same problems that are engaging our attention in the West, but viewed from a diametrically opposite angle.

NOTES

[1] Though beyond the scope of this book, it would be interesting in this connection to take up the whole question of ancient Greek mysticism, including the oracles and mysteries. We are convinced that this would disclose various points of contact with ancient China. It would, however, call for an approach to Ancient Greece from more than the all too one-sided rationalist point of view, which has been the rule hitherto.

[2] Jacob Burckhardt, *Weltgeschichtliche Betrachtungen.*

[3] Alfred Weber, *Abschied von der bisherigen Geschichte.*

[4] Quoted from Wilhelm Röpke, 'Kollektivschuld und deutscher Widerstand' (Neue Schweizer Rundschau, 1946).

[5] Graf Hermann Keyserling, *Das Reisetagebuch eines Philosophen.*

[6] *Maximem und Reflexionen.*

[7] Junyu Kitayama, *West-östliche Begegnung.*

[8] Ibid.

[9] Chang Hsiu-hai, 'The Intellectual Situation in Modern China' (Comptes Rendues des Séances de la Société des Sciences et des Lettres de Varsovie XXIV, 1936, Classe II).

[10] Kitaro Nishida, 'Goethe' (Quarterly of the Goethegesellschaft, 1938).

[11] Bernhard Bavink, *Die Naturwissenschaft auf dem Wege zur Religion.*

[12] Bertrand Russell, *The Problem of China.*

Chapter 10

SYNTHESIS AS THE COMMON TASK

WHEN we observe cosmic and terrestrial events we detect a process of continuous development—in the formation and history of planets and in the evolution of organisms. In the story of mankind we find an analogous process in the incidence of entirely new and previously unknown phenomena such as, for example, our applied science and technology.

Cyclic motion, on the other hand, is revealed in natural and terrestrial history, in the sequence of the seasons, the ebb and flow of the tides, the cyclical processes of geology; in the change from life to death and again from death to life, from seed to tree and from tree to seed. It appears also in history in the rhythmic alternations of peace and war, and of good and bad times; in the flowering and decay of cultures, and in the rise and fall of nations.

This once again reflects those two basic philosophical approaches to history, one of which sees things develop in a straight line, while the other stresses progression in cycles. Most other theories attempt to co-ordinate these two methods of progression, but even so one or other of the two basic approaches nearly always predominates.

Now that we have compared and contrasted East Asian with Western history and culture, we have reached the apparently inescapable conclusion that the two attitudes—the rationalist and the mystical, the concept of development and that of change—are both valid, provided that their spheres of application are appropriately restricted. Seen in this light the history of both human and terrestrial events—and that of the universe also—consists in the complementary interaction of these two phenomena.

In what follows we propose to confine ourselves to historical

319

considerations and to omit all reference to natural and cosmic processes.

*

Now, recurrent and irreversible development is exclusive to the history of civilization, the word 'civilization' being here understood to mean the emergence and development of rationally apprehensible things. Its necessary preliminary is psychic differentiation. We therefore also regard the increasing degree of psychic differentiation in human kind as a unique and irreversible process of development.

A view of history such as, for example, that of Spengler, whose basic ideas have a certain affinity with those of Plato and the I Ching, is therefore tendentious and misleading, in that it omits all reference to such development as has in fact taken place and is still going on. It is certainly not only possible but also instructive to compare, say, the period of the classical era in its decline, with the present, provided that in so doing certain quite definite limitations are set and reservations made. At the same time it is absurd to maintain that the events of that period must repeat themselves in fundamentally the same way, for our external conditions of life and the state of our psychic differentiation are, of course, quite different from those of classical days. Science and technology, for example, present us with some of the cardinal problems of our time, with phenomena which did not exist two thousand years ago. We are on a higher level of 'civilization' than the classical world; in this sense humanity has 'developed'. It therefore follows that the basic facts with which we have to come to terms are different from those obtaining at any previous time.

When we consider history from the human and cultural standpoint, we are unable to find any trace of progressive, non-recurrent development. Morals, religion, wisdom, knowledge and creative power are for ever alternately waxing and waning. We are neither wiser, more enlightened nor nearer perfection than were the men of former ages, and, in order to try to become so, must exert ourselves just as much as did all our antecedents. The attainment of perfection or—looked at in terms of human society—of peace, universal happiness and prosperity is just as difficult—just as possible or as impossible—whatever the level of civilization. In the human and cultural spheres we see eternal cycles of endeavour, of success, of failure, and fresh endeavour.

What, then, is the point of civilized progress if it is unable to assist man towards the solution of his chief problems, namely those concerning morality, wisdom, happiness and contentment?

The unique and non-recurring changes to which humanity and the universe are subject, fulfil in our view a necessary function in that they prevent life and all cosmic processes from coming to a halt. Without variation life stagnates; it likewise stagnates when this variation takes the form of perpetual repetition, when it is nothing but everlasting circular motion determined always by the same laws. We saw this danger clearly in East Asia, where life threatened to become formal and stereotyped, and thereby to lose its vital quality.

To retain his strength and vitality, man needs new tasks and problems against which to pit himself. A constantly repeated ebb and flow of life and death, of war and peace, of good harvest and of bad, of wise government and foolish, of happiness and unhappiness—none of this suffices. In the end man will learn to put up with it, philosophically and with resignation, for in this process of growth and decay he will come to see life's only purpose. And he will then have lost his chance of developing his latent faculties.

Psychical development, on the other hand, alteration in the conditions of life, science and technology, confront mankind perpetually with new situations, with the result that his vital energies are challenged and spurred on. If we care to consider technology in this light, it seems like a heaven-sent plaything given to man as an instrument for his own development. Man does not change qualitatively, the battle between perfection and imperfection goes on just the same inside him, but he requires changing tasks and situations to keep his vital interests alert.

*

History resembles a non-recurrent and irreversible process around which individual human beings, nations and cultures revolve rhythmically and spirally. Spiral motion resembles cyclic motion but is not identical with it, because its coils never return to the same point. The intervals between the individual coils may also be described as steps.

Since humanity moves forward in spiral motion it can never repeat its experiences, but finds itself always confronted with different situations. In this sense one can say that humanity is always experiencing something new. But we may assume spiral motion *per se* to remain the same, so we are constantly faced with the same situation: the need to come to terms with the conditions of the time, that is, to achieve perfection in constantly changing circumstances. In this sense humanity never in fact experiences anything new. From the point of view of human nature and morality there is no development, let alone 'upward' development. But should man prove inadequate to meet the tasks that this spiral process imposes upon him, he will be cast forth and perish.

The East Asians perceived only the circular motion of the spirals and, in so doing, disregarded the fact that the latter draw constantly further apart; for this reason they failed to detect any development. We, on the other hand, gave our attention so much to the 'steps', to the intervals between the coils, that we scarcely noticed the latter and regarded the whole as a process of moving forward in a straight line.

In the course of time man becomes more complex but not more perfect. He must seek perfection for the differentiated state just as his ancestors sought it for the more simple psyche. He must constantly re-seek his equilibrium, his 'centrum' and his way of approach to the Absolute. If he fails in this, the new complex structure will not stand the test of life. The structure of our conscious mind changes, but its task remains always the same: to comprehend the varying circumstances it encounters, and to grasp what is imperishable.

There seems here to be some affinity with certain biological problems, with the secret of the evolution of higher types of being, and the conditions under which they thrive or perish.

Each new coil in the spiral that we reach, each new step that we climb, is governed by its own peculiar laws, for an understanding of which all our acquired knowledge is unavailing. In this sense there is nothing that can be learnt from the past. But there is another, more important respect in which the past can very well afford us guidance, and that is in answering the question why we have to understand these peculiar governing laws, and where lies the goal of our endeavours; for this goal itself is something that does not change. Man plays a part in the self-realization of the world, but he must constantly bear in mind that this is no process of pointless unchecked growth, but that underlying everything there is a scheme or pattern which is related to that of the Absolute.

When Jacob Burckhardt says:[1] 'Every nation falls short of perfection and seeks to make up the deficiency—the more advanced the nation, the greater its efforts', he is referring to that urge towards self-realization which manifests itself in the progress of civilization. If cultures become more complex in structure, they nevertheless remain organisms with a content of ultimate and immutable truth.

If we consider history in terms of our spiral image it becomes clear that the part played by the Western world can only have served to drive the spiral a good distance onwards, in other words, to raise humanity to a new level of civilization. But in so doing we boldly and heedlessly extended the spiral to the point where it was in danger of breaking, and we are now compelled to turn to other nations for advice as to how best it can be made strong again.

In the history of civilization there is no way back, for its progress is irreversible. All nations must raise themselves to the new technical level, if they are not to be left behind and run the risk of collapse. The leap we hazarded during the last century or so was both a mighty and an absolute one. So comprehensive was it that even the peasantry, a class which until then had been very largely unaffected by history, was caught up in it. We need only think of the vast wheatlands of North America and Siberia which are today cultivated with the help of the tractor.

This concept of history, which is literally forced upon us by our comparison of the course of events in East Asia with that of the West, is no dualistic one, although it is possible that the distinction we have drawn between civilizing progress in a straight line and cultural recurrence of a cyclic nature might give the impression that it is. Both movements, as already mentioned, are however regarded as complementary. There is, in the last resort, no culture without civilizing progress, and this progress is in its turn dependent upon the presence of races having a natural aptitude for culture. There are instances in history where the development of these factors is unbalanced, and others where neither thrives; but taken all in all it is these two elements which combine to give history a meaning.

*

Hitherto, theories of history have paid little attention to the interaction of these two elements; they tended, according to the circumstances, to see them both as one, or to let the one factor emerge from the other.

Both the cyclic and the 'rectilinear' conceptions were represented in ancient Greece, as well as combinations of the two; in general, though, it was the cyclic, whose typical representatives were Hesiod and Heraclitus, that was predominant. Modern Western evolutionary theories, however—and in particular the natural sciences and rationalist 'Enlightenment', —preferred to take as their point of departure the 'rectilinear' thinkers of ancient Greece; not only Democritus and the Epicureans, but also Aristotle. Plato's complex picture of man's destinies and history has, we believe, an overall cyclic pattern. Despite the wide range of his thought, the conception of 'rectilinear' development is nowhere to be found in it. He sees nations developing concurrently and successively, without the one, however, influencing the other. Cultures originating in this way differ from one another because each nation incorporates one or the other of the 'eternal ideas'. Perhaps it is possible to see in this conception a certain affinity with the theory of development, but nothing more; for it is sharply distinguished from the concept of 'rectilinear' development by the fact that it does not see each nation beginning where the other left off, but making an entirely fresh start as regards not only culture but also civilization.

The conception of history as a unique and irreversible process made its first decisive impact on the world with the advent of Christianity. In a sense one could even say that it was Christianity that first created history.

According to the Christian faith, history runs in a straight line from the Creation, by way of the Fall of Man and the Revelation, to the Last Judgment. Furthermore, it requires the whole human race to follow this course; the destinies of individual peoples and cultures are disregarded. 'Cyclic' thinkers have admittedly made their appearance from time to time in Christianity; but the foregoing has been the prevailing conception.

The determining factor in the triumphant progress of this view of history has been religious feeling—the belief in God and the unique world of his creation, and also in the destiny he has ordained for the latter. To the extent that this view of history has been given a rational and philosophical foundation, this was designed to serve a specific purpose, i.e. the tenets of this faith were accepted as something incontrovertible, with the result that the activities of Christian thinkers served merely, in the last resort, to make it even more inflexible and opened up no fresh paths. The rationalist evolutionary theories that made their appearance later on under the aegis of reason, then proceeded—seduced by the objects of their consideration, namely such things as lay, or as were held to be, within the grasp of reason—to transfer the principle of progressive evolution, which was discernible in the sphere of the natural sciences and civilization, to the broader canvas of universal history. In this way the narrow belief in progress ultimately attained at least a temporary position of dominance.

We believe that the 'spiral' view of history can be combined with the Christian conception. Thus we could imagine the beginning and end of the spiral, about which we have so far not enquired, as corresponding to the Creation and Last Judgment. To this end we should, indeed, have to avail ourselves of the idea of 'inward' time so as to conceive of the Creation and the Last Judgment as not separate in time, but as eternally present and eternally active. But our enquiry is concerned, basically, only with the relatively short span of time taken up by the history of human affairs, in so far as it is known to us. Relating to this ascertainable period we have propounded the thesis that two complementary factors are at work, and that in their interaction is to be found the meaning of history.

*

Now the question arises as to whether the principle of synchronism, already mentioned several times, can be reconciled with the above conception. This principle postulates the existence, all over the world, of an influence emanating from the same time-quality.

In broad outline we can in fact discern a certain simultaneity of events in East Asia and in the West. Even though things have developed quite differently and independently in the West, it nevertheless often seems as though Europe and Asia possessed a common invisible root, a common and subterranean primal source from which flow effects of a like nature; as though some distant master were intervening in events or controlling the springs of action without the nations observing that it was not they alone who were subject to these influences.

In concrete terms, does not the mystery perhaps lie in the fact that the nomadic tribes of Central Asia broke out simultaneously at certain periods of history both eastwards and westwards, to effect considerable changes in both regions? The first of the advanced cultures of the West originated at about the same time as those of East Asia (between the fourth and the third millennium B.C.), and this can be attributed to the incursions of nomadic tribes who mixed with the indigenous population. This gave new impetus to established cultures, and more advanced forms resulted from this synthesis. In later times it happened repeatedly that both East Asia and Europe were simultaneously afflicted and thrown into confusion by nomadic invasion—for example, at the time of the great migrations of the Western peoples, and of Ghengis Khan; at the same time we can, with the best will in the world, attribute only partial responsibility for these parallel phenomena to such trouble-makers.

How are we to explain the fact that the great philosophers and founders of religions in both East and West—from Buddha to Christ and from Lao Tse to Aristotle—all make their appearance in the last five centuries B.C.? How strange that these saints, sages and philosophers should all simultaneously become so dissatisfied with the state of the world, that they longed— and would fight—for a new and better one! And how can we account for the fact, noted by Richard Wilhelm, that the stylistic epochs in Chinese art correspond roughly to our own? Is it coincidence that the great Roman roads and aqueducts had their origin in the same epoch as the Chinese irrigation works? And finally—are not both Asia and the West being simultaneously affected by the modern spiritual crisis and attendant outbreaks of war and violence?

A more critical study of history reveals, however, that these— at least approximate—parallelisms are offset by notable instances of non-simultaneity. Thus the development of technology in China had virtually come to an end at a very early period. China can show nothing analagous to the tremendous progress made by the West in this respect during the last two hundred years (whilst the Greek rationalists and the Chinese Mohists belonged roughly to the same period of antiquity!). But most noteworthy of all is the fact that a period, during which China marked time culturally, produced in Europe two entirely different cultures: the Classical and the modern Western. Many of the disparities can be traced back to this fact; for example, the periods of the feudal ages, of the establishment of unified empires, of the religious wars, etc.

Despite these contradictions, it nevertheless seems to us that the influence of 'concrete time' is something that, in itself, cannot be denied. It is not unreasonable to assume that it impinges equally upon all nations, but that their reactions to it vary according to the national character. Some have readily and courageously attempted to master the temporal element, whilst those who were more timid and 'wise' did their best to eschew contact with it altogether. The former, in their concern for the temporal, ran the risk of forgetting altogether the eternal verities, whilst the latter failed to perceive that the eternal can only be realized in terms of what is temporal.

Man is not the helpless, will-less servant of concrete time. One can either devote oneself to it, adjusting oneself to, and thereby trying to master it like the Westerners—or one can repudiate it like the East Asians. In our view these divergent attitudes go to explain the unequal historical influence exercised by 'concrete time' in the East Asians and upon ourselves. Concrete time wears away and 'devours' nations; eternal values sustain them.

The conception of concrete time expounded here is identical in most respects with that long held by the Chinese. The only point of variance is that the Chinese in the ultimate analysis regard the process of time as taking the form of a circle, whilst we see it as transforming the circular into spiral motion as a result of its tendency to move forwards in a straight line.

What is more, the Chinese are convinced that man is not a helpless victim of the currents of time: they are no fatalists. The Chinese—at least if he belongs to the educated class—consults oracles and the stars, not in order to resign himself, blindly and submissively, to the workings of destiny, but rather to discover with what currents, with what good or evil tendencies he has to contend. Once he has learnt the judgment of the oracle or of the stars, he determines his independent course of action on the basis of his own deliberations.

Varied are the ways in which the nations seek to counter the effects of concrete time, and equally various are therefore their respective destinies. A classic example of this is the way in which the Chinese took their stand against Mohism and stemmed the religious tide that rose about 2,000 years ago.

It is also significant that, during the pre-Christian era, such parallels were more striking than during the Christian era. It has only been since the Birth of Christ that the Western attitude has gradually developed into one diametrically opposed to that of the East Asians.

*

East Asia and the whole 'history-less' world are today in the grip of a profound disquiet, for the old ideals have begun to totter. Such of these nations as are susceptible to change and new ideas are beginning to realize that no Gandhi could have the power to arrest this development; they perceive that, at the most, he could only delay and retard it. These nations today stand prepared for the great exertions involved in scaling the heights of the new technology; but it is not their intention to climb onward and upward without respite. Their goal is the attainment of a new stage of 'history-lessness'.

This is a type of endeavour the East Asians have not hitherto known, for such 'history-lessness' they took as a matter of course. It could only become a *goal* at the moment when the East Asians were compelled to abandon their old attitude. The

22

Western world, however, which has never known a state of
repose, has always yearned for the advent of this 'history-less'
condition—a yearning which, from Christianity to Marxism,
has taken many forms.

Today all nations have set themselves this goal; some hope
soon to regain the static condition which they have just surrendered, whilst the others cherish the belief that the moment
of the realization of their century-old dreams is at last drawing
near.

That in this respect the Russians are, in fundamentals, ranged
on the side of the East Asians might well be inferred from the
foregoing (cf. p. 316). But how do the Americans stand with
regard to these problems? It is possible to observe two strongly
divergent tendencies among them which serve to make America,
as it were, a downright caricature of Europe: highest dynamic
qualities and active participation in world politics in a leading
rôle, are in their case coupled with a most ardent and genuine
desire for peace and lasting quiet; consciousness of world-wide
responsibilities is grafted on to the strongest isolationist tendencies. American isolationism has the same psychological roots
as the East Asians' former endeavours to cut themselves off from
the world, and as the Russians' policy of the 'Iron Curtain'.
Nor is our argument affected by the fact that during the last
few years isolationism has been out of favour with the majority
in America.

The Americans—though less exhausted and out of breath than
we—will not continue for ever to chase along the spiral at the
same breakneck tempo as heretofore. Nor in point of fact do
they really want to do so, for the 'history-less' tendency was
always strong and active among them and will get the upper
hand when the time is ripe for it.

Jacob Burckhardt,[2] after discussing the thesis that 'history-
lessness' and barbarism are identical, has this to say of the
Americans: 'Further, the historical factor is renounced by
Americans, i.e. by people of an unhistorical culture, who are
however, by reason of their associations with the old world,

not able to get history out of their system altogether.' Thus he numbers the Americans among the barbarians; not indeed explicitly, but the point is implicit. We reproduce this judgment of Burckhardt's merely to show that the 'history-less' tendency has always been felt as something typically American, although we cannot, in other respects subscribe to his opinion. Of the many witnesses who could be produced to testify to the anti-historical and at the same time pacifist tendency of the Americans, we need mention only Ralph Waldo Emerson whom the Chinese like to look upon as someone spiritually akin to themselves. Hence the opinion of Ku Hung-Ming[3] that Emerson's conception of non-government and non-resistance fully corresponds to the ideals of the Chinese, and those of Confucianism in particular.

*

Neither the static nor the dynamic attitude are panaceas for staving off downfall. Egypt perished because it could not overcome its collectivist-static outlook, and was therefore unable to fall in with the dynamically individualistic tendency of the Graeco-Roman era which gradually gained the upper hand. India and East Asia would today equally be condemned to insignificance and would probably come increasingly under foreign influence, were they now endeavouring to adjust themselves to the new developments brought about by the West. The dangers for the modern world inherent in the dynamic attitude hardly need mentioning here: they are those of becoming a completely spent force and, ultimately, of possible self-destruction as the result of carrying this attitude to ridiculous extremes. It is the duty of the nations to comprehend the truth, i.e. the inherent meaning of time. Only he who knows the secret of change is proof against the rhythmic oscillations of history.

In this connection, Walter Schubart[4] has the following to say: 'Western culture yearns for its own annihilation. All things mortal perish, but the manner of its decline is peculiarly its own. It is not being overwhelmed by foreign invaders as was that of the Incas or Aztecs. Nor is it dying of old age and debility as did that of Rome. It is killing itself in the excess of its own power. This suicide of a culture is a unique phenomenon in the story of mankind.' In this trenchant summing-up, Schubart surely describes accurately the danger inherent in our dynamic culture; and the events of the last decades have to some extent justified his view. Nevertheless it seems to us that these very events (Nazism, Fascism, etc.) have in fact led to a higher degree of self-communion and in this way, too, have helped to avert the danger. The situation today is different from that between the first and second World Wars in that, by reason of our new experiences, we now recognize the chief problems of the time more clearly and distinctly than we did then. Above all we recognize today the possibility that the age of technology may be working towards a purposeful end. The 'yearning for self-annihilation', which was doubtless present, is yielding to the wish for active participation in the creation of a new world— a world, static, tranquil and of an altogether different kind. At the same time it cannot be denied that purely material factors might now give rise to a new and general European defeatism: this would be the more tragic since, as we believe, the intellectual crisis—European nihilism—has been so nearly overcome.

It cannot readily and convincingly be proved that the rise and fall of nations and cultures takes place to a set pattern and always in accordance with the same laws. The interaction of the two components of history, to which must be added the third element of racial genius, leaves room for a wide range of very different possibilities. We have only to think of the unique part played by the Jews, a rôle which few will deny has for thousands of years been one of the most important in history. But we cannot easily dispute questions of quality and vitality, since our judgments on these matters are determined principally by our subjective emotions and our subjective attitude.

*

What then are the future tasks of Europe and East Asia in the modern world? If we can shed even a little light on this problem then we shall already have accomplished a great deal.

Everything that has happened in recent decades has had for good or for ill its political and economic, as well as its spiritual and intellectual roots in Europe or Asia. Politically and economically these regions no longer represent the strongest world powers, but they none the less continue to be the centres of culture. It was in Europe that the most hard-fought and tragic intellectual battles took place, struggles in which people strove to master the problems of the day. The ideology of the democratic countries originated in Europe just as much as those of the Fascists and Communists.

The East Asians, on the other hand, were the first to make a great effort to throw off Western influence and culture. Apart from all purely temporary political factors, it is in this that we perceive the true meaning of the Japanese upsurge. It was an attempt to drive back and weaken the political power of the white nations in order to lay the foundations for a free Asia. Asia, thus liberated, was to be independent of the restless and intrusive, dynamic and changeable spirit of the West; it was once again to live according to its own ideal of stability, concord and harmony, as it had in former ages. An attempt would probably have been made to seal off this Asia from outside, and thus protect it from the noxious and 'barbaric' influences of the white man, since the latter would not yet have been brought to his knees but only forced to withdraw. Millions of Asians in all countries thought these thoughts and to some extent still think them today. Let us not forget how complete and powerful a break we forced upon them, and with what bitterness, sadness and longing they have had to stand by and see the demise of their ancient traditions which they had hitherto managed to preserve intact.

The Japanese did, indeed, commit a fundamental error. They —not to mention the other Asian peoples—were themselves insufficiently advanced in a technical sense to think of reverting to a state of tranquillity. Mighty efforts are still required of them in order to equal us in this respect. No one can cheat his way through history.

The Chinese have for decades carried on exactly the same struggle as the Japanese, but with quite different means. The Sino-Japanese conflict was not fought primarily to decide whether China or Japan should rule in Asia, but to decide by what method the white races should be expelled. The reactions of the Chinese seemed too tardy and indecisive to the Japanese: the latter feared that such indolent methods would in the end jeopardise their existence because, left to themselves, they would scarcely have been in a position to keep the Western nations indefinitely at bay.

They wanted to compel the Chinese to adopt the Japanese tempo. That is where they badly miscalculated. Not a single Japanese, not even the most narrow-minded general, at any time thought in terms of a 'conquest' of China. The Chinese, who were not inwardly ready and did not yet feel themselves fully equipped to deal with the mighty tasks of the day, were neither able nor willing to submit to Japanese dictation in the matter of how they should act and how they should come to terms with the whites. They feared, and rightly, that this would of necessity involve them, on account of the disorganized and infirm state of the country, in Japanese political and economic tutelage. This, China was unwilling to accept.

The 'War for a Greater East Asia' (as the second World War was called by the Japanese) and the Sino-Japanese conflict must remain incomprehensible if one fails to realize this: it was a question of coming to terms with the whites and their civilization. Both wars, as well as the rise of Communism in China, number among the events which are ushering in a new era; as, to a certain extent, was the catastrophic war in Europe.

Perhaps the age of the atomic bomb will see further catastrophes: this cannot, however, in any way affect the goals for which we are striving. Europe and East Asia, the bearers of the ancient cultures that have created these situations and problems, are, when all is said and done, responsible for the present state of world affairs: in East Asia it is not only the Japanese, but also the Chinese; in Europe it is not only the Germans but also the other nations. The guilt for that which we have caused or allowed to happen, will not be lifted from our shoulders because we no longer wield political or economic power. The spiritual responsibility persists. We cannot shift it to the shoulders of America or Russia, who now have the power that once was ours. Our main task must be to help prepare the way spiritually for the reconstruction of the world; and this is not only the task of the Europeans, but also of the East Asians.

In order to do this, however, we should be clear in our minds about the two components of history, and understand which of them must be cultivated. From this follows the necessity for intellectual exchange and mutual enlightenment.

*

Nowhere, unless it be in India, can we learn as much that is worth knowing as in East Asia. Some consider Russia to be the coming power that will set the tone both spiritually and culturally, and point to the robust and, indeed, spiritual vitality of its people. This spiritual power and the future potentialities of Russia are things that cannot be gainsaid, but at the same time we cannot overlook the fact that we are dealing here with something undeveloped, something unformed and incomplete. The 'older' nations can certainly learn from the 'younger', but by and large it is the older that do most of the giving.

Our culture did not originate as the antithesis of the Russian: it is much more a case of the Russians having developed in a way that is the antithesis of ours. The author feels convinced that not in Russia shall we of the West find a distinct and fertile antipole, but in India and East Asia. Many things that in Russia are blurred and indistinct, have already for ages existed in clear and mature form in East Asia. Why should we preoccupy ourselves with Russian mysticism when we can learn much more about mysticism and its methods from the Indians and the East Asians? Russia has, moreover, no philosophy which can be compared to Christian concepts in the West, or to those of Buddhism in India or China; no traditional social forms that are of special interest, and no all-pervading popular culture. What we see taking shape in Russia are things that in a robust and talented nation hold out possibilities for the future—but with the best will in the world one can learn nothing from mere potentialities! Those people who want to throw themselves unreservedly into the arms of Russia—and we are not here speaking of the Communist régime—are insufficiently aware of the fact that this would mean for us nothing more than a process of reverting to a primitive intellectual state. Should we do this, Spengler would prove right, for we should then revert to the 'primordial soul' and be 'reborn', not as proper Russians, but probably as poor and ineffectual copies of them. And this would, in any case, involve the suicide of our culture. As I see it, however, the West, despite the powerful place the Russians today occupy, has not ceased to influence them spiritually. The Russians are much more likely to need us in matters of the spirit than vice versa. As we have already pointed out, Russia's aims in this sphere are, in the ultimate analysis, the same as our own; namely, to master the dynamic era of technology and to bring it to a significant conclusion. For this reason we shall certainly, at some later date, reach a more satisfactory mutual relationship with the Russians. But on the way there, Europe will have much of importance to say.

*

East Asia offers us stimuli but no ready-made solutions for our problems. These stimuli are nevertheless of the greatest significance, since they can focus our minds on the viewpoint that is complementary and opposite to our own. They help us towards the discovery and rediscovery of things in our own tradition of which we had already almost lost sight. To make the detour through East Asia would be beneficial in that it could prevent us time and again from slipping, without our consciousness or volition, into a purely rationalist view of things.

This detour will loosen us up intellectually, for, even though we have not become mentally rigid like the East Asians, we have gone like blind folk along prescribed pathways without looking to right or left. The study of things East Asian will help us towards a new 'formative experience' (to use a somewhat old-fashioned expression), and one that derives from the times: it shows us that many of the so-called 'formative experiences' which still linger on in odd corners of our humanistic education are now superseded and valueless, and are spinning out a lifeless and abstract existence.

Furthermore, it provides us with the opportunity of seeing Christianity in a new light and of acknowledging the fact that here, too, an excessively narrow tradition has been fostered. Should greater stress come to be laid on the 'total' mystic element in Christianity, many of the problems bound up with religion and our outlook on life would, as it were, solve themselves. Thus, the natural sciences have long since been ready for incorporation into a revised Christian concept of the world. A large number of the present younger generation in Europe have already instinctively outgrown the old dualistic approach which still has the decisive say in the books of many of our more elderly scholars. Where are the 'Church Fathers' who can adapt and assimilate the many external stimuli to which the Church is now subject?

Though their outward manifestations are different, the problems faced today by the two world religions, Christianity and Buddhism (we need not go into the question of the significance of Islam), are essentially the same. The task of the present day, particularly our own task, lies in self-communion, and not in mutual strife.

As we have seen, many of the 'total' East Asian ideas seem to fit in better with our new scientific conception of things than with our traditional dualistic one. The Western world had to make a very considerable detour in order to perceive the relativity of dualistic notions. Intellect has finally defeated itself. Goethe, who in the course of a long life gave expression to so many contradictory ideas, gave his allegiance as he grew older ever more unambiguously to the organic—'total' view of life. And so, from our point of view, he was a forerunner. Had we, then, started to live our lives in accordance with his views, we should have been spared many sorrows and many disasters, but our development, too, would have come to an abrupt end. The specialists, whom Goethe admired so little, have carried this development to its conclusion by serving the spirit of objectivity and neglecting to cultivate what is essentially human. These sacrifices on the altar of Work have not been altogether without their significance.

We of today can find consolation and a sense of reconciliation above all by realizing that all past events have served to raise mankind to a new level of development. What matters now is the strengthening of the coils of the spiral, so that it does not come apart.

NOTES

[1] Jacob Burckhardt, *Weltgeschichtliche Betrachtungen.*
[2] Ibid.
[3] Ku Hung Ming, *Chinas Verteidigung gegen Europäische Ideen.*
[4] Walter Schubart, *Europa und die Seele des Ostens.*

INDEX

INDEX

PUBLISHER'S NOTE

In the case of books by authors writing in German, reference is made throughout to the original editions and the wording of quotations is the present translators'. Quotations from Lafcadio Hearn are rendered from the German-language editions used by the author. Quotations from all other English sources are from the originals.